CABLE BY GERRY DUGGAN VOL. 1. Contains material originally published in magazine form as CABLE (2020) #1-4. First printing 2020. ISBN 978-1-302-92178-1. Published by MARVEL WORLDWIDE, INC., a subsidiary of MARVEL ENTERTAINMENT, LLC. OFFICE OF PUBLICATION: 1290 Avenue of the Americas, New York, NY 10104. © 2020 MARVEL No similarity between any of the names, characters, persons, and/or institutions in this magazine with those of any living or dead person or institution is intended, and any such similarity which may exist is purely coincidental. **Printed in Canada.** KEVIN FEIGE, Chief Creative Officer; DAN BUCKLEY, President, Marvel Entertainment; JOHN NEE, Publisher; JOE QUESADA, EVP & Creative Director; TOM BREVOORT, SVP of Publishing; DAVID BOGART, Associate Publisher & SVP of Talent Affairs; Publishing & Partnership; DAVID GABRIEL, VP of Print & Digital Publishing; JEFF YOUNGQUIST, VP of Production & Special Projects; DAN CARR, Executive Director of Publishing Technology; ALEX MORALES, Director of Publishing Operations; DAN EDINGTON, Managing Editor; RICKEY PURDIN, Director of Talent Relations; SUSAN CRESPI, Production Manager; STAN LEE, Chairman Emeritus. For information regarding advertising in Marvel Comics or on Marvel.com, please contact Vit DeBellis, Custom Solutions & Integrated Advertising Manager, at vdebellis@marvel.com. For Marvel subscription inquiries, please call 888-511-5480. **Manufactured between 9/23/2020 and 10/20/2020 by SOLISCO PRINTERS, SCOTT, QC, CANADA.**

10 9 8 7 6 5 4 3 2 1

Writer:	Gerry Duggan
Artist:	Phil Noto
Letterer:	VC's Joe Sabino
Cover Art:	Phil Noto

Head of X:	Jonathan Hickman
Design:	Tom Muller
Assistant Editors:	Annalise Bissa &
	Lauren Amaro
Editor:	Jordan D. White

Collection Editor:	Jennifer Grünwald
Assistant Managing Editor:	Maia Loy
Assistant Managing Editor:	Lisa Montalbano
Editor, Special Projects:	Mark D. Beazley
VP Production & Special Projects:	Jeff Youngquist
SVP Print, Sales & Marketing:	David Gabriel
Editor in Chief:	C.B. Cebulski

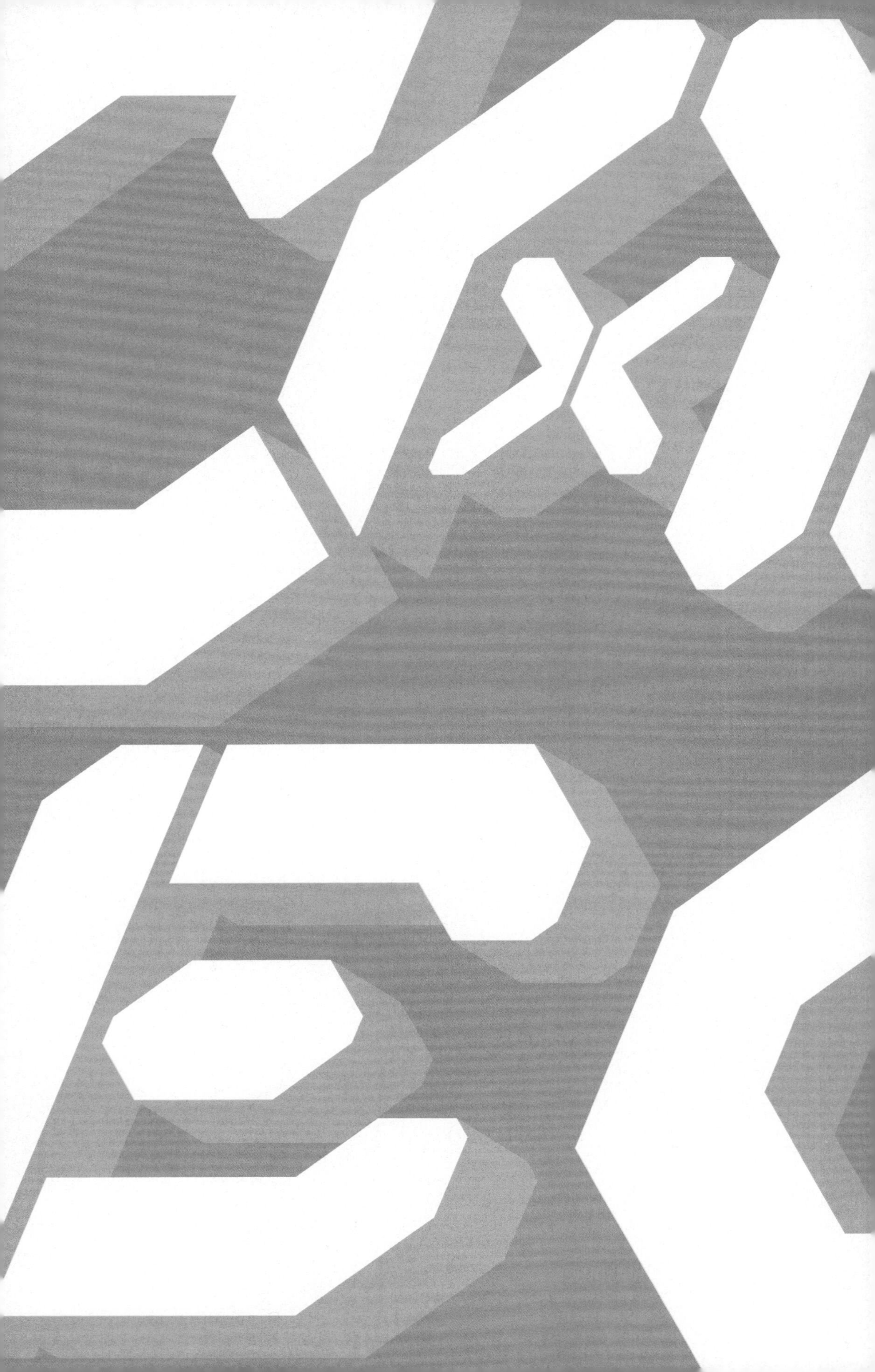

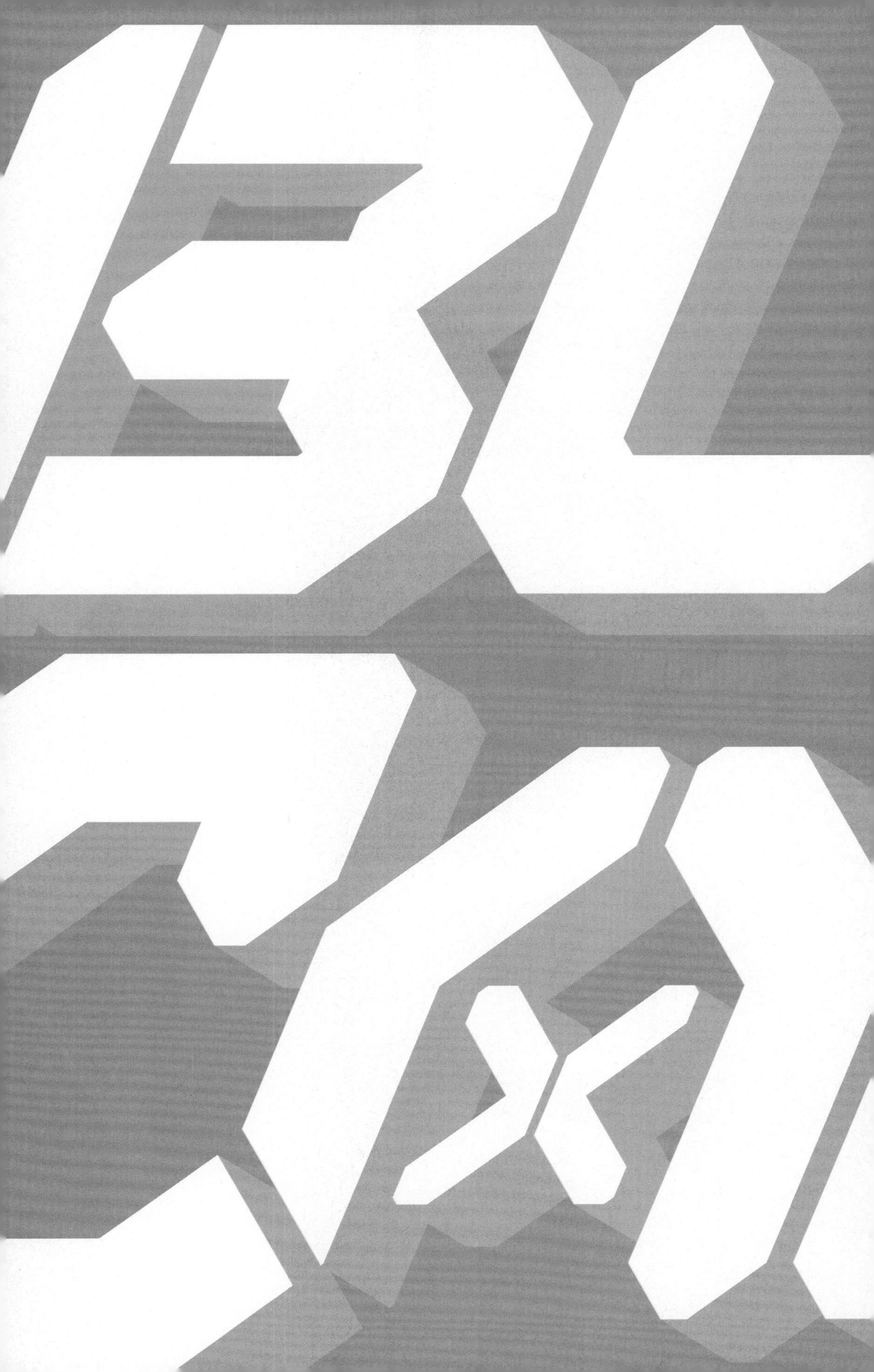

[dawn_of_x]

[guns_&_]
[swords_]

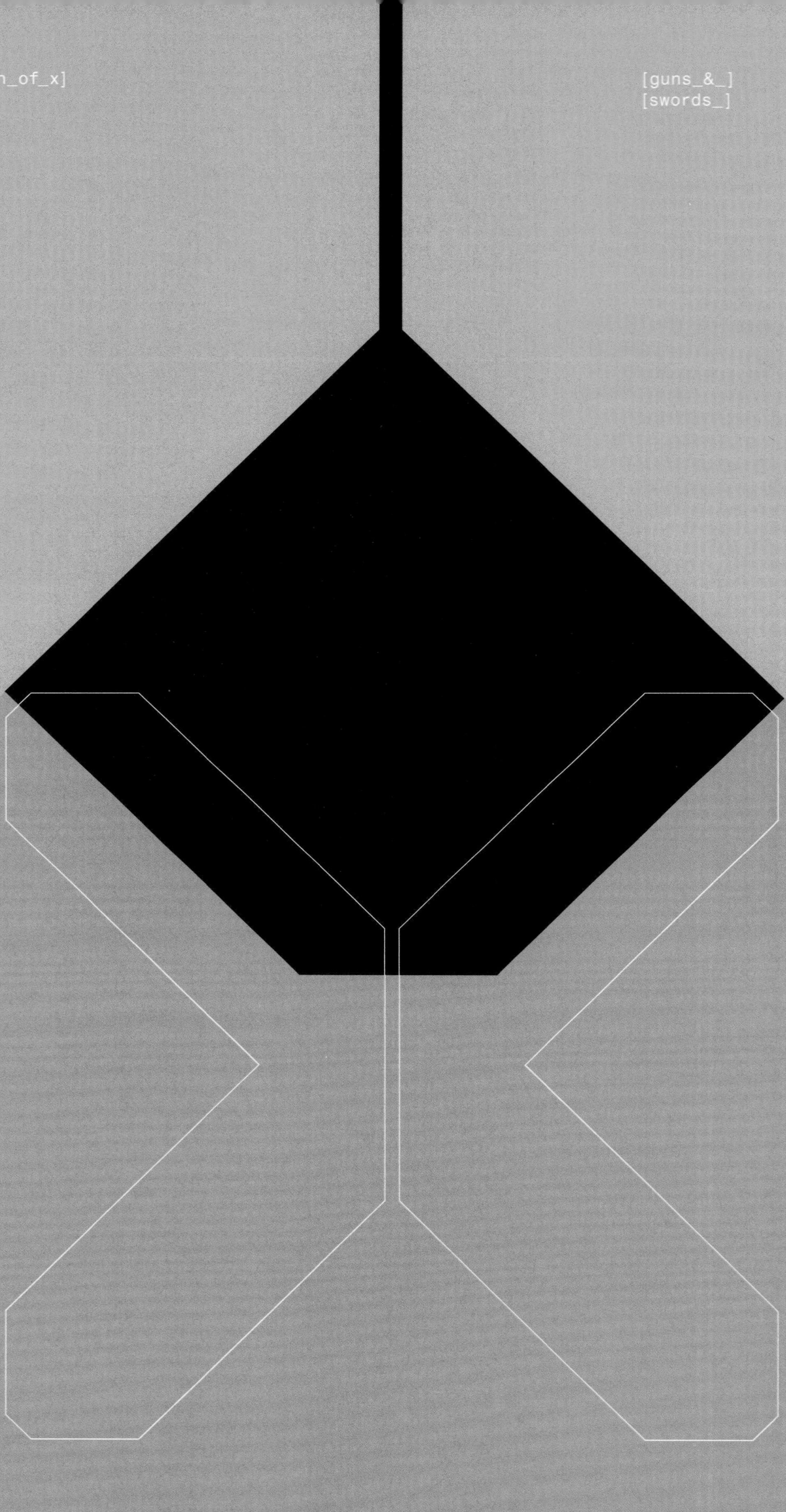

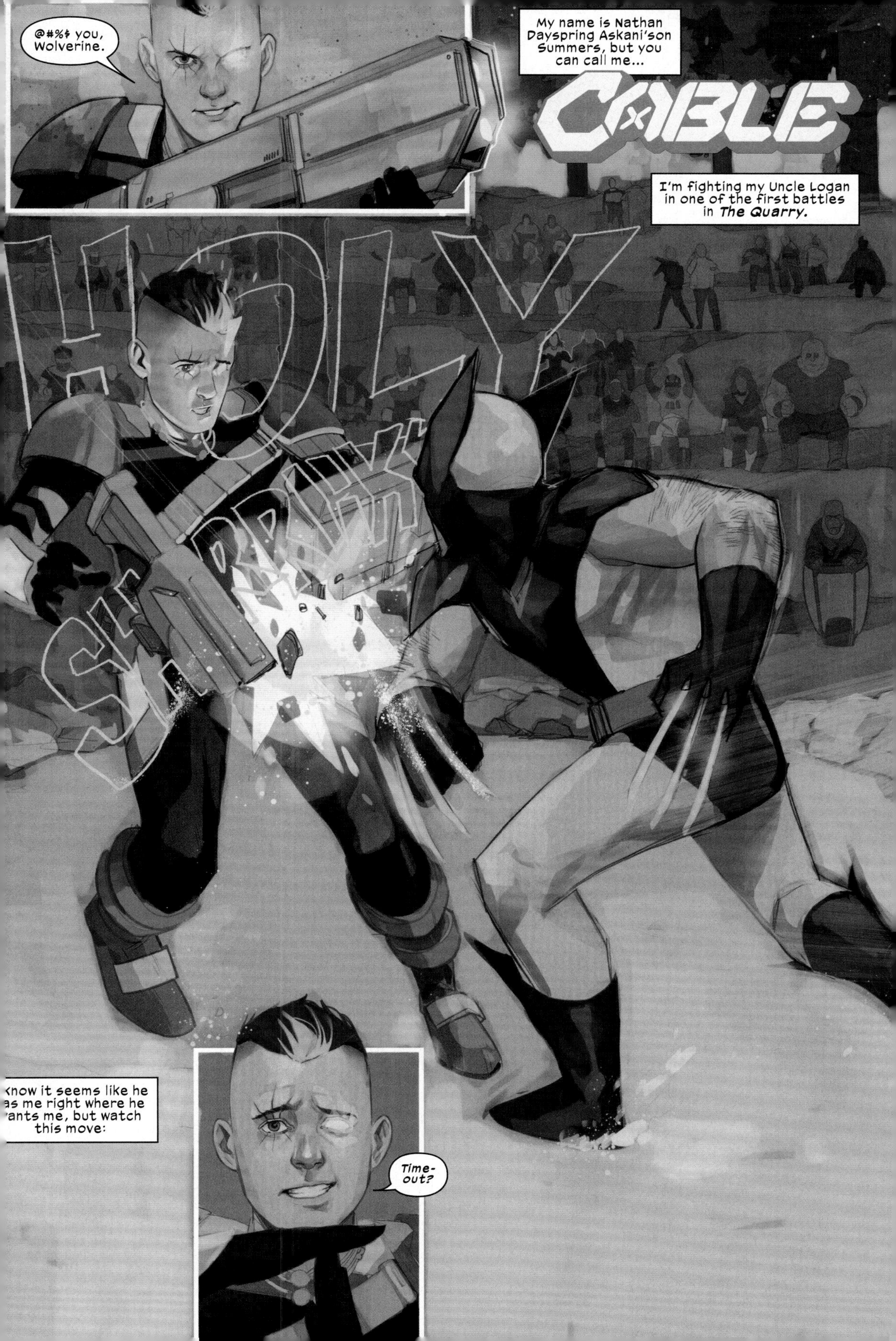
@#%$ you, Wolverine.
My name is Nathan Dayspring Askani'son Summers, but you can call me...
CABLE
I'm fighting my Uncle Logan in one of the first battles in *The Quarry.*
know it seems like he as me right where he ants me, but watch this move:
Time-out?

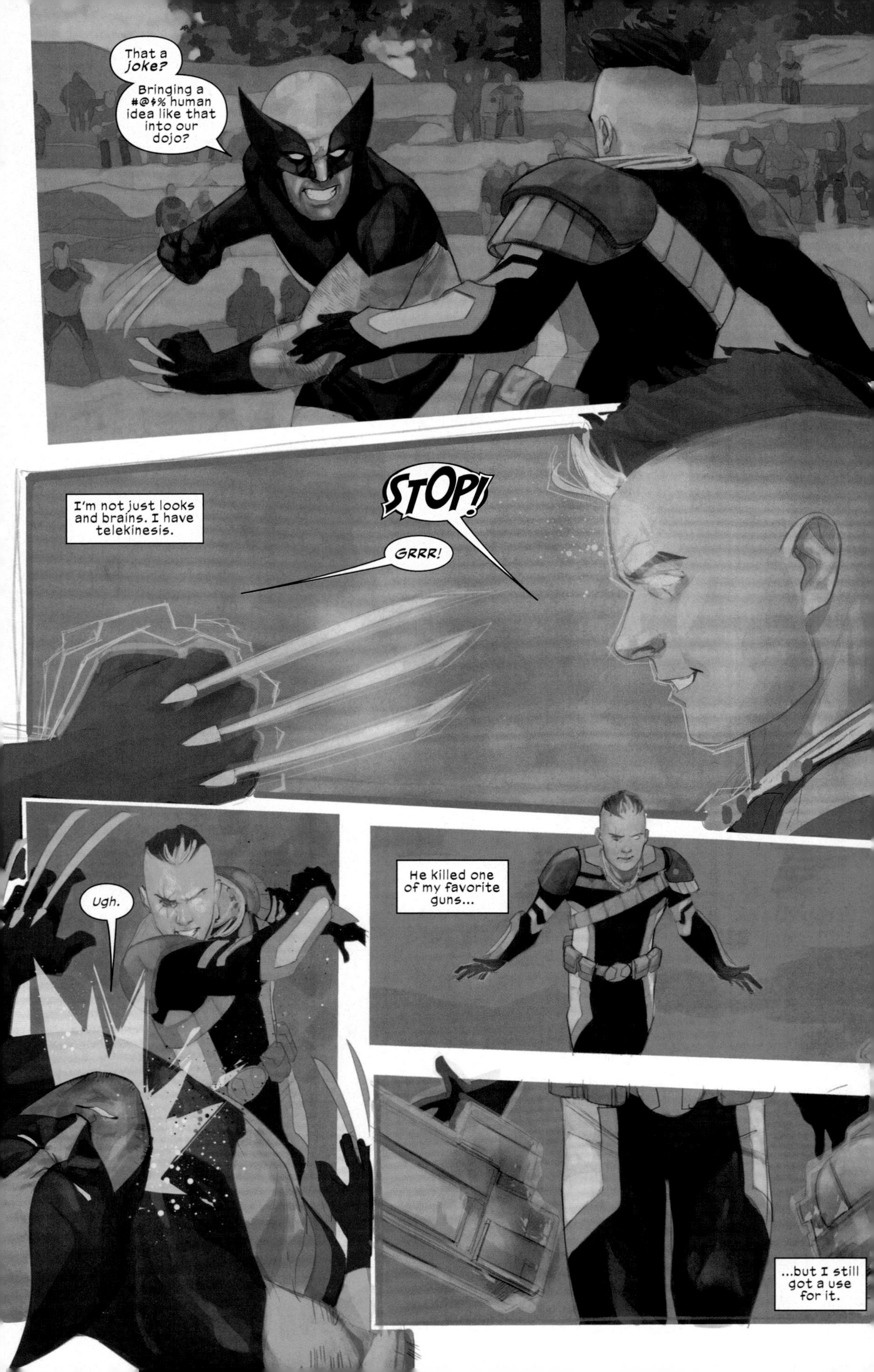

That a *joke?*
Bringing a #@$% human idea like that into our dojo?
I'm not just looks and brains. I have telekinesis.
STOP!
GRRR!
Ugh.
He killed one of my favorite guns...
...but I still got a use for it.

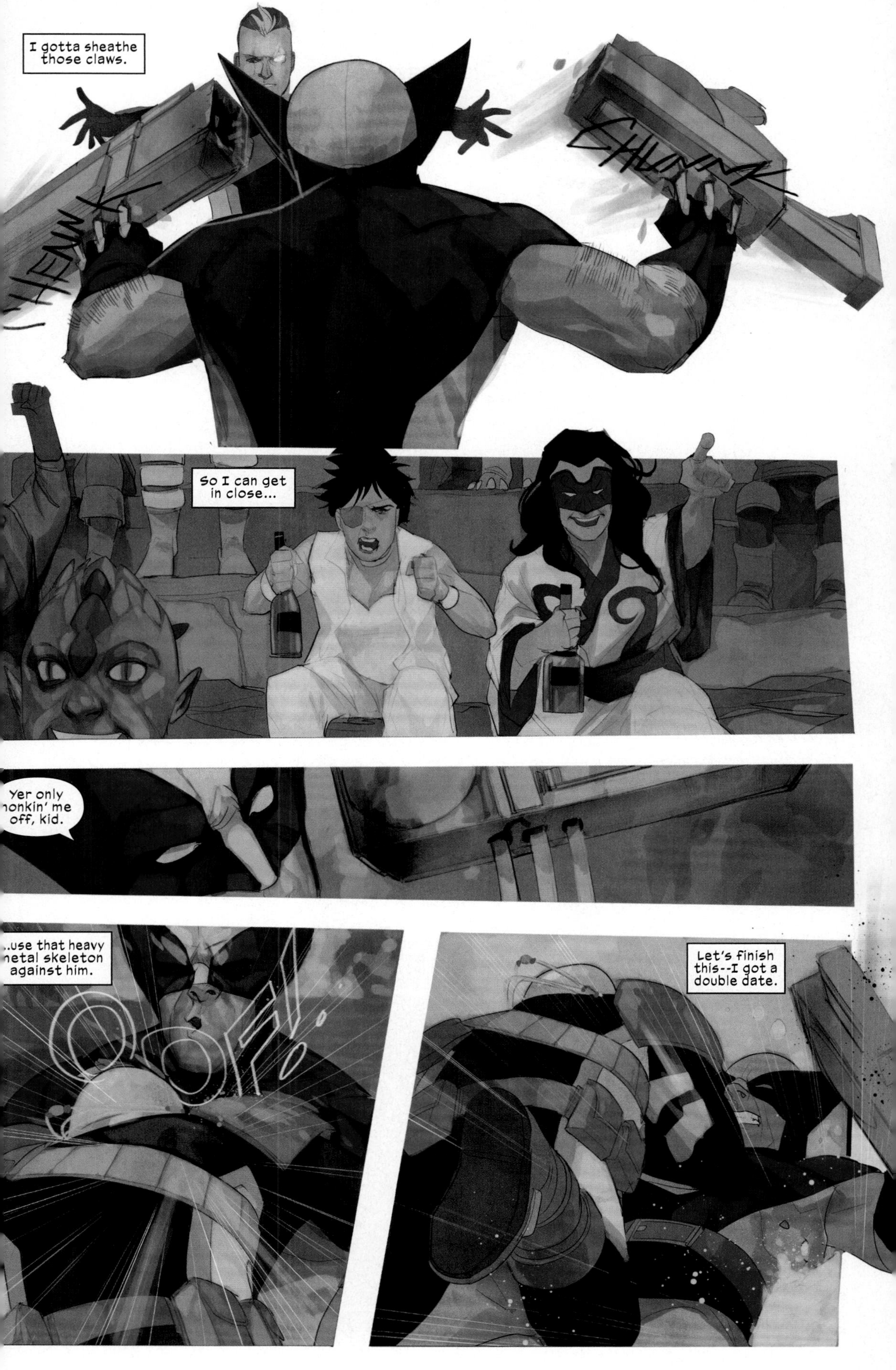

I gotta sheathe those claws.
CHUNK
SHENK
So I can get in close...
Yer only honkin' me off, kid.
...use that heavy metal skeleton against him.
OOF!
Let's finish this--I got a double date.

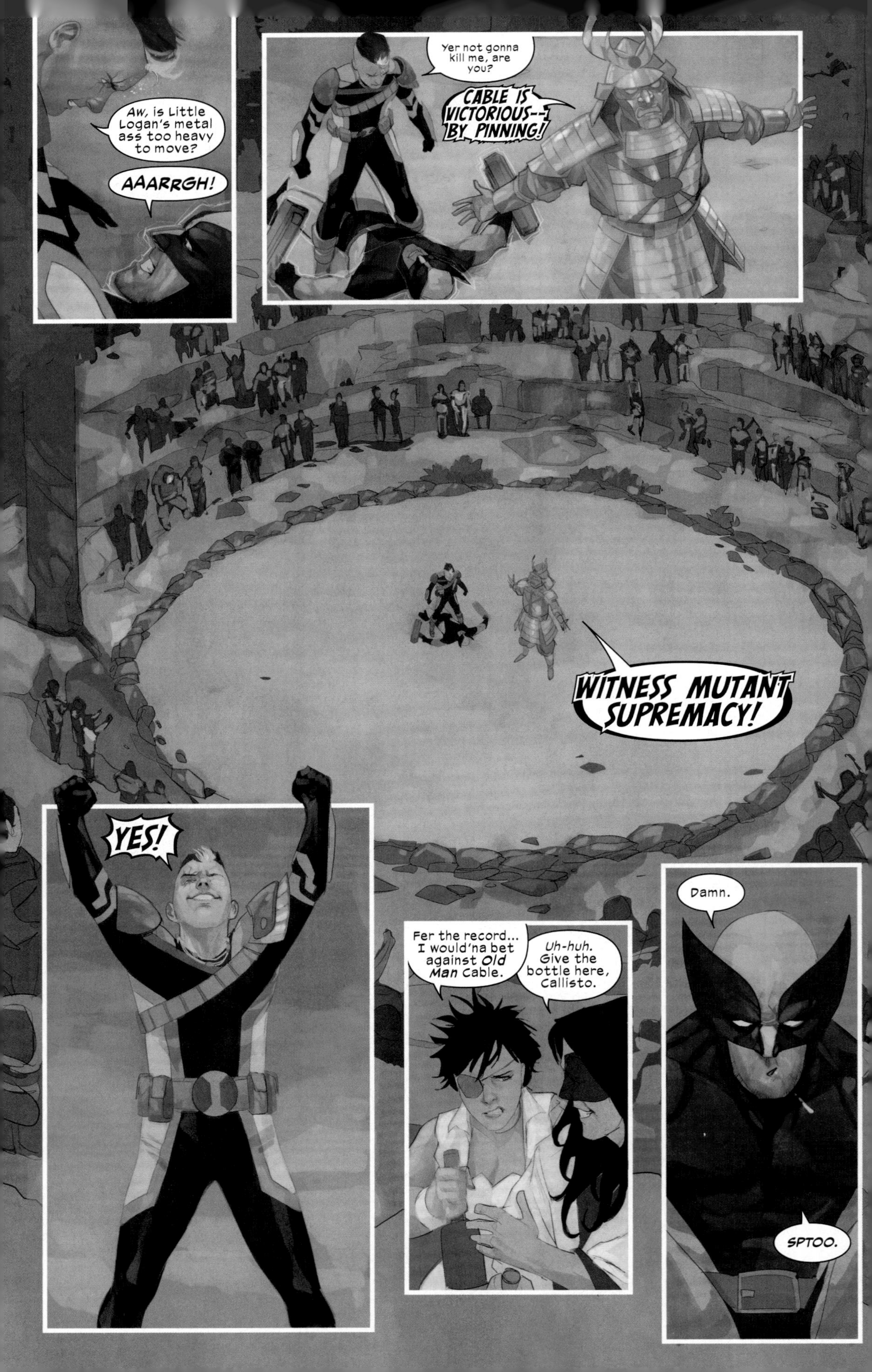
Aw, is Little Logan's metal ass too heavy to move?
AAARRGH!
Yer not gonna kill me, are you?
CABLE IS VICTORIOUS--BY PINNING!
WITNESS MUTANT SUPREMACY!
YES!
Fer the record... I would'na bet against Old Man Cable.
Uh-huh. Give the bottle here, Callisto.
Damn.
SPTOO.

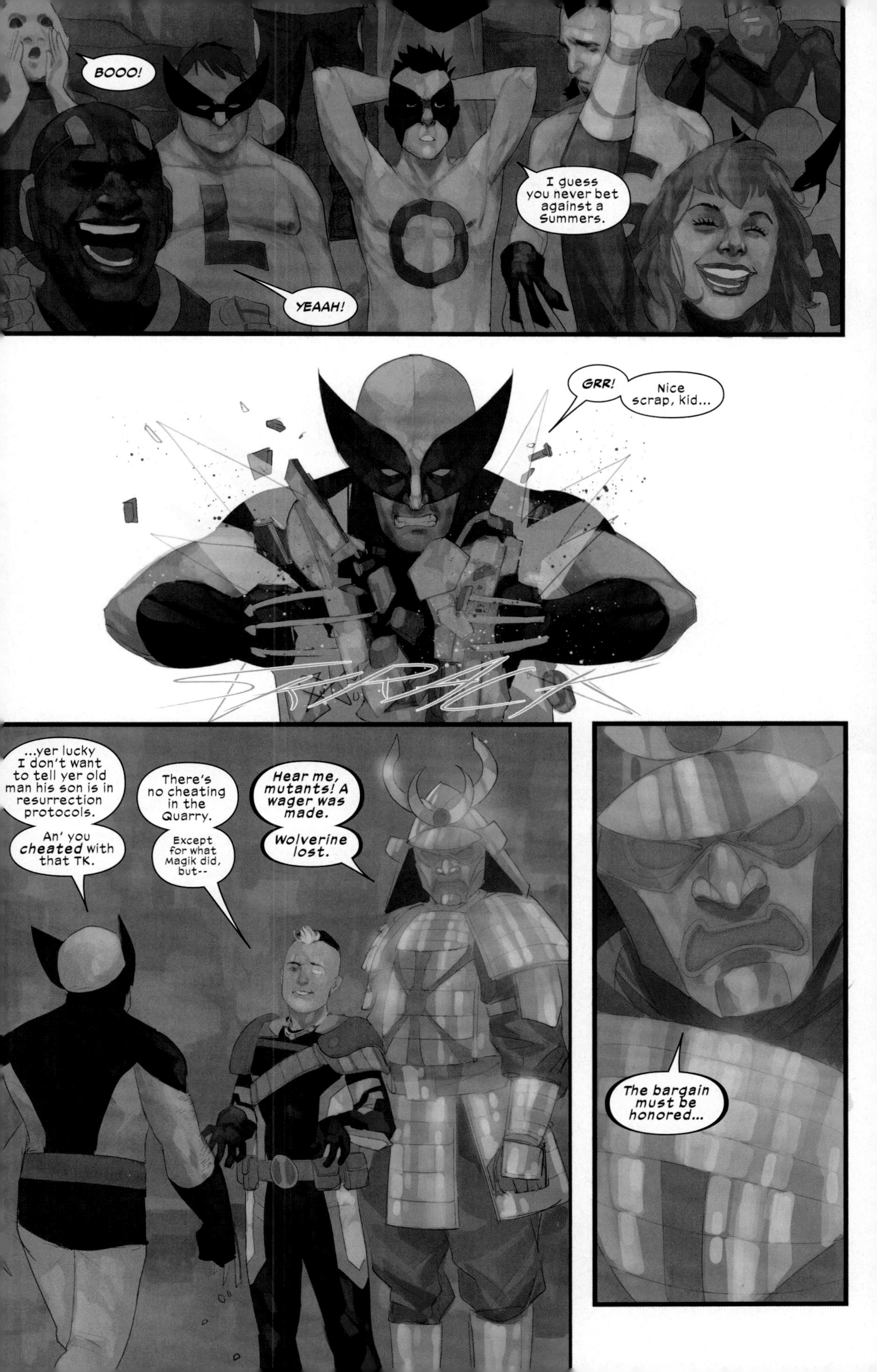
BOOO!
I guess you never bet against a Summers.
YEAAH!
GRR!
Nice scrap, kid...
...yer lucky I don't want to tell yer old man his son is in resurrection protocols.
An' you *cheated* with that TK.
There's no cheating in the Quarry.
Except for what Magik did, but--
Hear me, mutants! A wager was made.
Wolverine lost.
The bargain must be honored...

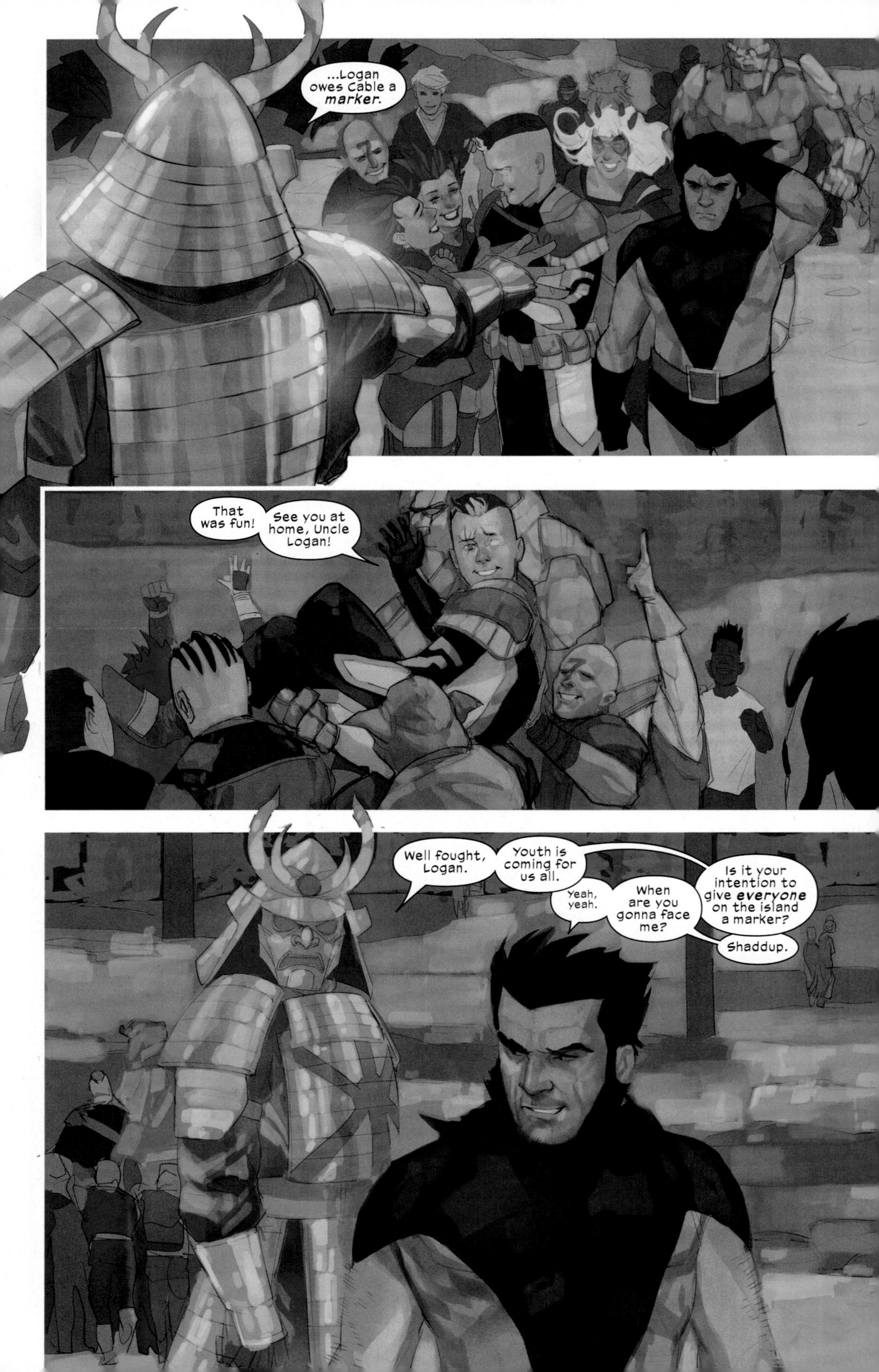
...Logan owes Cable a *marker*.
That was fun!
See you at home, Uncle Logan!
Well fought, Logan.
Youth is coming for us all.
Yeah, yeah.
When are you gonna face me?
Is it your intention to give *everyone* on the island a marker?
Shaddup.

THE OFFICIAL RECORD OF COMBAT IN THE QUARRY

This journal is the living record of single combat in the Quarry. It is the property of all mutants. Matches are officiated and records are maintained by the Silver Samurai.

[013]	(W)	Cable	(L)	Wolverine
[012]	(W)	Callisto	(L)	Jumbo Carnation
[011]	(W)	Callisto	(L)	Fish
[010]	(W)	Callisto	(L)	Pyro
[009]	(W)	Leech	(L)	Artie
[008]	(W)	Dazzler	(L)	Jubilee
[007]	(W)	Wolfsbane	(L)	Pyro
[006]	(W)	M	(L)	Bishop
[005]	(W)	Magma	(L)	Firestar
[004]	(W)	Rogue	(L)	Havok
[003]	(W)	Esme Cuckoo	(L)	Irma Cuckoo
[002]	(D)	Nightcrawler	(D)	Blink
[001]	(W)	Gorgon	(DQ)	Magik

(W) **Win**
(L) **Loss**
(D) **Draw**
(DQ) **Disqualified**
(DNF) **Did Not Finish**

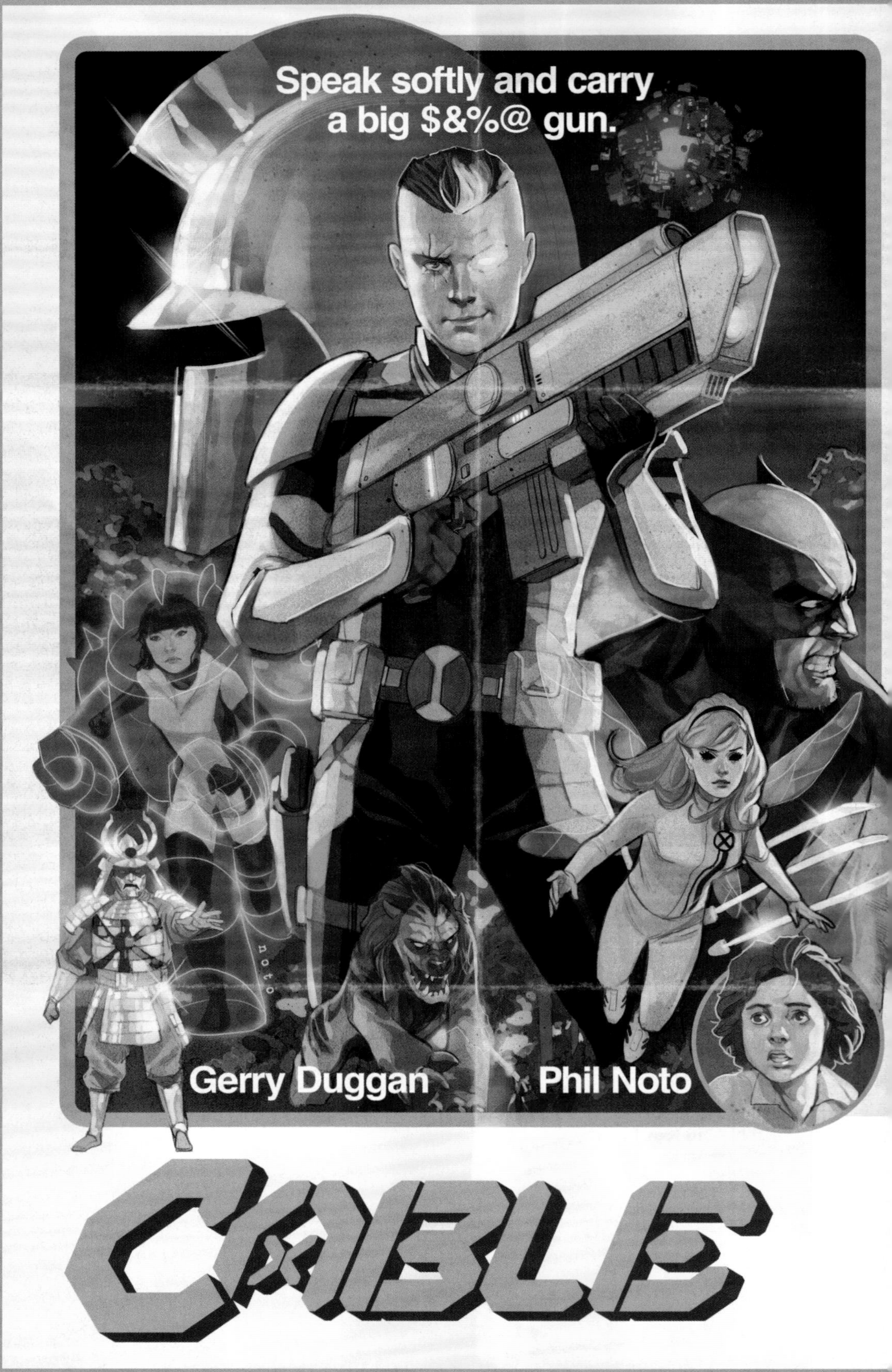

Speak softly and carry a big $&%.@ gun.
noto
Gerry Duggan
Phil Noto
CABLE

Big Guns

1

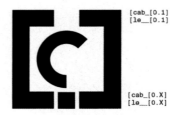

[cab_[0.1]
[le__[0.1]

[cab_[0.X]
[le__[0.X]

A NEW START

No longer the grizzled time-traveling fighter, the young CABLE is ready to make the most of life on the mutant island-nation of Krakoa. Luckily, there's plenty of trouble to get into...

Cable

Wolverine

Pixie

Armor

Silver
Samurai

Curse

Fauna

[cab_[0.0]..]
[le__[0.0]..]

[...young...]

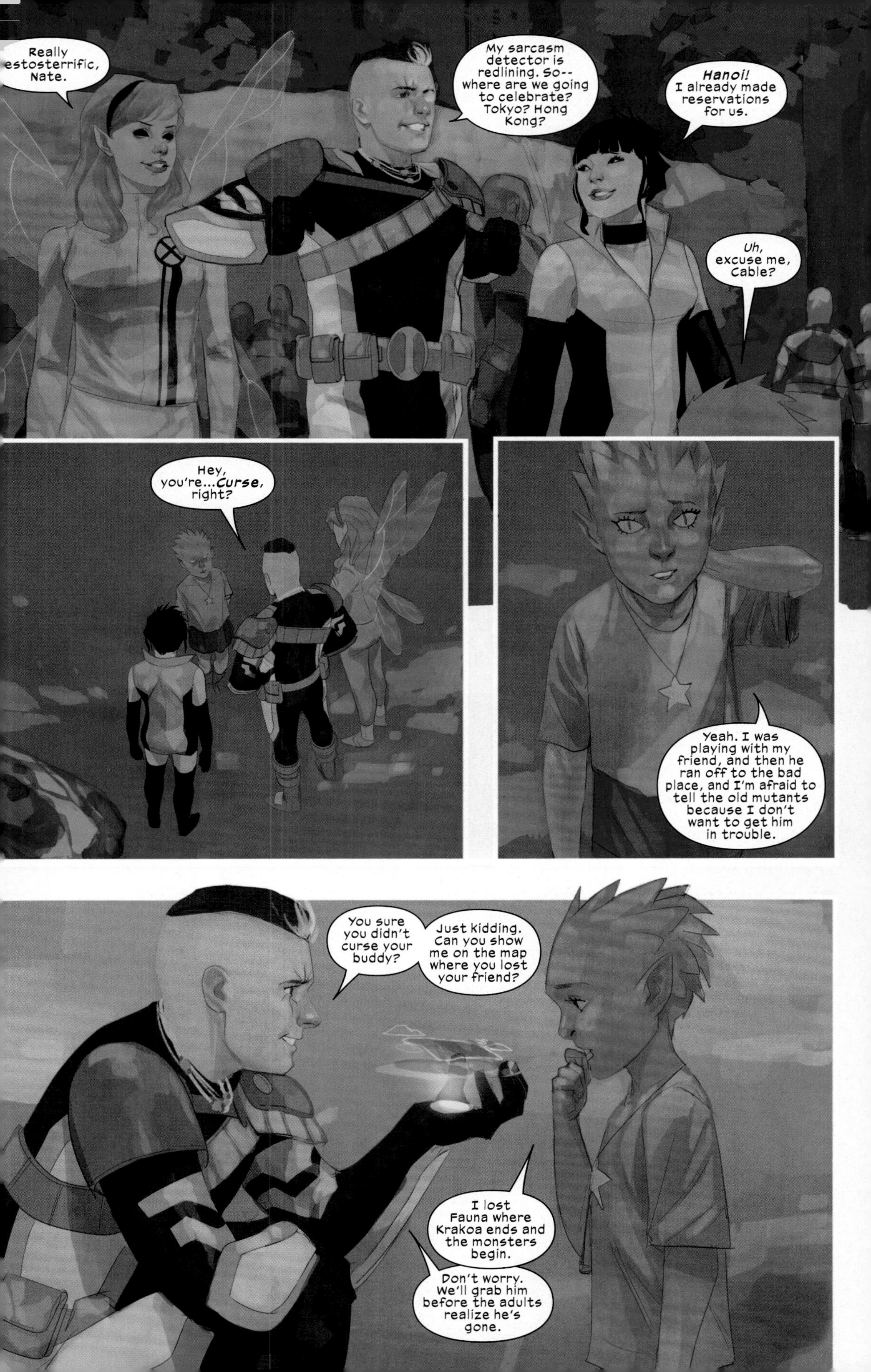

Really
estosterrific,
Nate.
My sarcasm detector is redlining. So-- where are we going to celebrate? Tokyo? Hong Kong?
Hanoi! I already made reservations for us.
Uh, excuse me, Cable?
Hey, you're...*Curse*, right?
Yeah. I was playing with my friend, and then he ran off to the bad place, and I'm afraid to tell the old mutants because I don't want to get him in trouble.
You sure you didn't curse your buddy?
Just kidding. Can you show me on the map where you lost your friend?
I lost Fauna where Krakoa ends and the monsters begin.
Don't worry. We'll grab him before the adults realize he's gone.

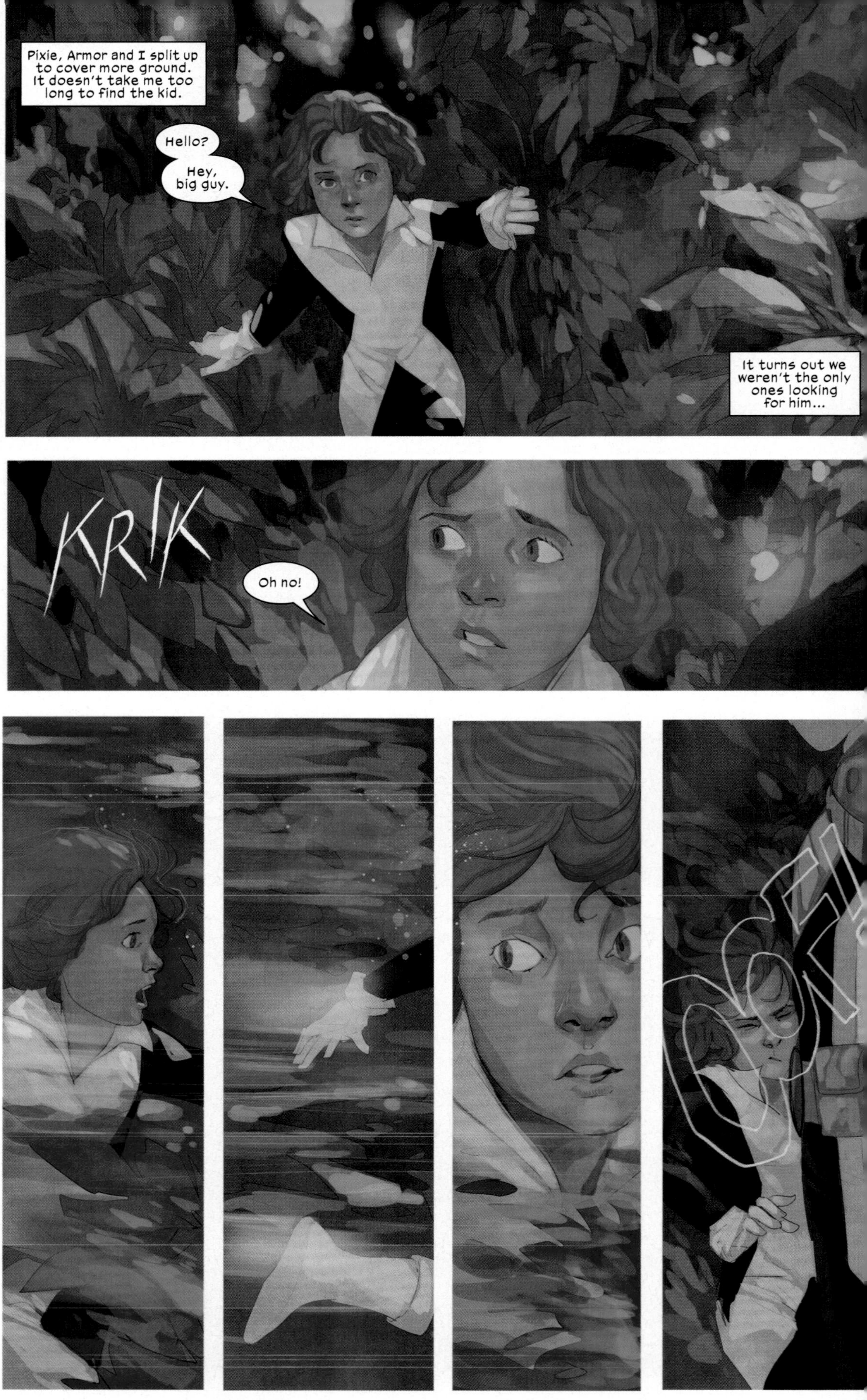
Pixie, Armor and I split up to cover more ground. It doesn't take me too long to find the kid.
Hello?
Hey, big guy.
It turns out we weren't the only ones looking for him...
KRIK
Oh no!

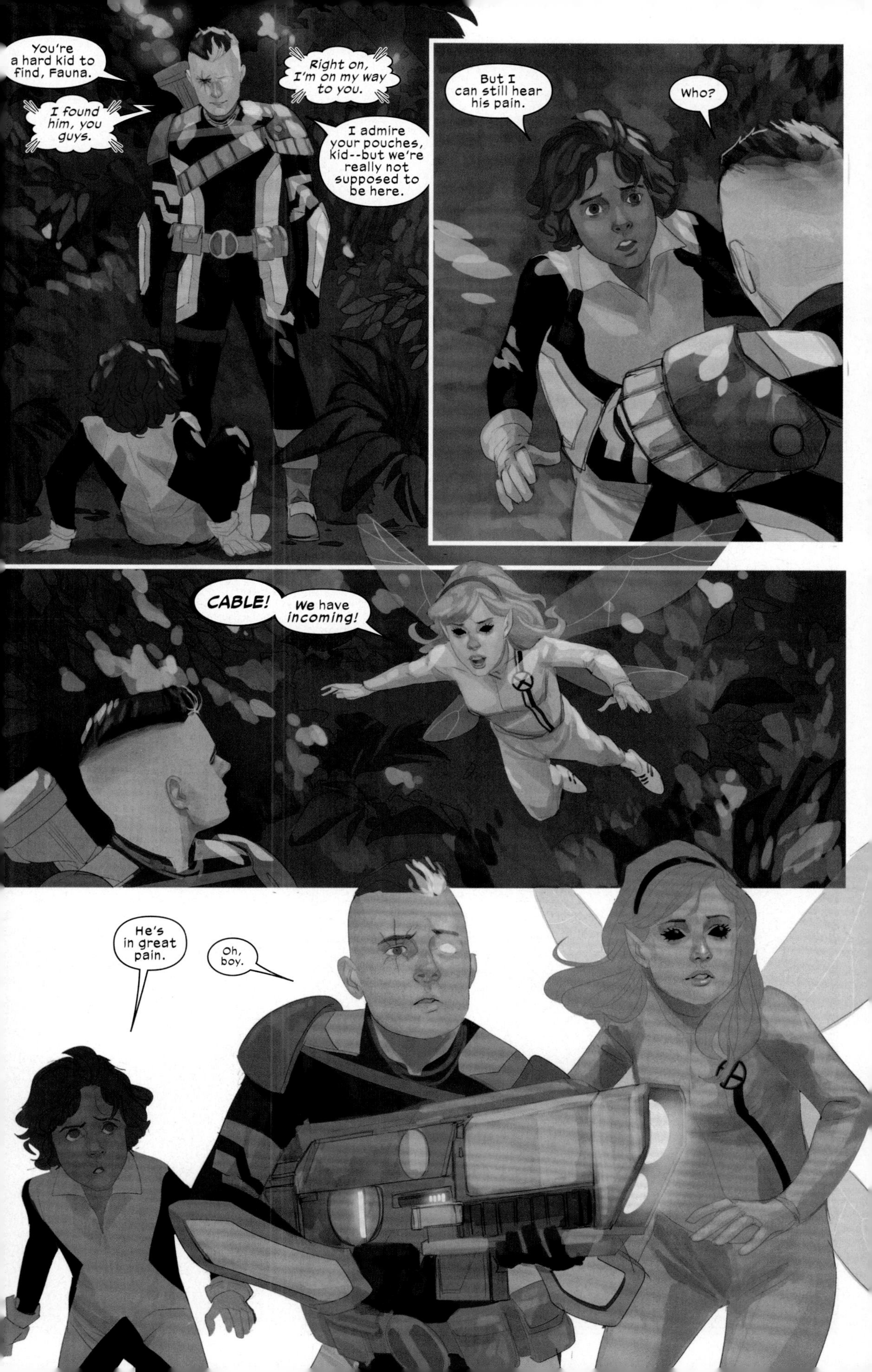
You're a hard kid to find, Fauna.
I found him, you guys.
Right on, I'm on my way to you.
I admire your pouches, kid--but we're really not supposed to be here.
But I can still hear his pain.
Who?
CABLE!
We have incoming!
He's in great pain.
Oh, boy.

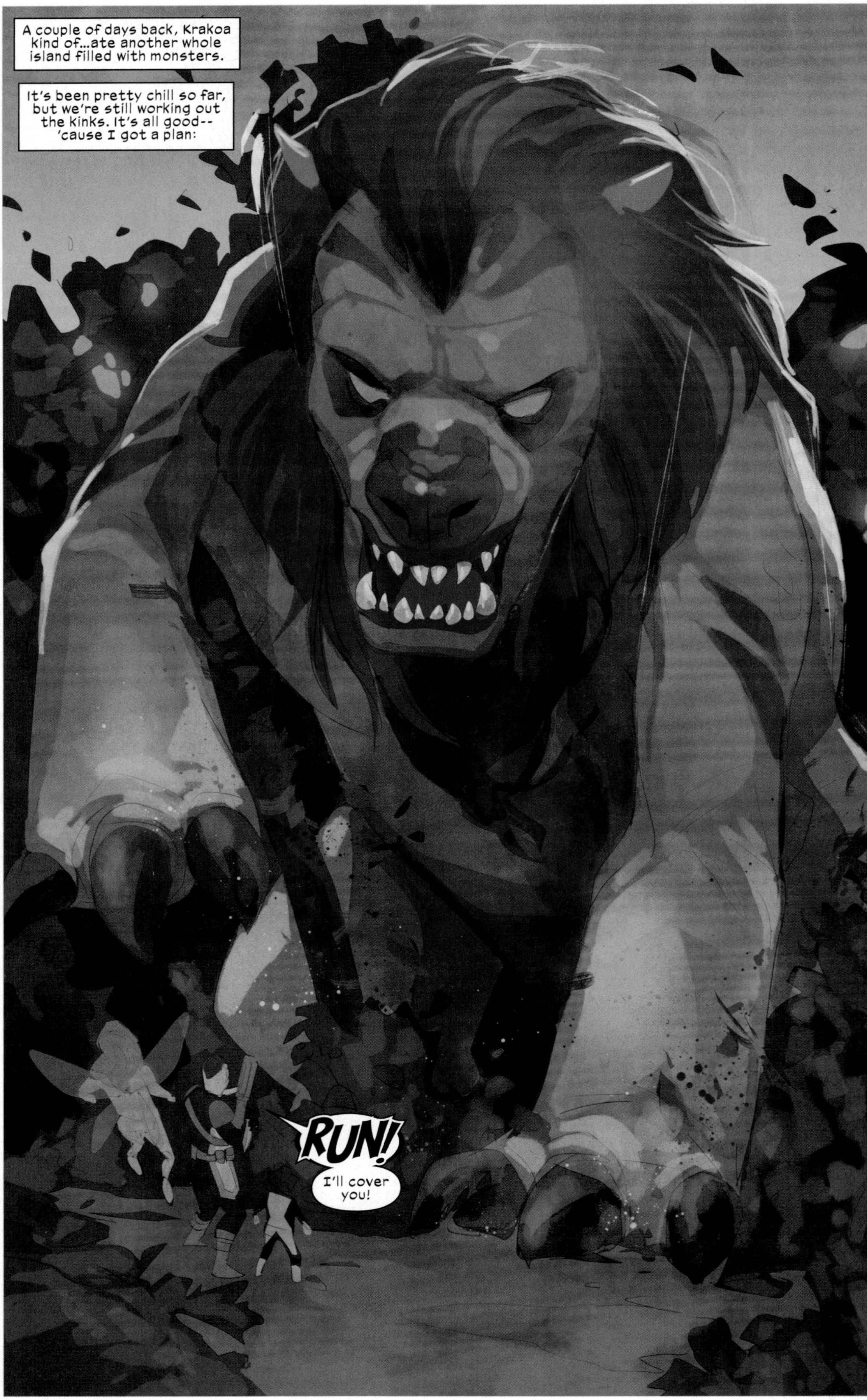
A couple of days back, Krakoa kind of...ate another whole island filled with monsters.
It's been pretty chill so far, but we're still working out the kinks. It's all good--'cause I got a plan:
RUN!
I'll cover you!

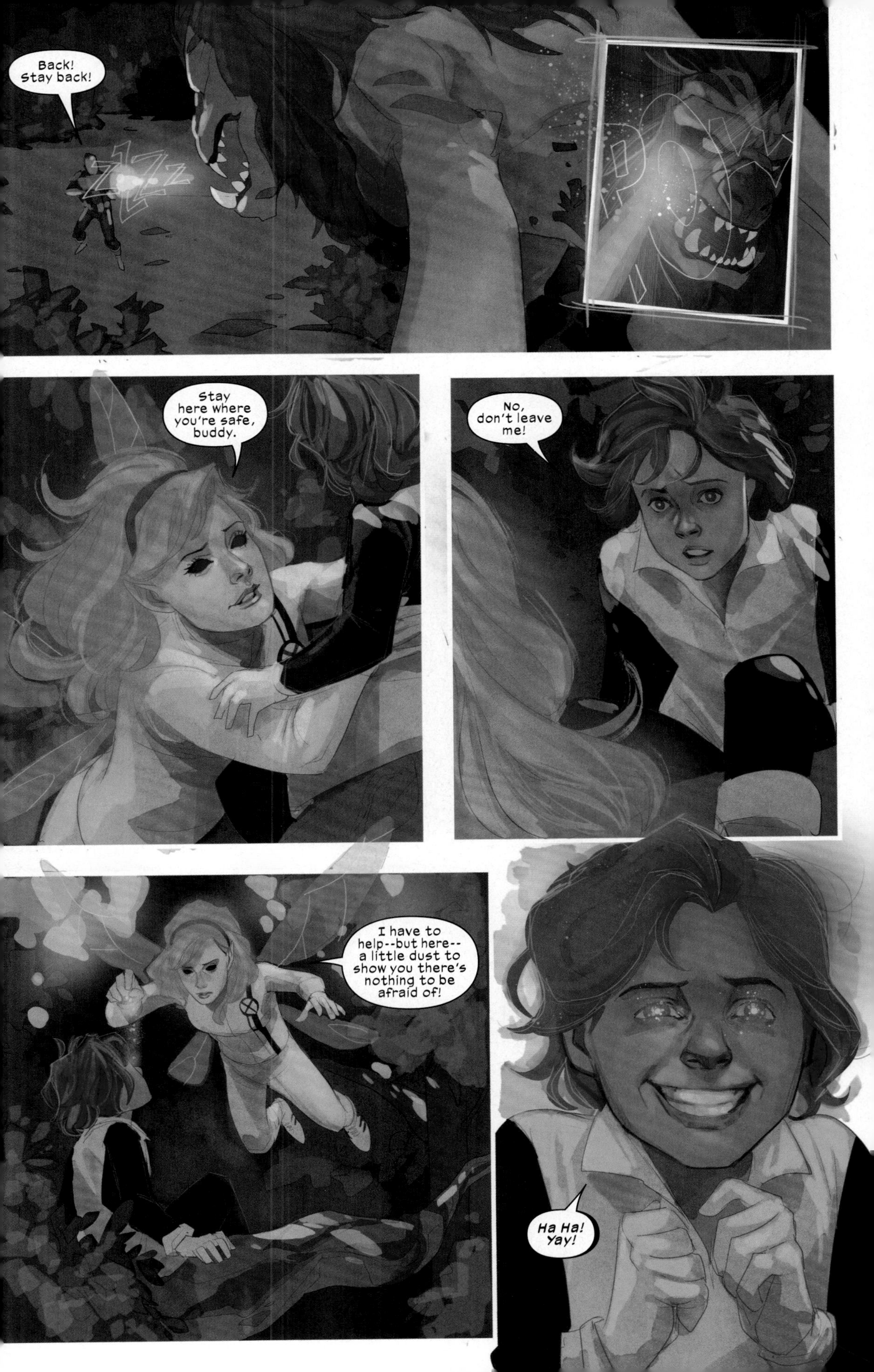
Back! Stay back!
ZZZ
POW
Stay here where you're safe, buddy.
No, don't leave me!
I have to help--but here--a little dust to show you there's nothing to be afraid of!
Ha Ha! Yay!

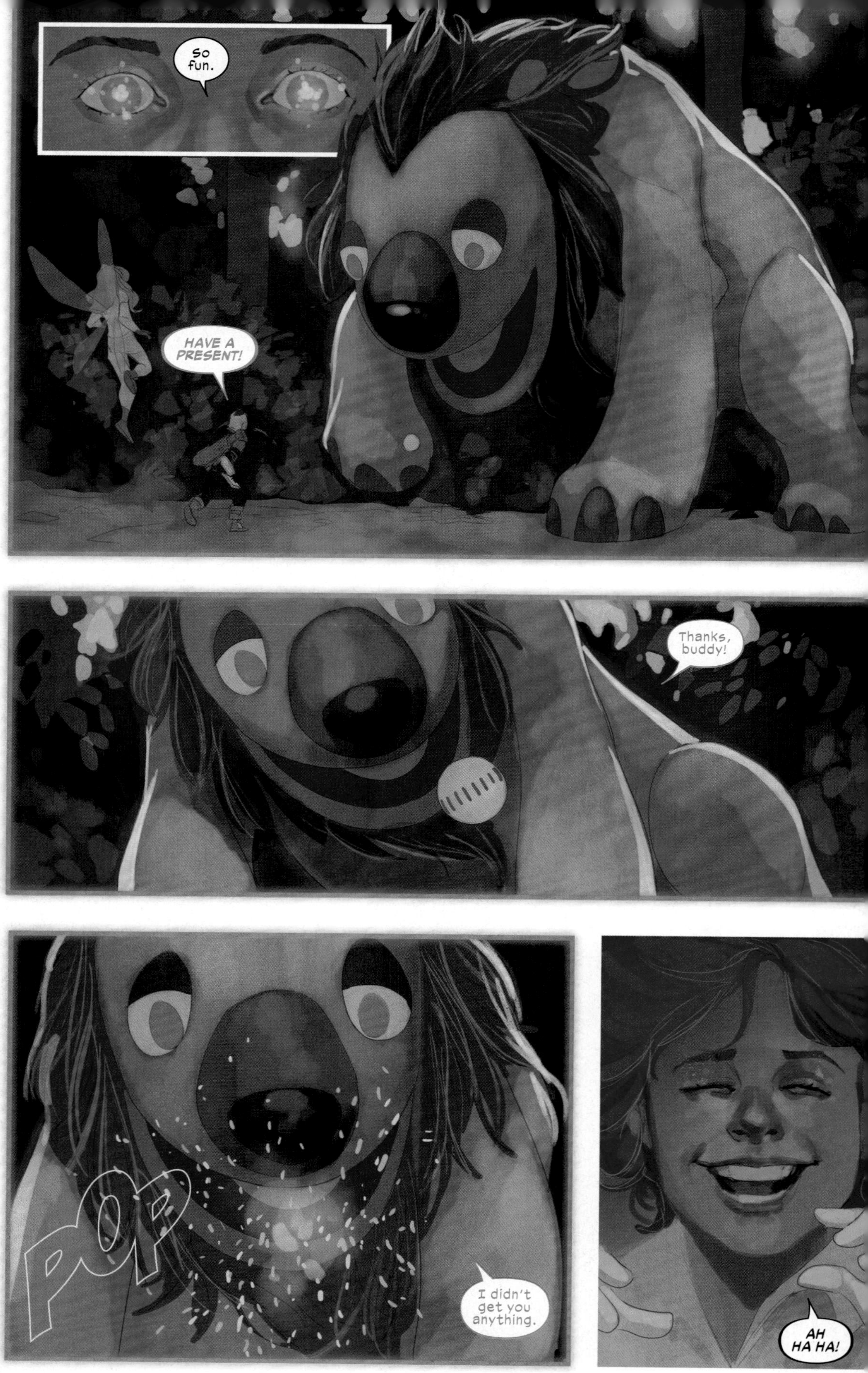
So fun.
HAVE A PRESENT!
Thanks, buddy!
POP
I didn't get you anything.
AH HA HA!

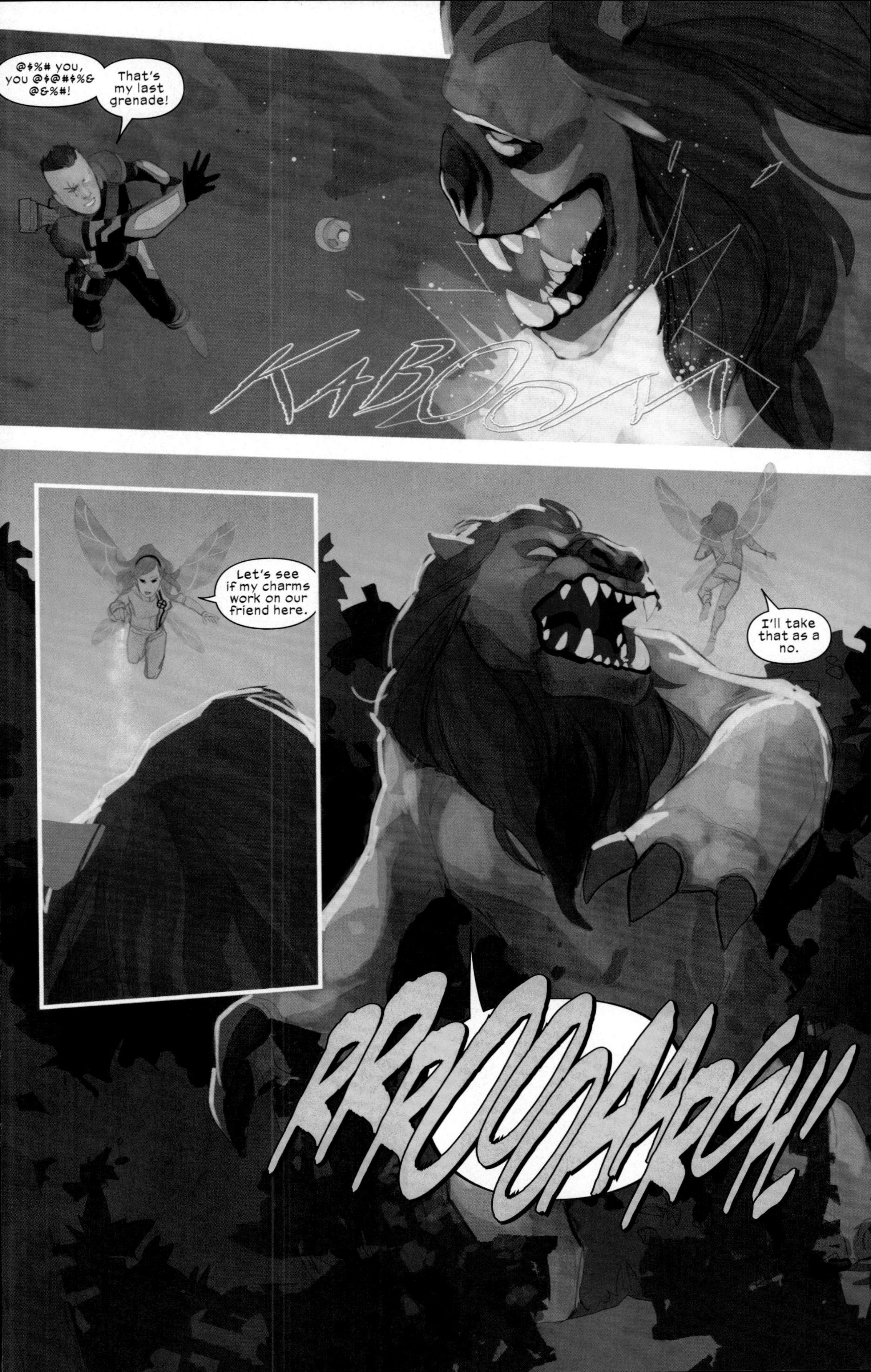

@$%# you, you @$@#$%& @&%#!
That's my last grenade!
KABOOM
Let's see if my charms work on our friend here.
I'll take that as a no.
RRROOOAARRGH!

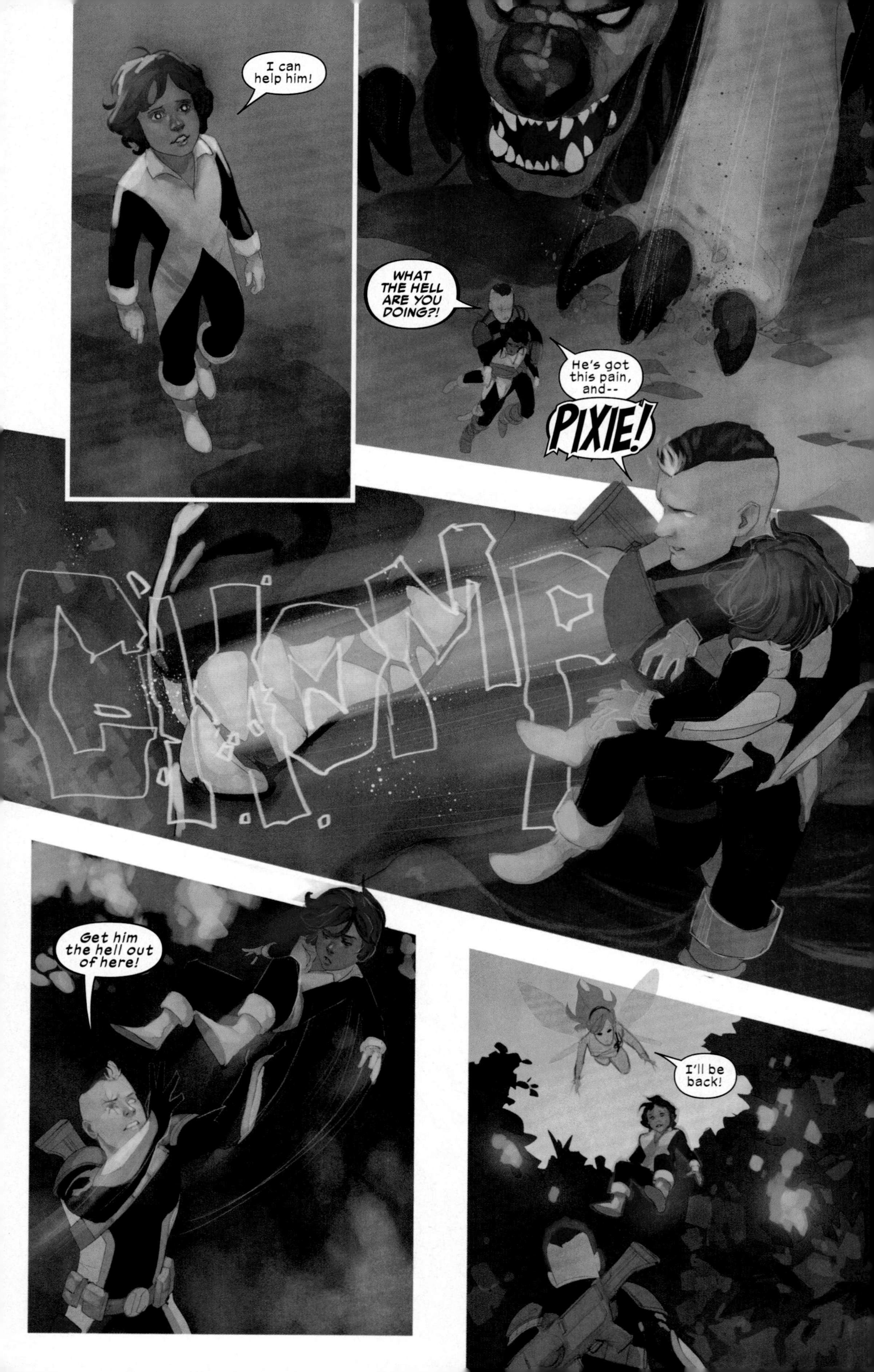
I can help him!
WHAT THE HELL ARE YOU DOING?!
He's got this pain, and--
PIXIE!
CHOMP
Get him the hell out of here!
I'll be back!

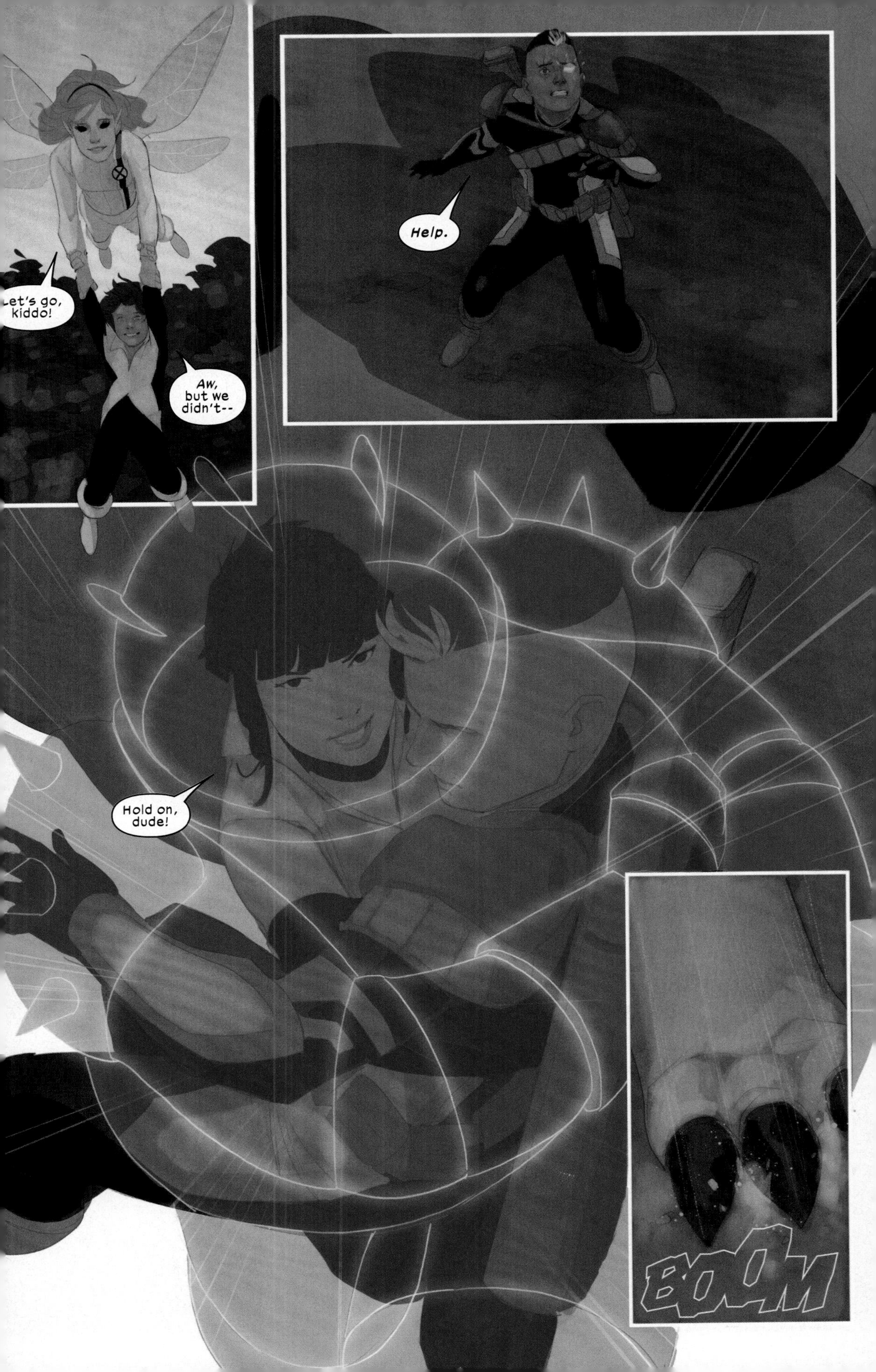
Let's go, kiddo!
Aw, but we didn't--
Help.
Hold on, dude!
BOOM

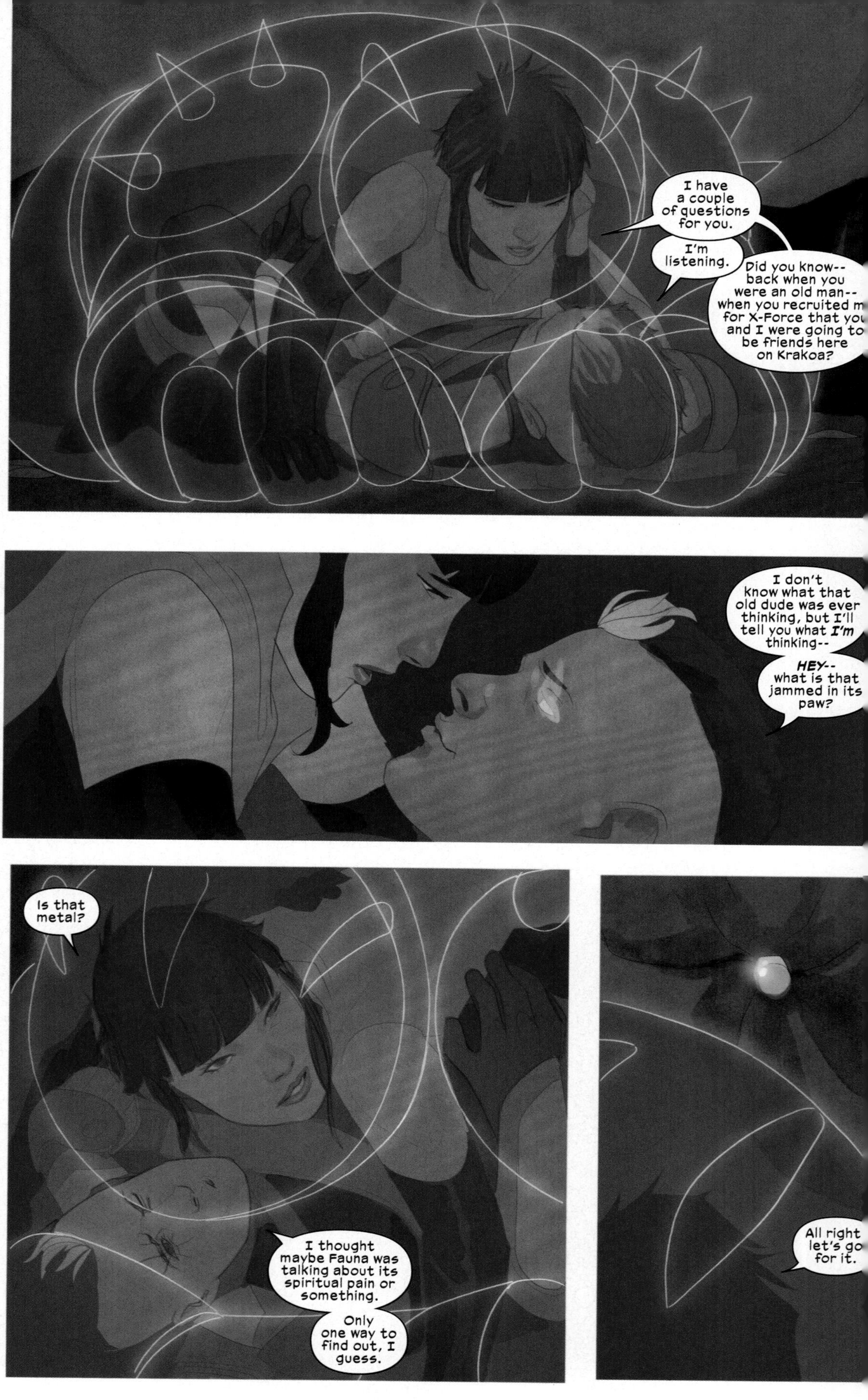
I have a couple of questions for you.
I'm listening.
Did you know-- back when you were an old man-- when you recruited m for X-Force that you and I were going to be friends here on Krakoa?
I don't know what that old dude was ever thinking, but I'll tell you what *I'm* thinking--
HEY-- what is that jammed in its paw?
Is that metal?
I thought maybe Fauna was talking about its spiritual pain or something.
Only one way to find out, I guess.
All right let's go for it.

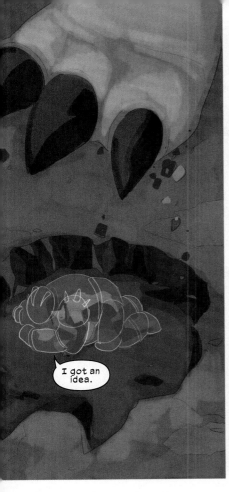

I got an idea.

Think you're strong enough to hold that leg up for a moment?

Of course.

How are we going to teach it to stand up?

With a really big gun.

HERE, BOY!

Sorry about this.

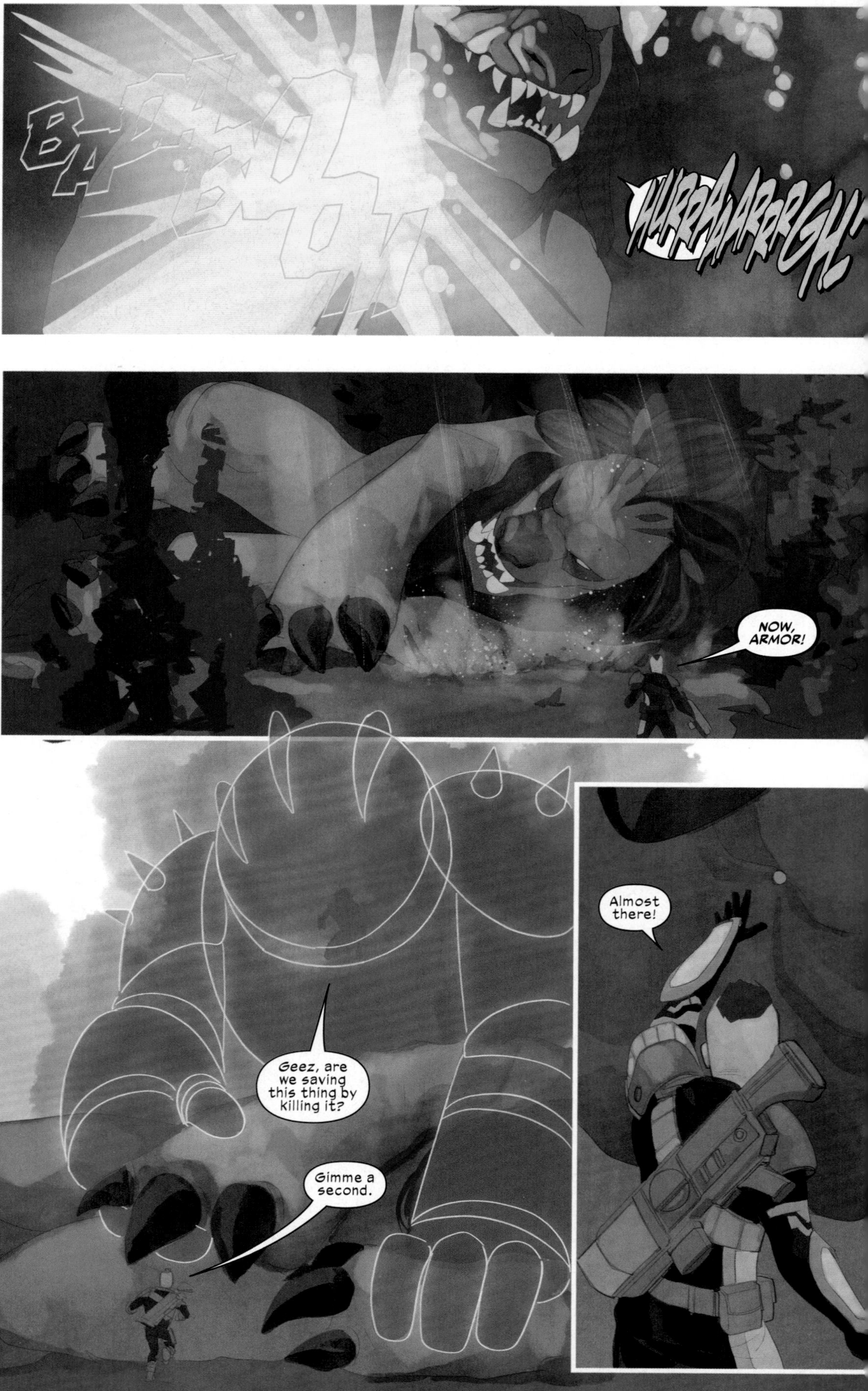
HURRAAARRRGH
NOW, ARMOR!
Almost there!
Geez, are we saving this thing by killing it?
Gimme a second.

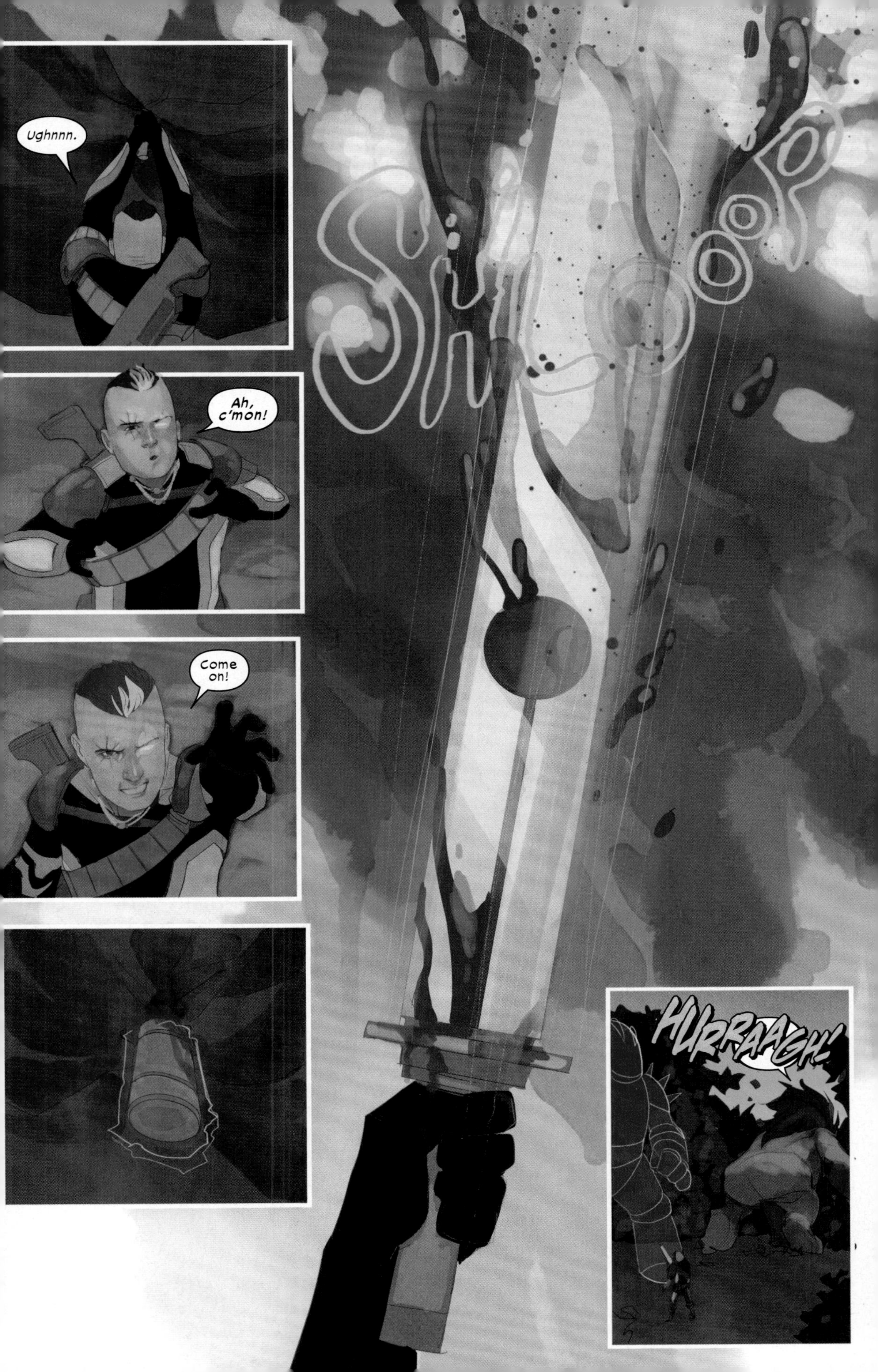
Ughnnn.
Ah, c'mon!
Come on!
SHLOOOP
HURRAAGH!

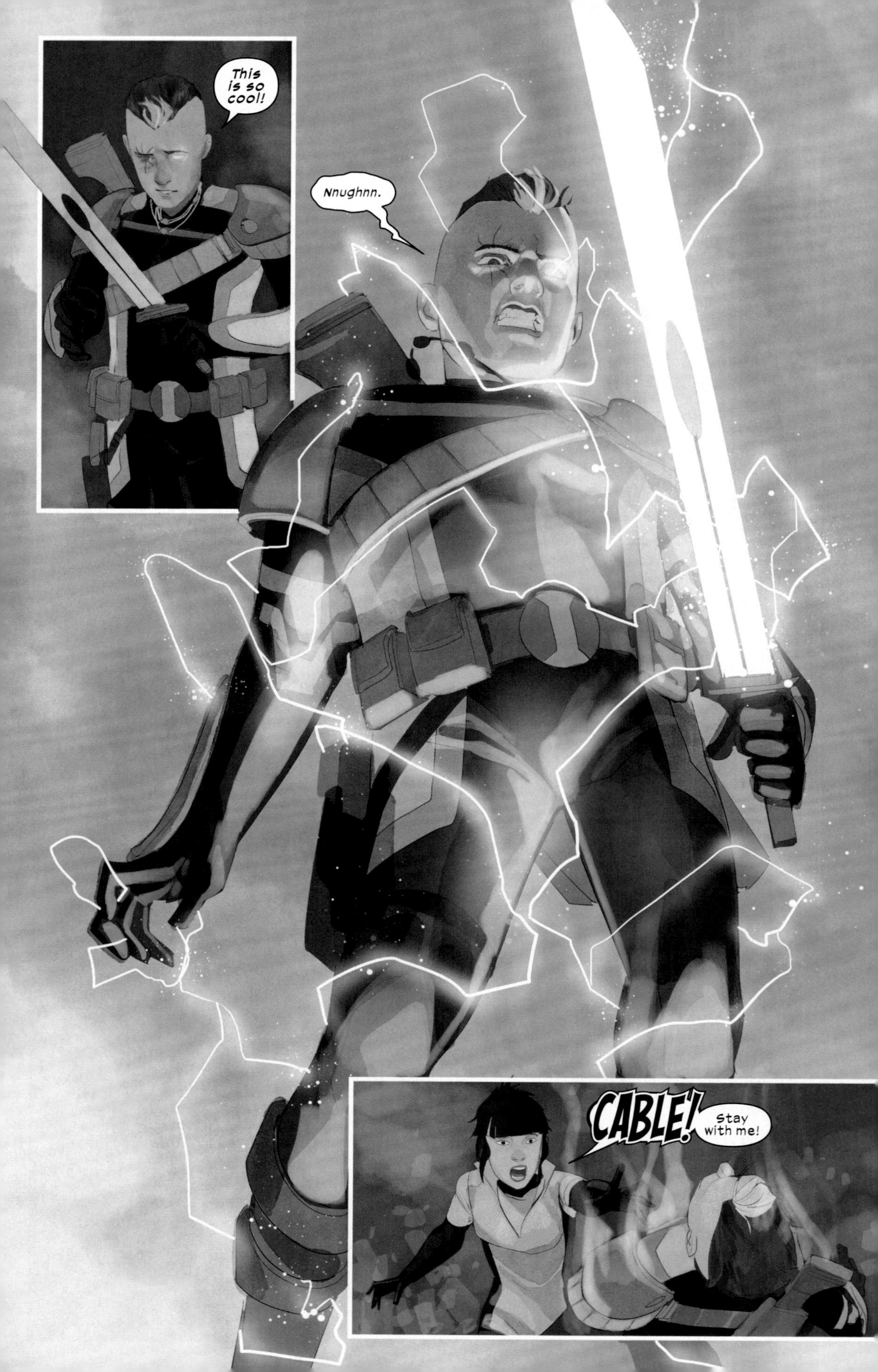
This is so cool!
Nnughnn.
CABLE!
Stay with me!

I hear Armor, but I can't respond. I'm millions of miles away...in the past. I'm in armor of my own... I'm a Spaceknight named *Morn*.

I'm the first of my kind. A progenitor for a new type of warrior, and I wield the *Light of Galador.*

I pursue monsters across the galaxy...

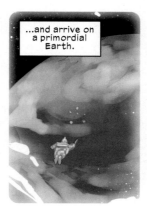

...and arrive on a primordial Earth.

The fight ends like all my others...

...but there is *bigger* prey here.

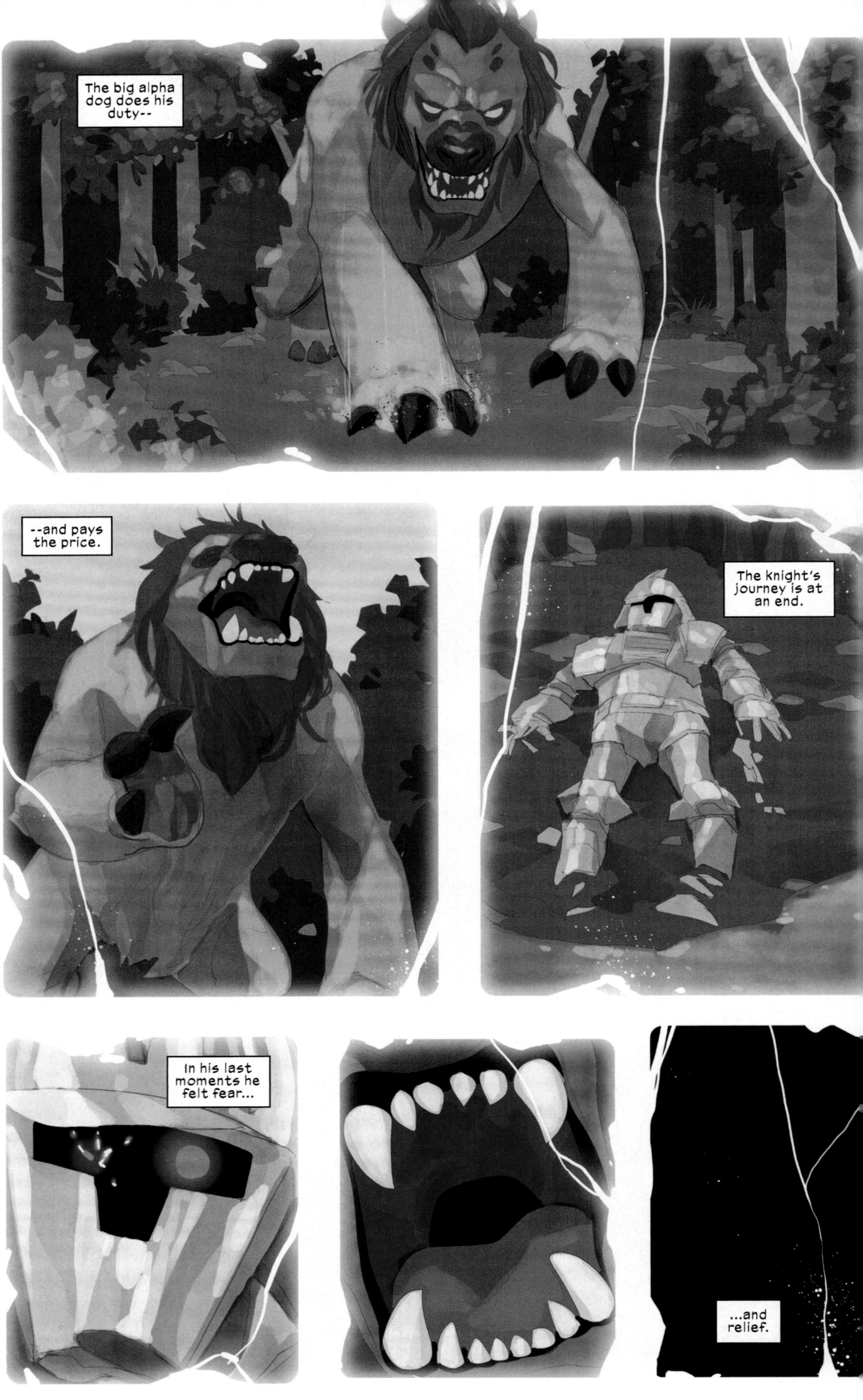
The big alpha dog does his duty--
--and pays the price.
The knight's journey is at an end.
In his last moments he felt fear...
...and relief.

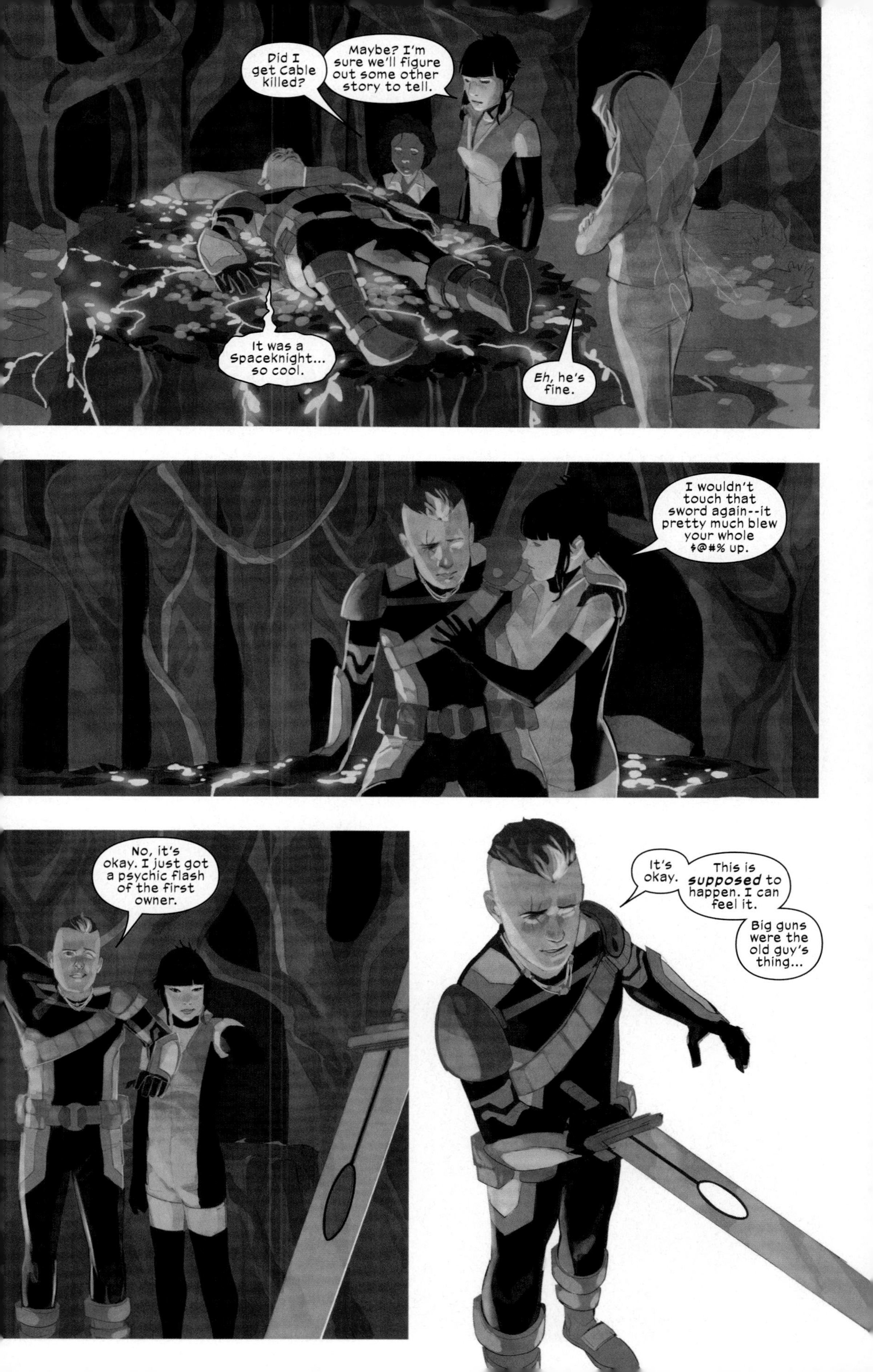
Did I get Cable killed?
Maybe? I'm sure we'll figure out some other story to tell.
It was a Spaceknight... so cool.
Eh, he's fine.
I wouldn't touch that sword again--it pretty much blew your whole $@#% up.
No, it's okay. I just got a psychic flash of the first owner.
It's okay.
This is ***supposed*** to happen. I can feel it.
Big guns were the old guy's thing...

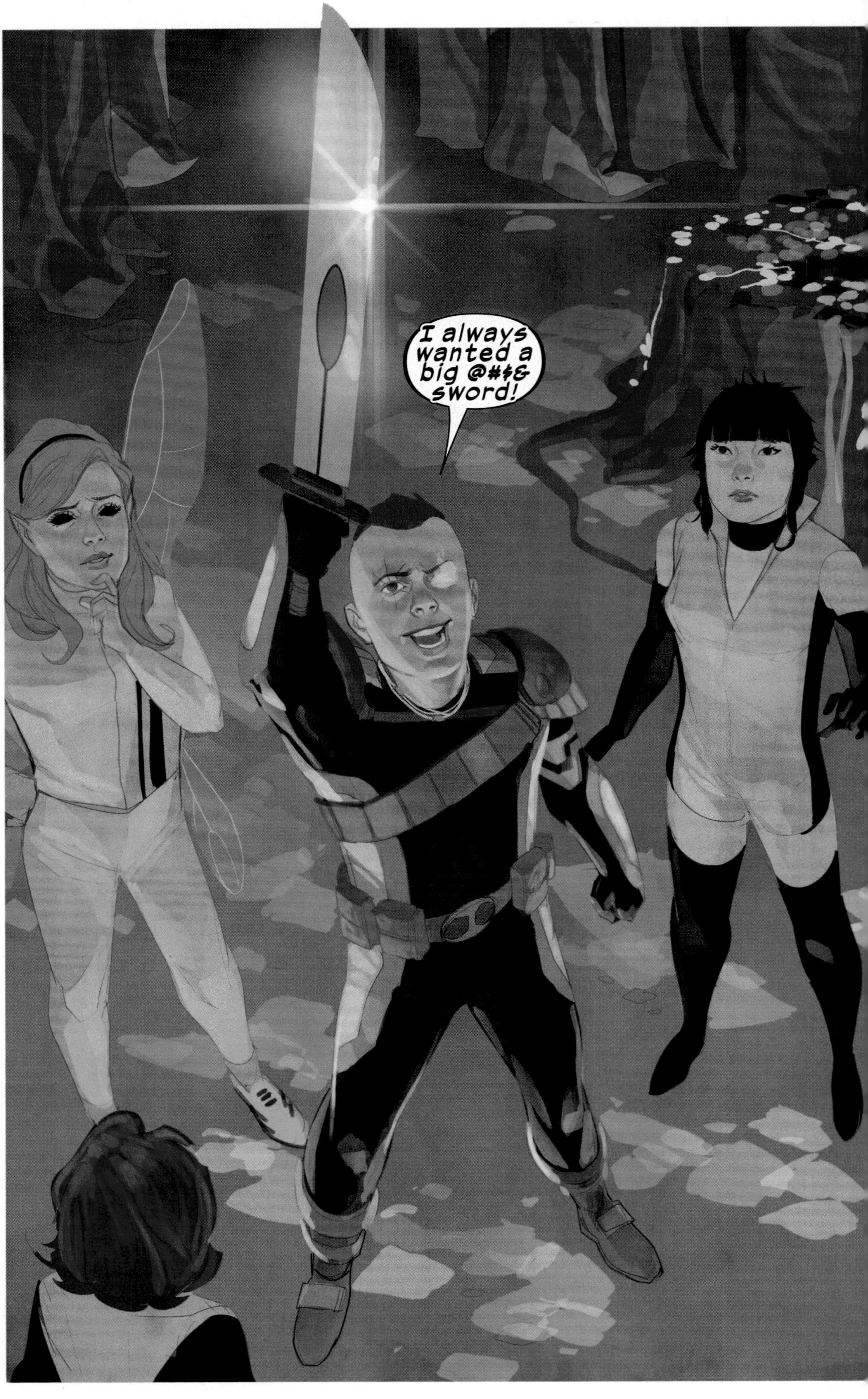
I always wanted a big @#$& sword!

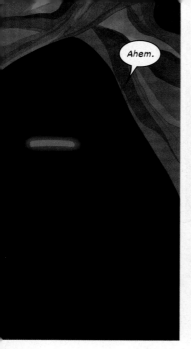

Ahem.

I thought everyone was crystal clear. *No. Monster. Island.*

It was all Cable's idea.

Hi, Dad.

See ya, Cable!

w cool is this? It was stuck in the paw of this huge beast, nd I pulled it out of this wound that wouldn't heal, and when I touched it with my metal arm I got a flash of a knight fighting these dog-like monsters--but it was like a robot knight, not a human.

Hmm.

I think this metal is too *light* to be from Earth...

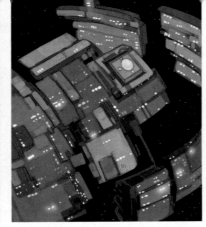

"...I wonder where it came from."

"Welcome to the Bachgigian Museum to Lost Civilizations.

"Even the star we orbit is dying, but don't worry. It won't collapse for a few million years..."

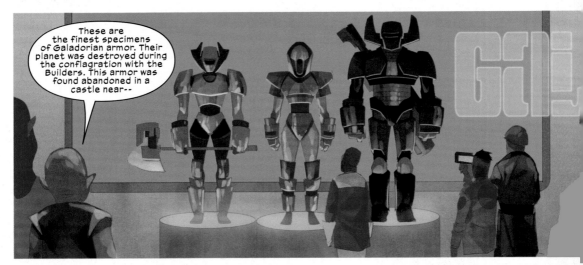

These are the finest specimens of Galadorian armor. Their planet was destroyed during the conflagration with the Builders. This armor was found abandoned in a castle near--

The blade--

--The Light of Galador!

It has been found!

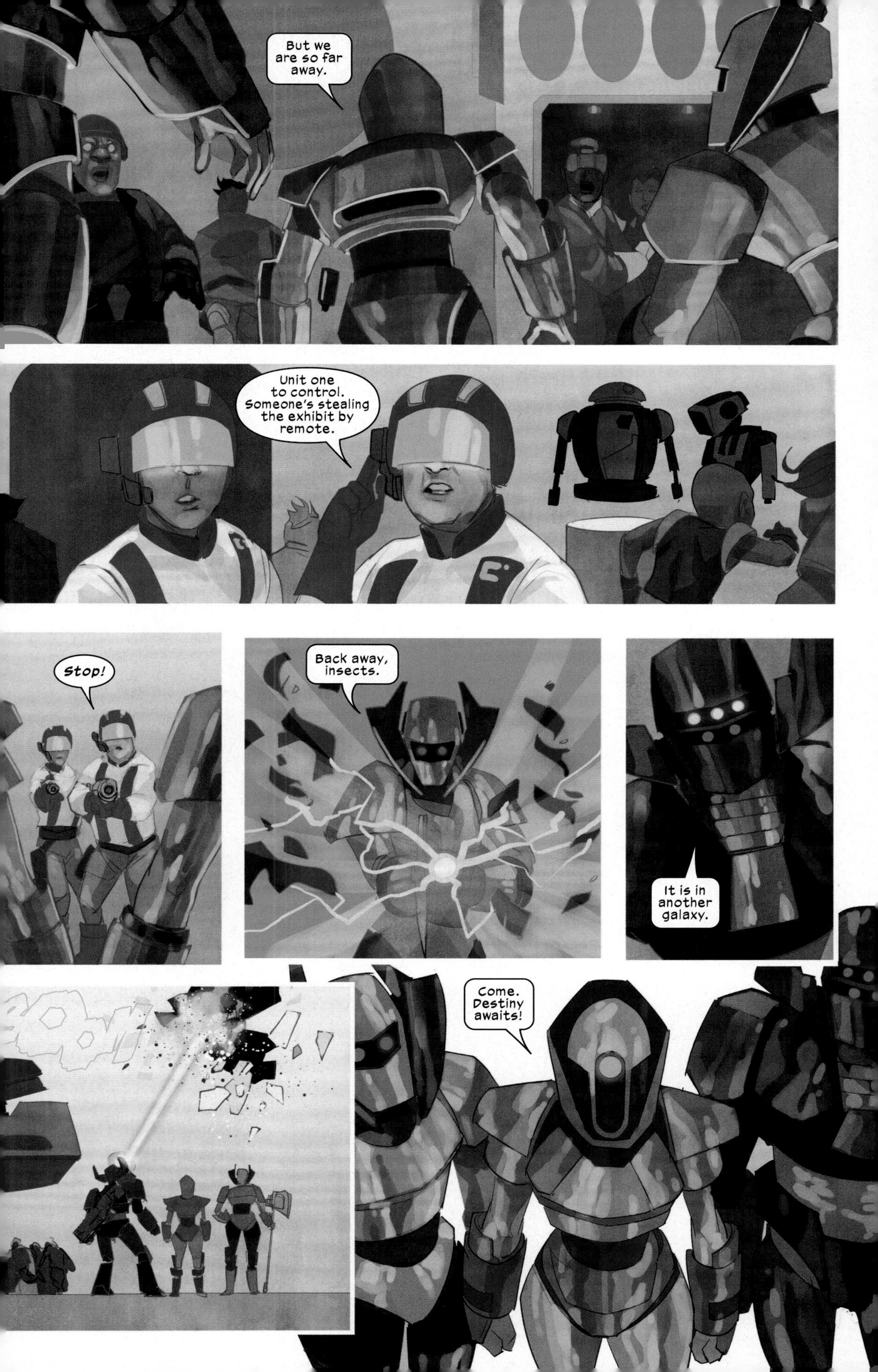

But we are so far away.
Unit one to control. Someone's stealing the exhibit by remote.
Stop!
Back away, insects.
It is in another galaxy.
Come. Destiny awaits!

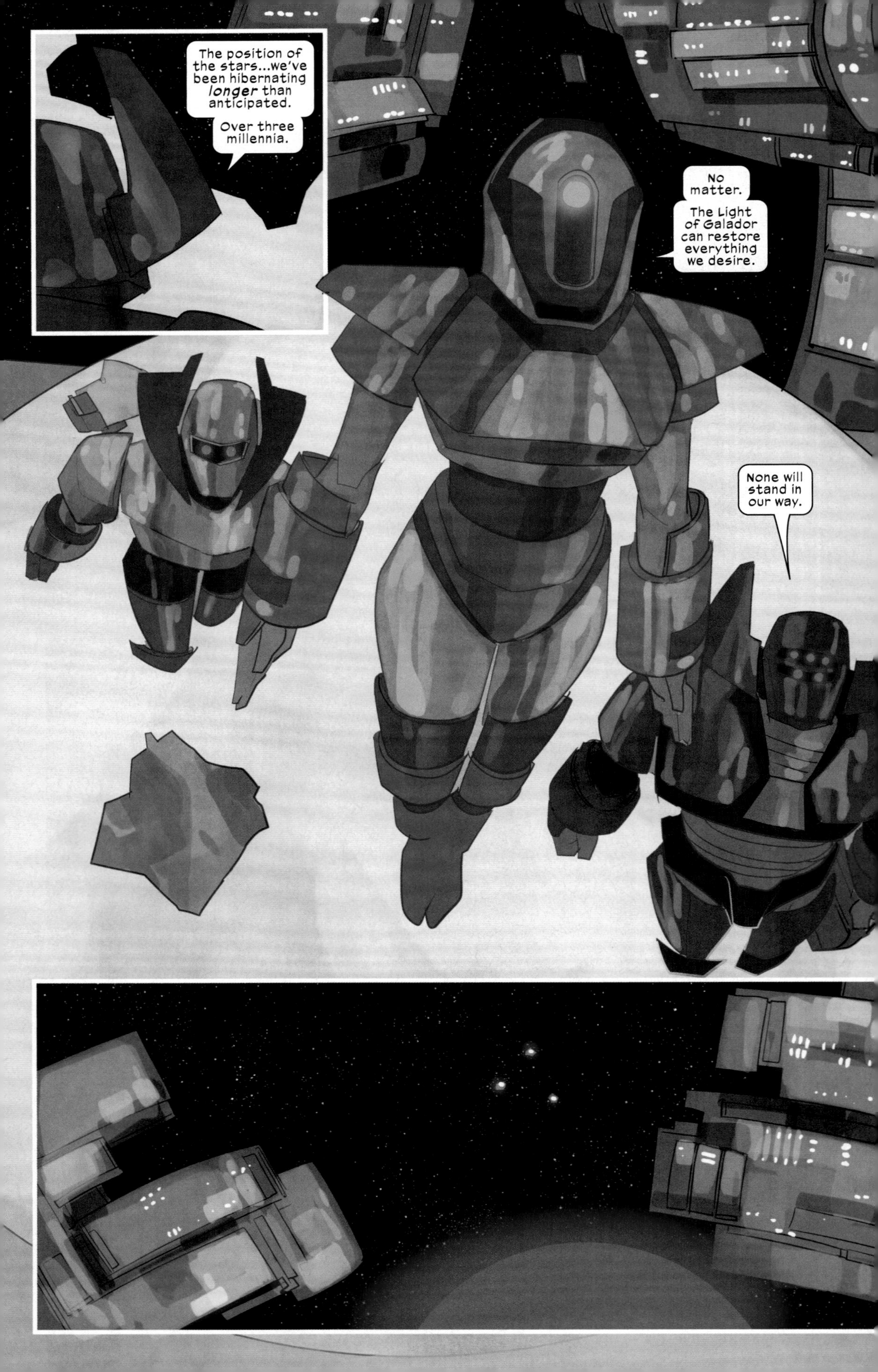

The position of the stars...we've been hibernating *longer* than anticipated.
Over three millennia.
No matter.
The Light of Galador can restore everything we desire.
None will stand in our way.

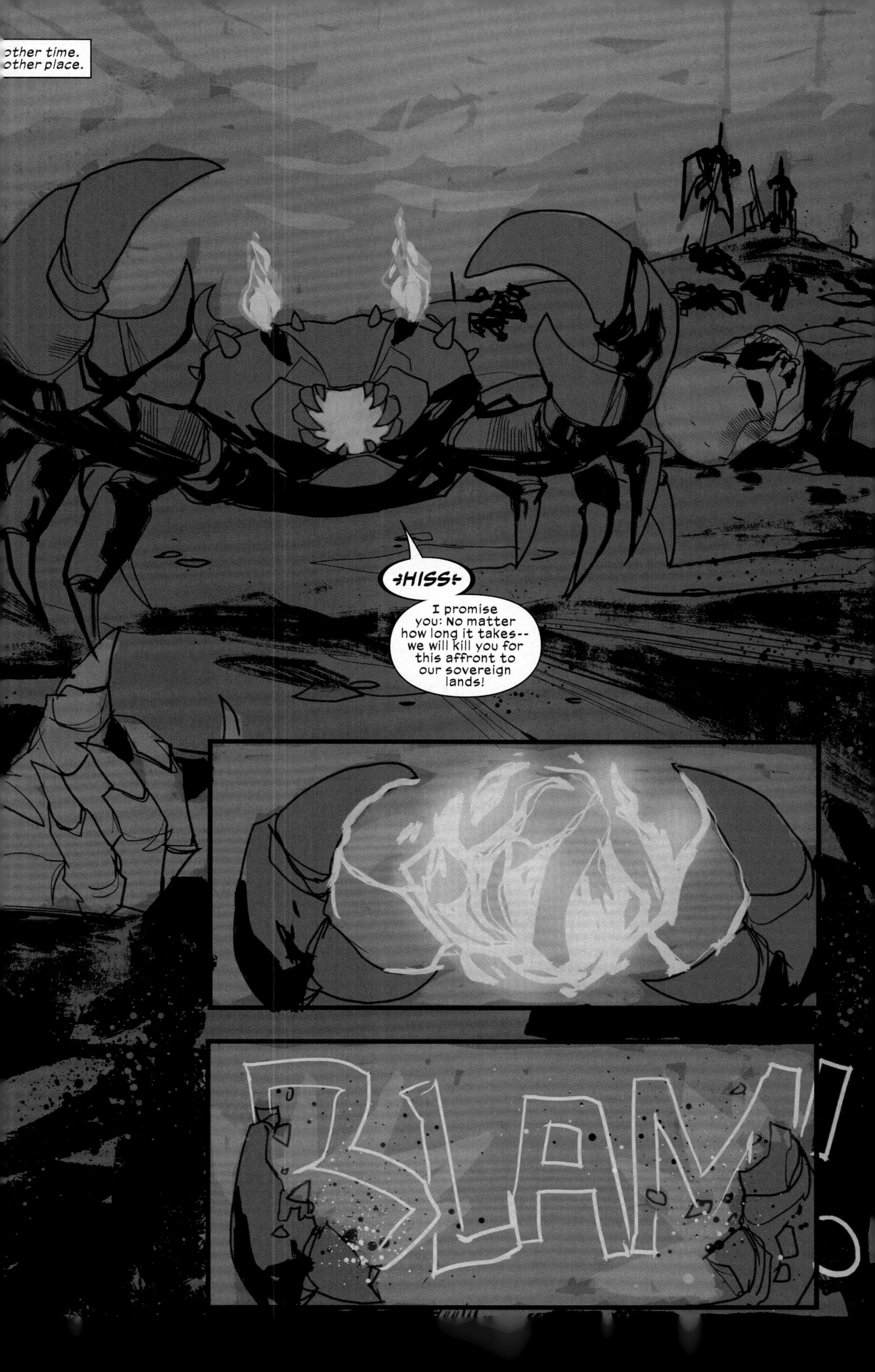
other time.
other place.
HISS
I promise you: No matter how long it takes-- we will kill you for this affront to our sovereign lands!
BLAM!

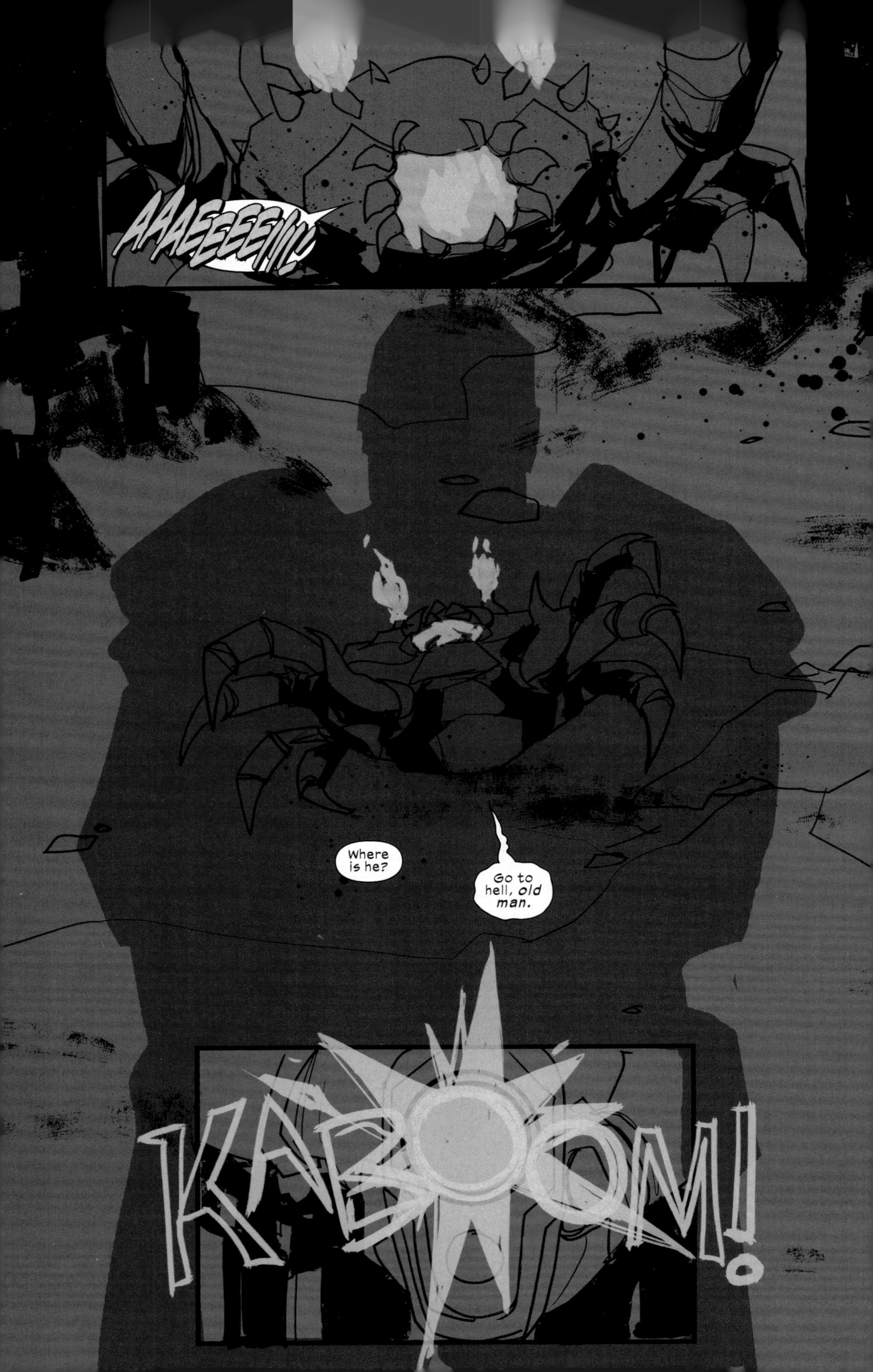
AAAEEEEEIIII!!
Where is he?
Go to hell, *old man.*
KABOOM!

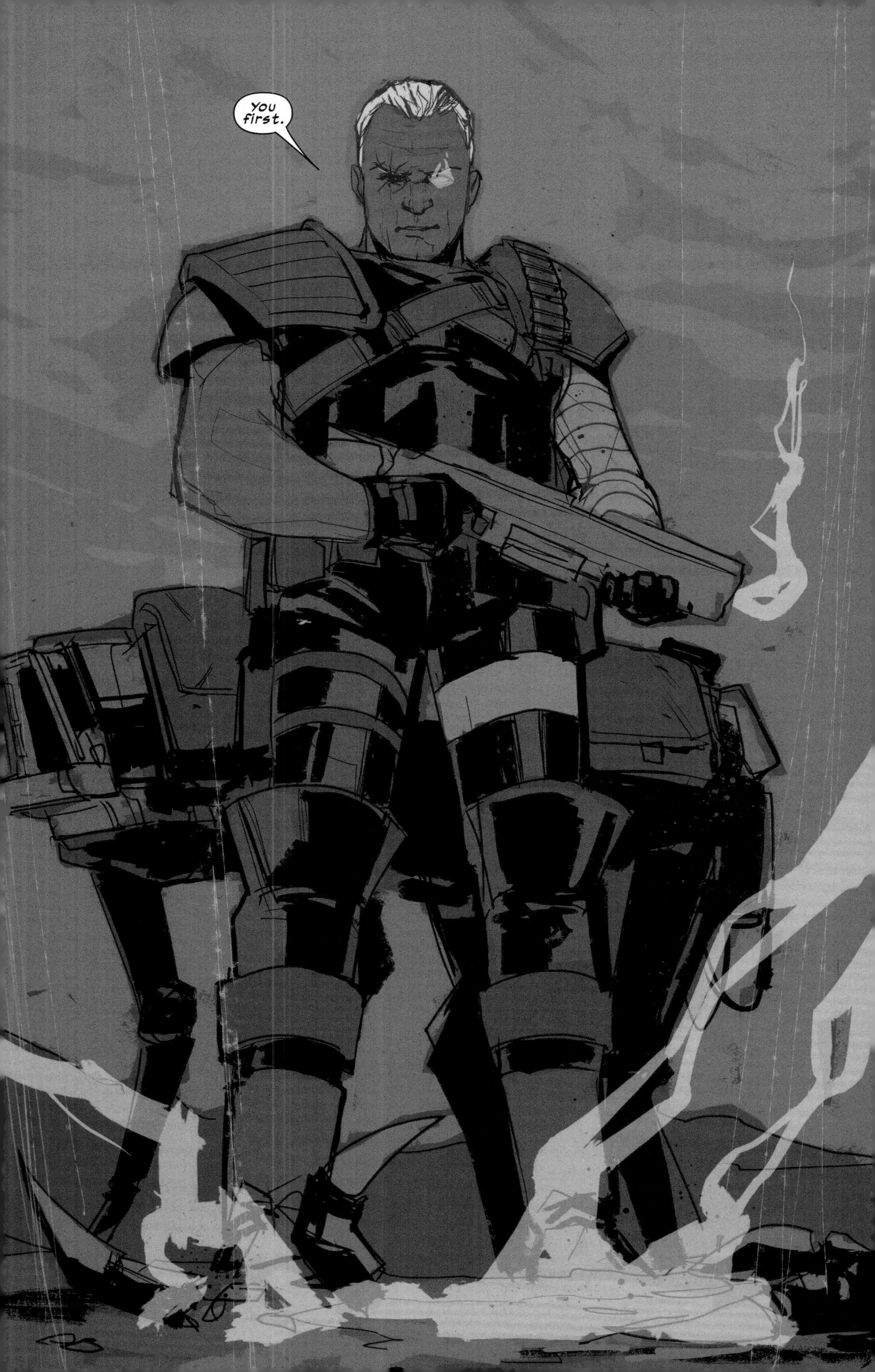
You first.

THE HUNT

Entry 001

I will continue to update this log to include all pertinent details of the hunt in the unlikely event that I fail.

I have rooted out the legion of demons on Earth, but they have fled off-world with hostages. They've cursed me and sworn they will have vengeance. I don't believe in curses, but I do believe in vengeance, so I have arranged transpo to their territory and will pursue them until the job is done.

The lives of the hostages will remain my top priority, but I cannot guarantee their safety or mine.

I am marking my path through this hell with arrows formed of rocks. The locals fear they are magic that they don't understand and are giving them wide berths.

Time is short for the hostages and for Earth. I suspect that the demons are attempting to replicate the old spell that caused Earth to nearly burn in an inferno of Hellfire.

-C

[guns_&_]
[swords_]

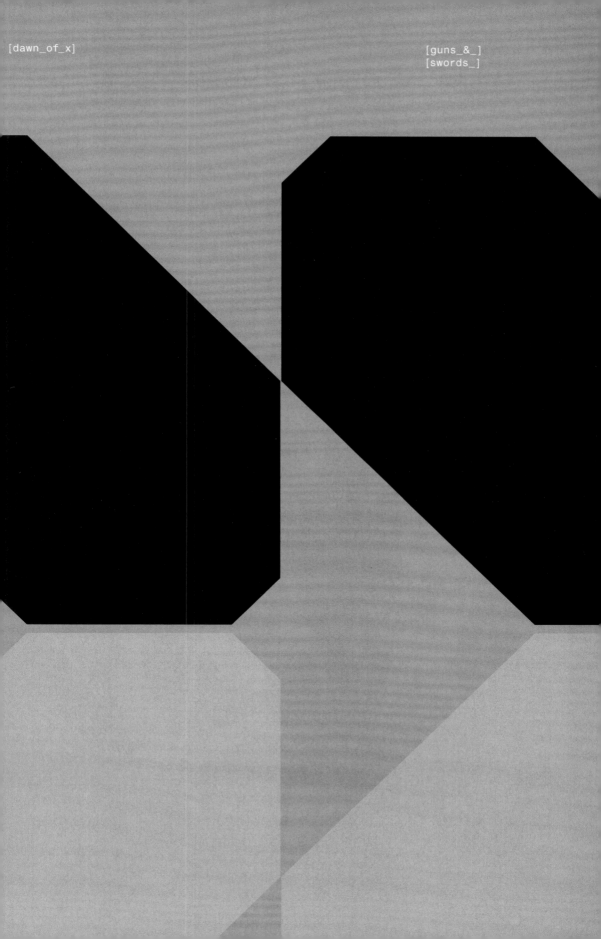

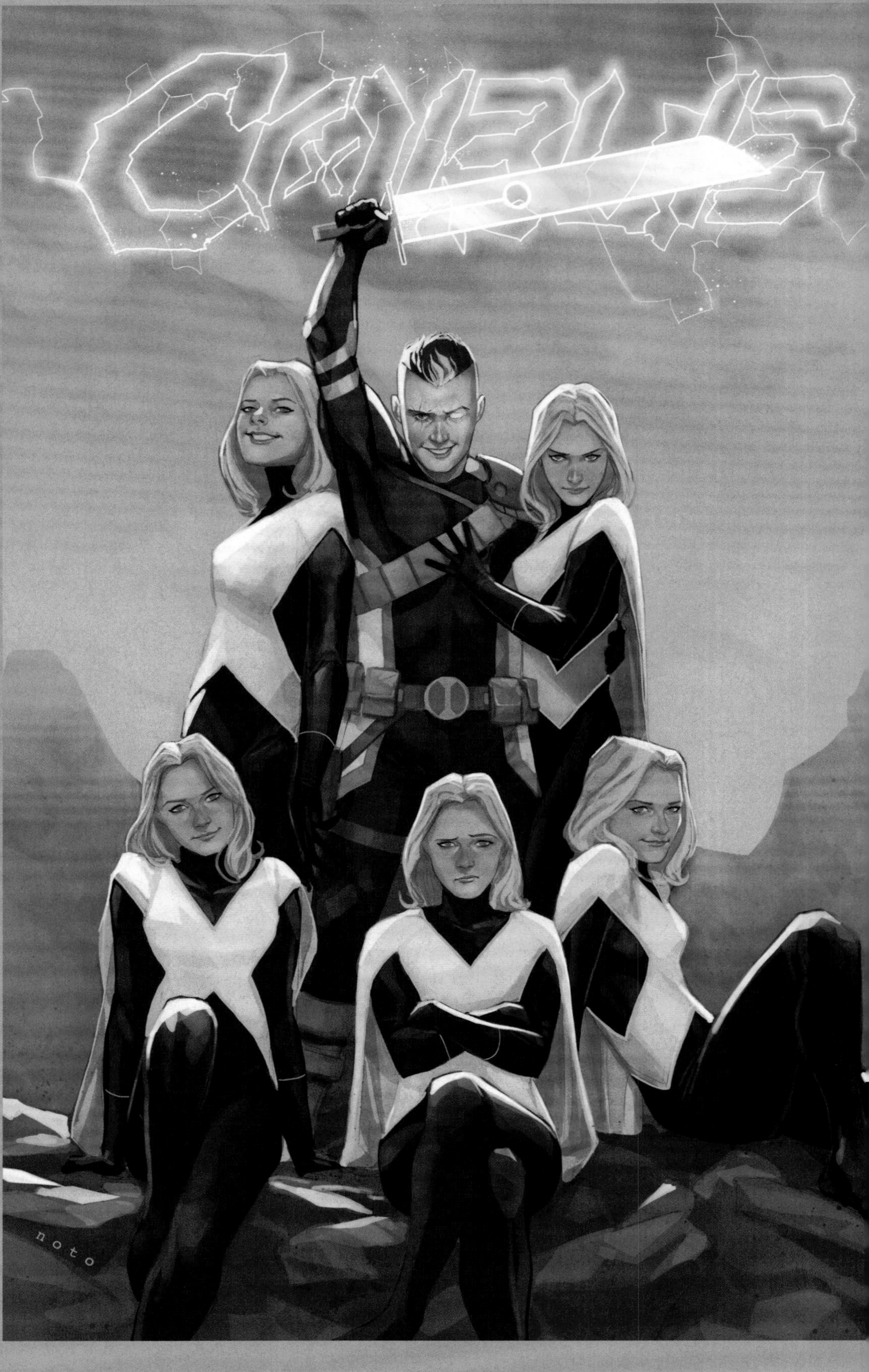
noto

The Five in One

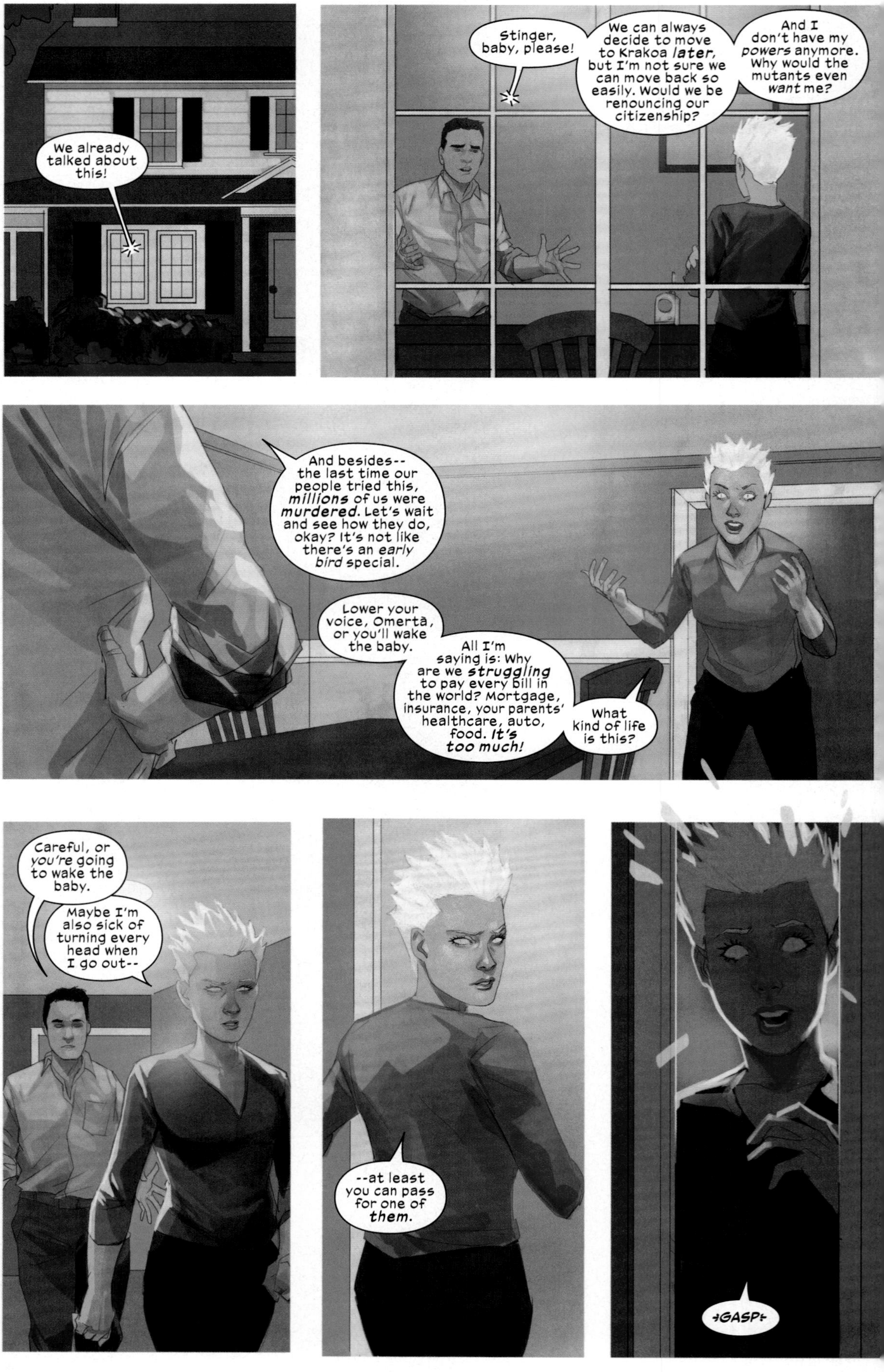
We already talked about this!
Stinger, baby, please!
We can always decide to move to Krakoa *later*, but I'm not sure we can move back so easily. Would we be renouncing our citizenship?
And I don't have my *powers* anymore. Why would the mutants even *want* me?
And besides-- the last time our people tried this, ***millions*** of us were ***murdered***. Let's wait and see how they do, okay? It's not like there's an *early bird* special.
Lower your voice, Omertà, or you'll wake the baby.
All I'm saying is: Why are we ***struggling*** to pay every bill in the world? Mortgage, insurance, your parents' healthcare, auto, food. ***It's too much!***
What kind of life is this?
Careful, or *you're* going to wake the baby.
Maybe I'm also sick of turning every head when I go out--
--at least you can pass for one of ***them***.
GASP

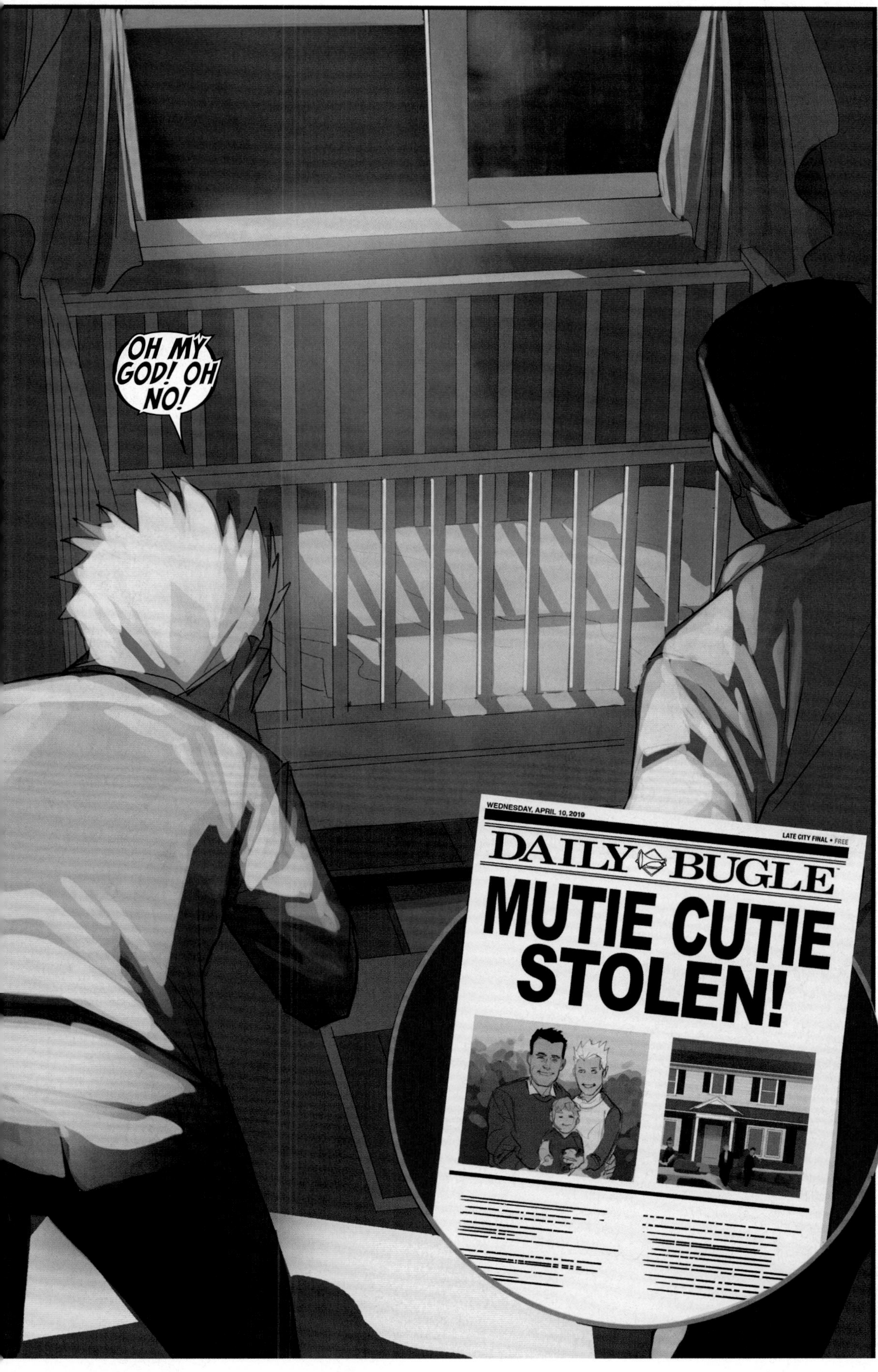
OH MY GOD! OH NO!
WEDNESDAY, APRIL 10, 2019
LATE CITY FINAL • FREE
DAILY BUGLE
MUTIE CUTIE STOLEN!

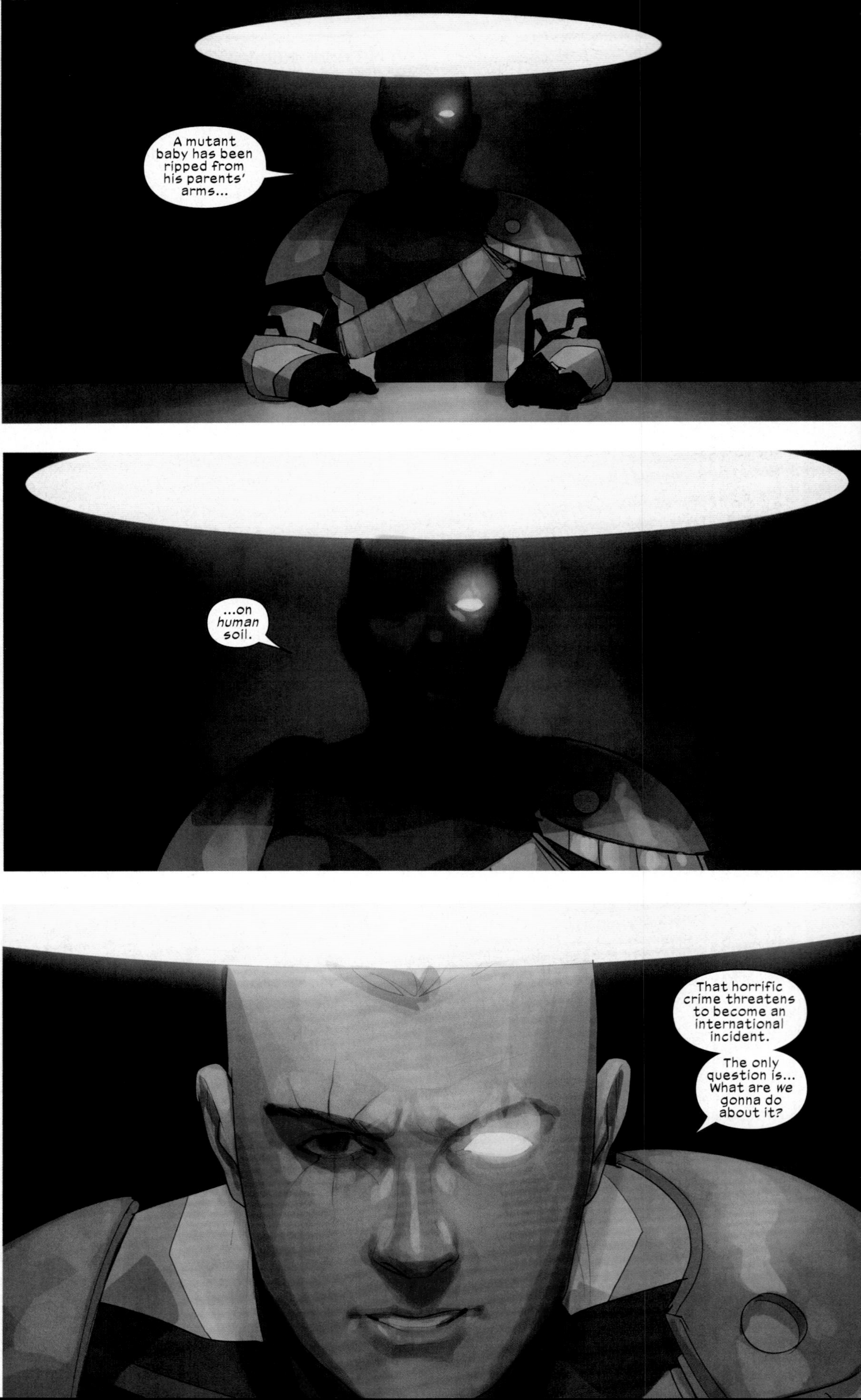

A mutant baby has been ripped from his parents' arms...
...on *human* soil.
That horrific crime threatens to become an international incident.
The only question is... What are *we* gonna do about it?

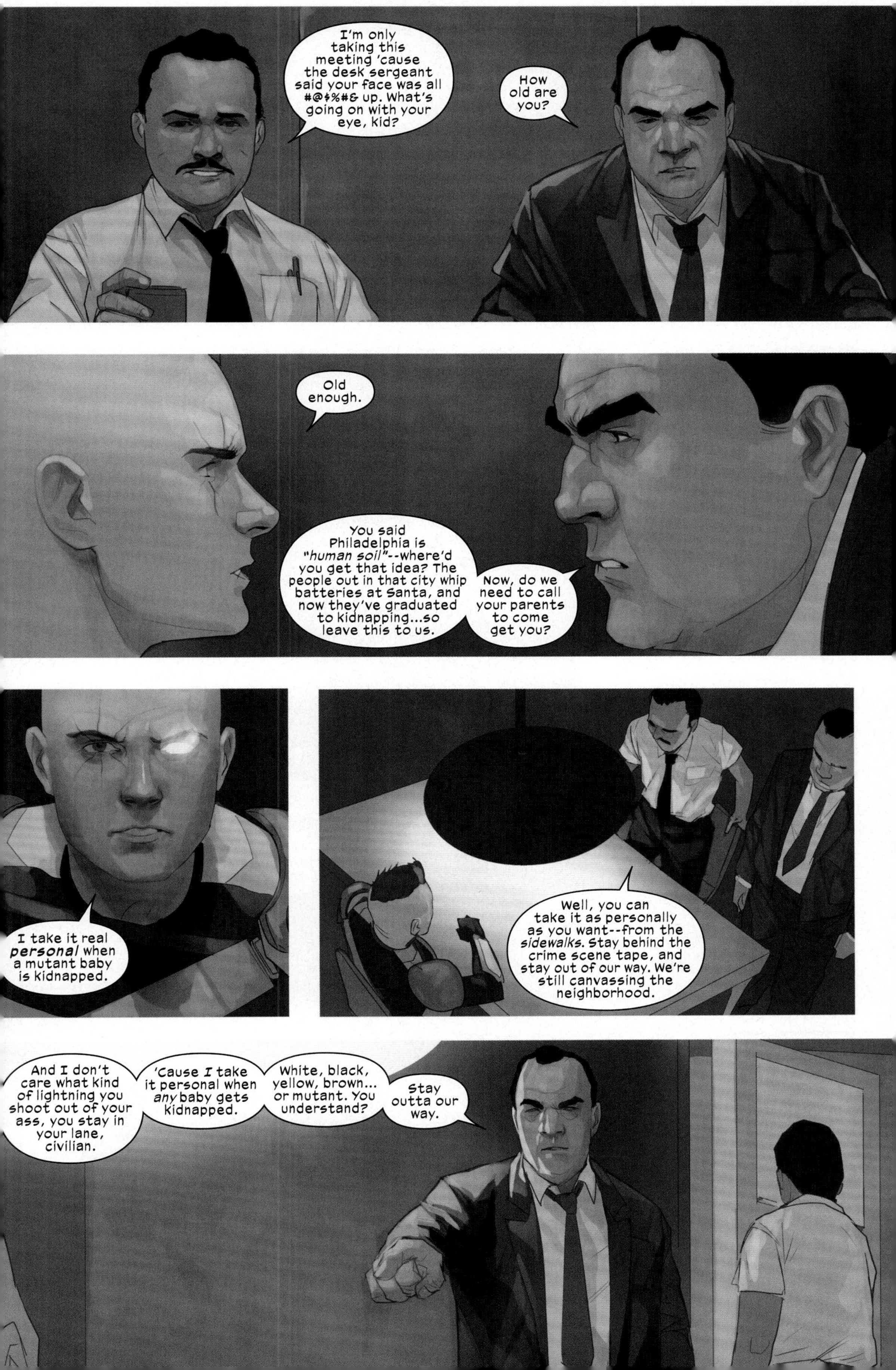
I'm only taking this meeting 'cause the desk sergeant said your face was all #@$%#& up. What's going on with your eye, kid?
How old are you?
Old enough.
You said Philadelphia is "*human soil*"--where'd you get that idea? The people out in that city whip batteries at Santa, and now they've graduated to kidnapping...so leave this to us.
Now, do we need to call your parents to come get you?
I take it real ***personal*** when a mutant baby is kidnapped.
Well, you can take it as personally as you want--from the *sidewalks*. Stay behind the crime scene tape, and stay out of our way. We're still canvassing the neighborhood.
And I don't care what kind of lightning you shoot out of your ass, you stay in your lane, civilian.
'Cause *I* take it personal when *any* baby gets kidnapped.
White, black, yellow, brown... or mutant. You understand?
Stay outta our way.

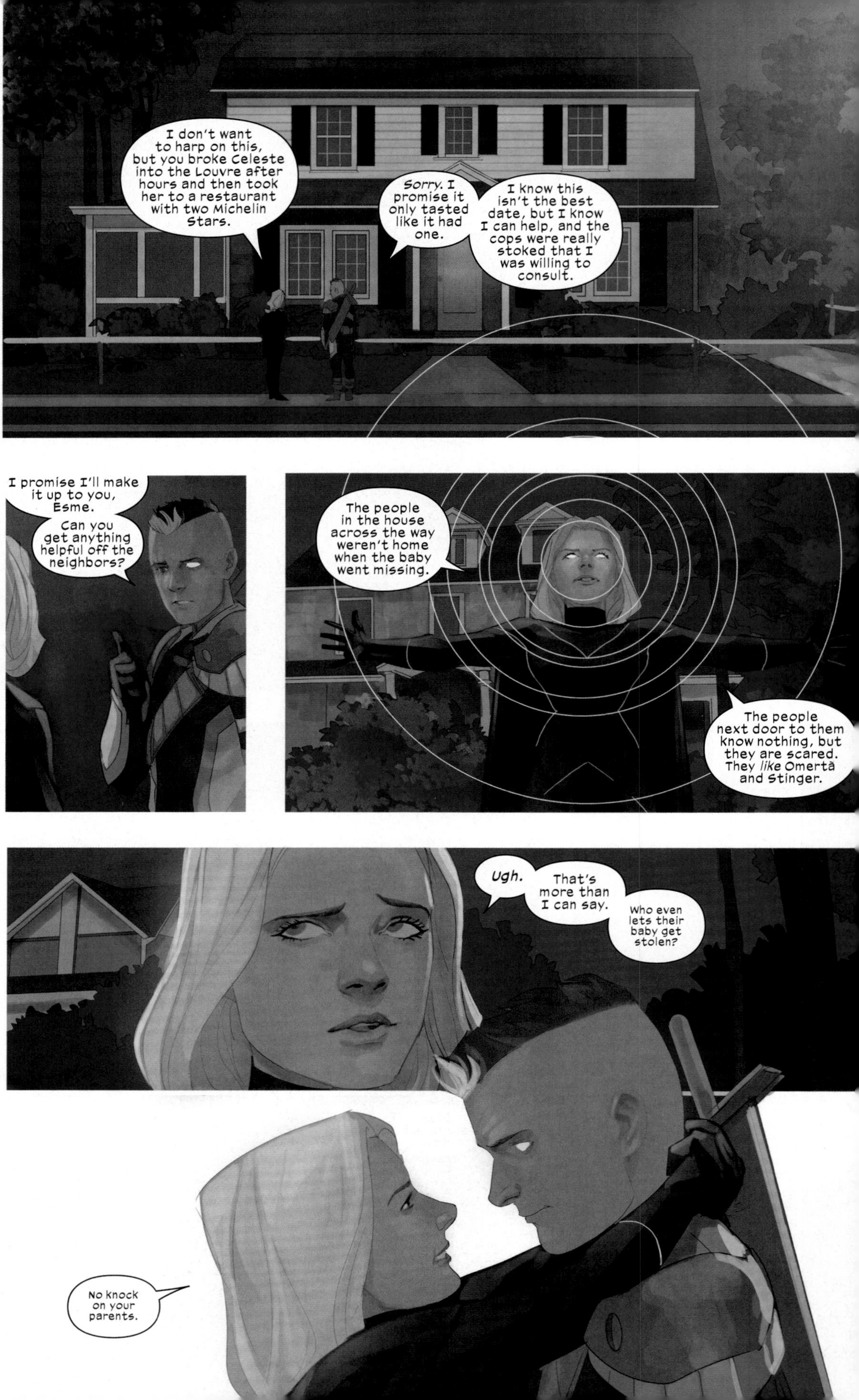
I don't want to harp on this, but you broke Celeste into the Louvre after hours and then took her to a restaurant with two Michelin Stars.
Sorry. I promise it only tasted like it had one.
I know this isn't the best date, but I know I can help, and the cops were really stoked that I was willing to consult.
I promise I'll make it up to you, Esme.
Can you get anything helpful off the neighbors?
The people in the house across the way weren't home when the baby went missing.
The people next door to them know nothing, but they are scared. They *like* Omertà and Stinger.
Ugh.
That's more than I can say.
Who even lets their baby get stolen?
No knock on your parents.

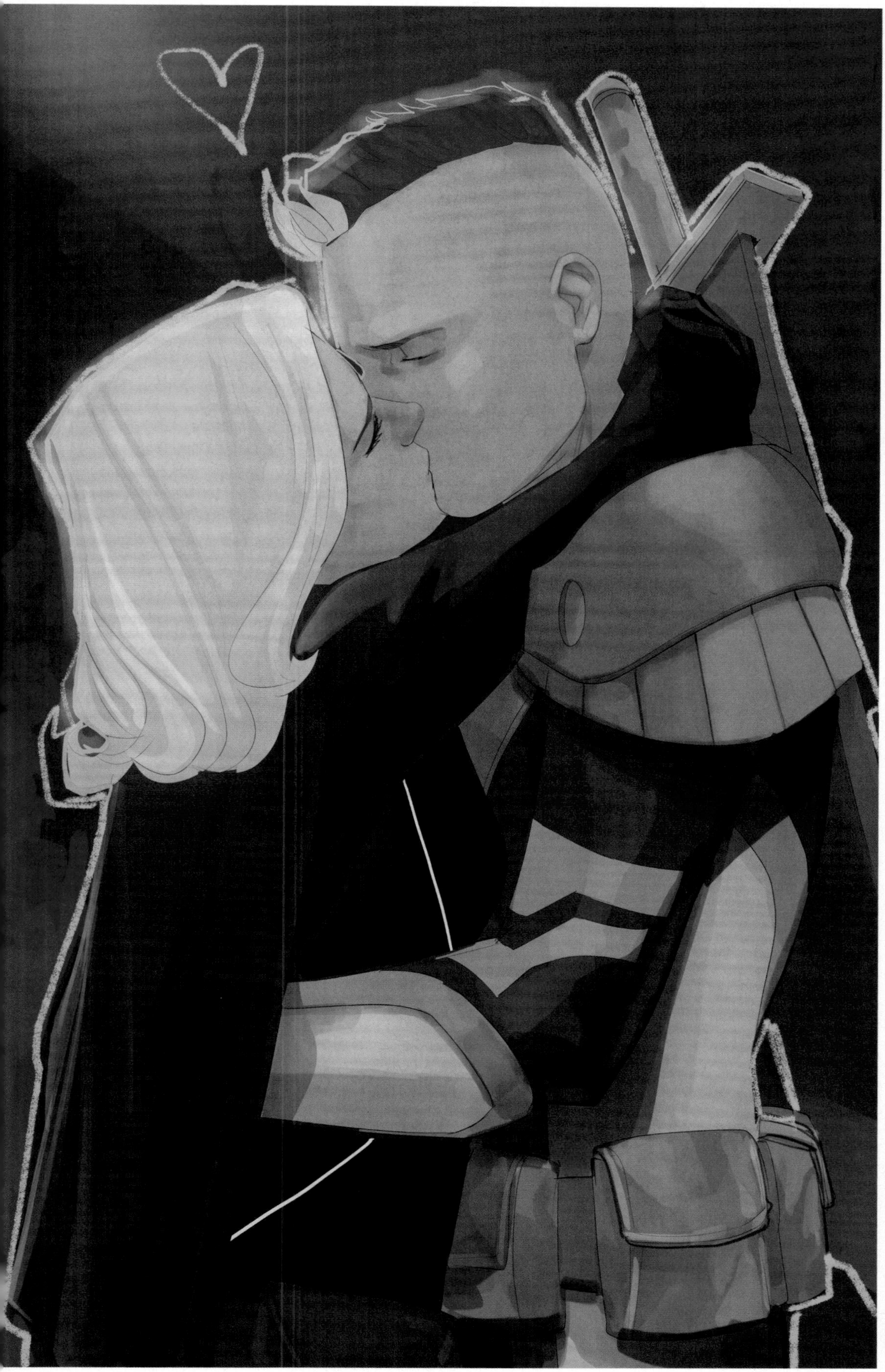

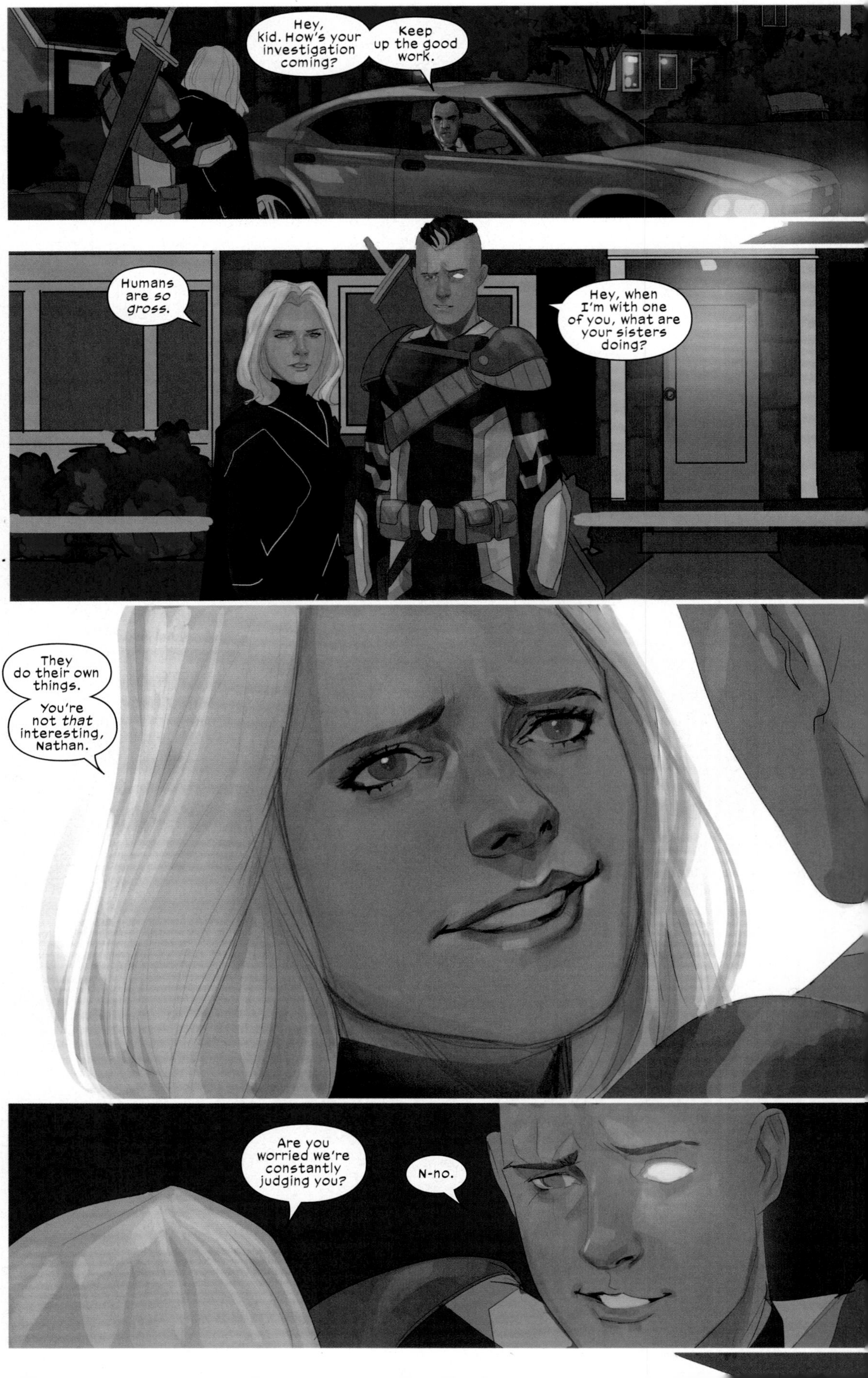

Hey, kid. How's your investigation coming?
Keep up the good work.
Humans are so *gross.*
Hey, when I'm with one of you, what are your sisters doing?
They do their own things.
You're not *that* interesting, Nathan.
Are you worried we're constantly judging you?
N-no.

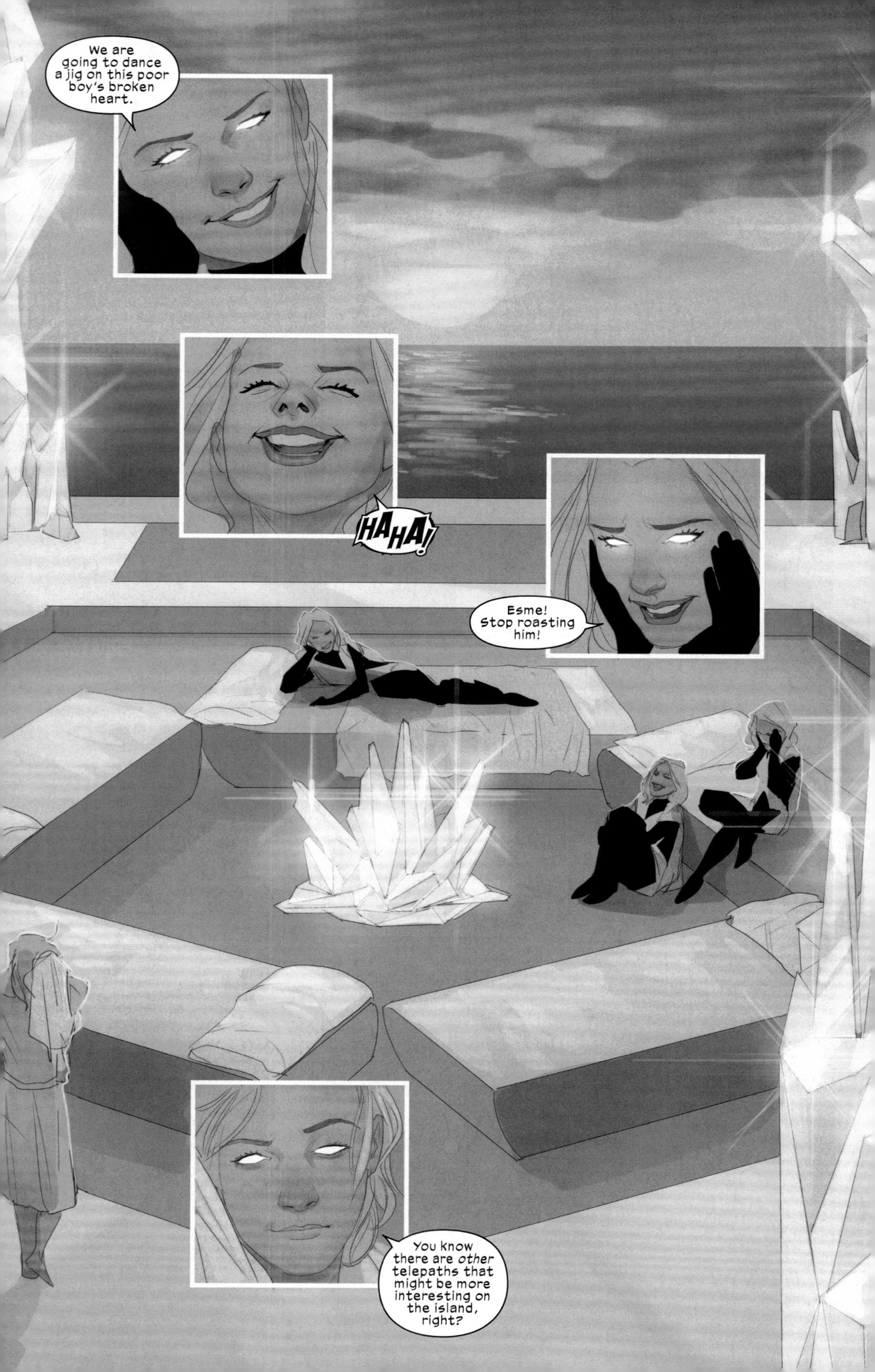
We are going to dance a jig on this poor boy's broken heart.
HAHA!
Esme! Stop roasting him!
You know there are *other* telepaths that might be more interesting on the island, right?

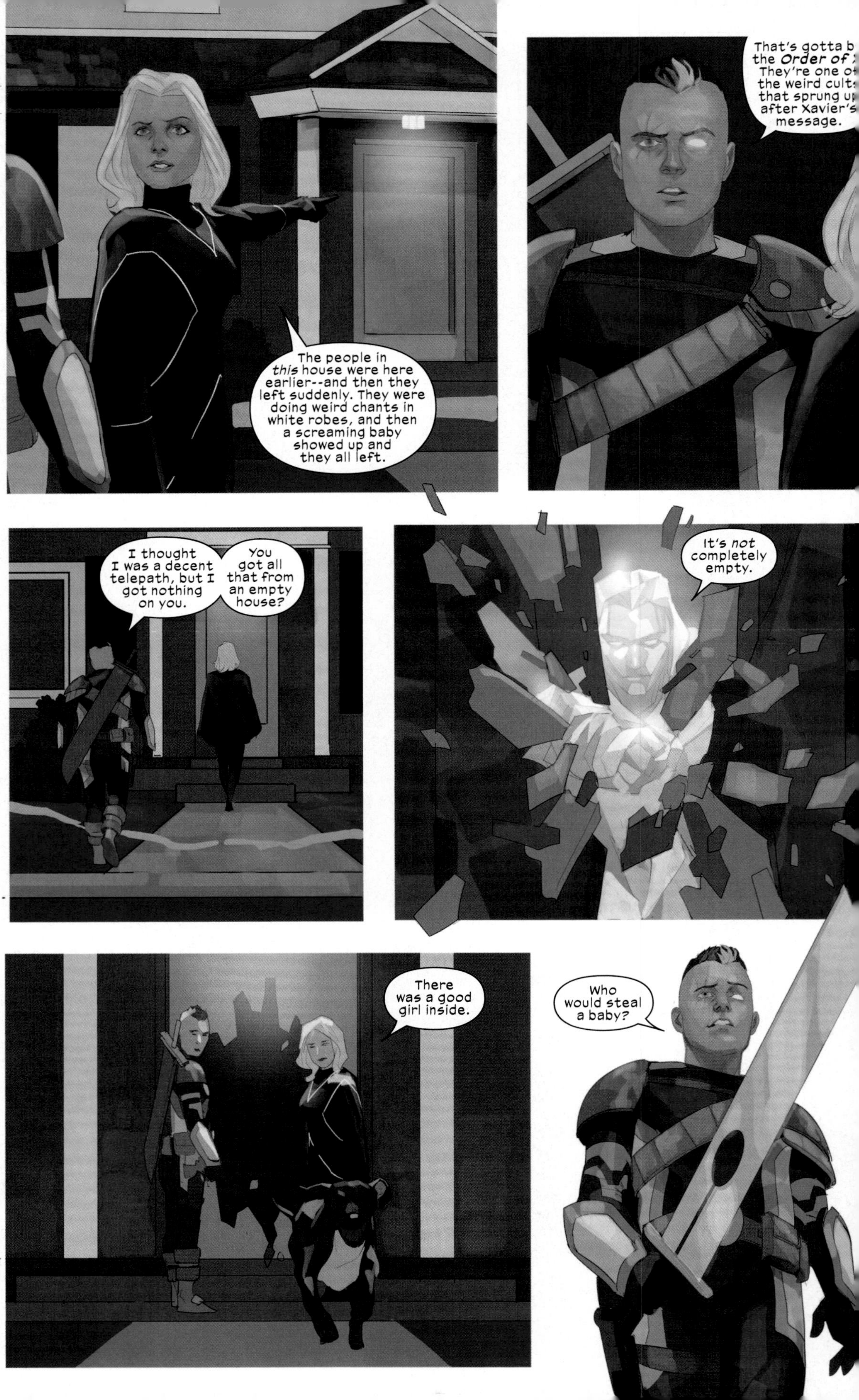
The people in *this* house were here earlier--and then they left suddenly. They were doing weird chants in white robes, and then a screaming baby showed up and they all left.
That's gotta b the *Order of* They're one o the weird cult that sprung u after Xavier's message.
I thought I was a decent telepath, but I got nothing on you.
You got all that from an empty house?
It's *not* completely empty.
There was a good girl inside.
Who would steal a baby?

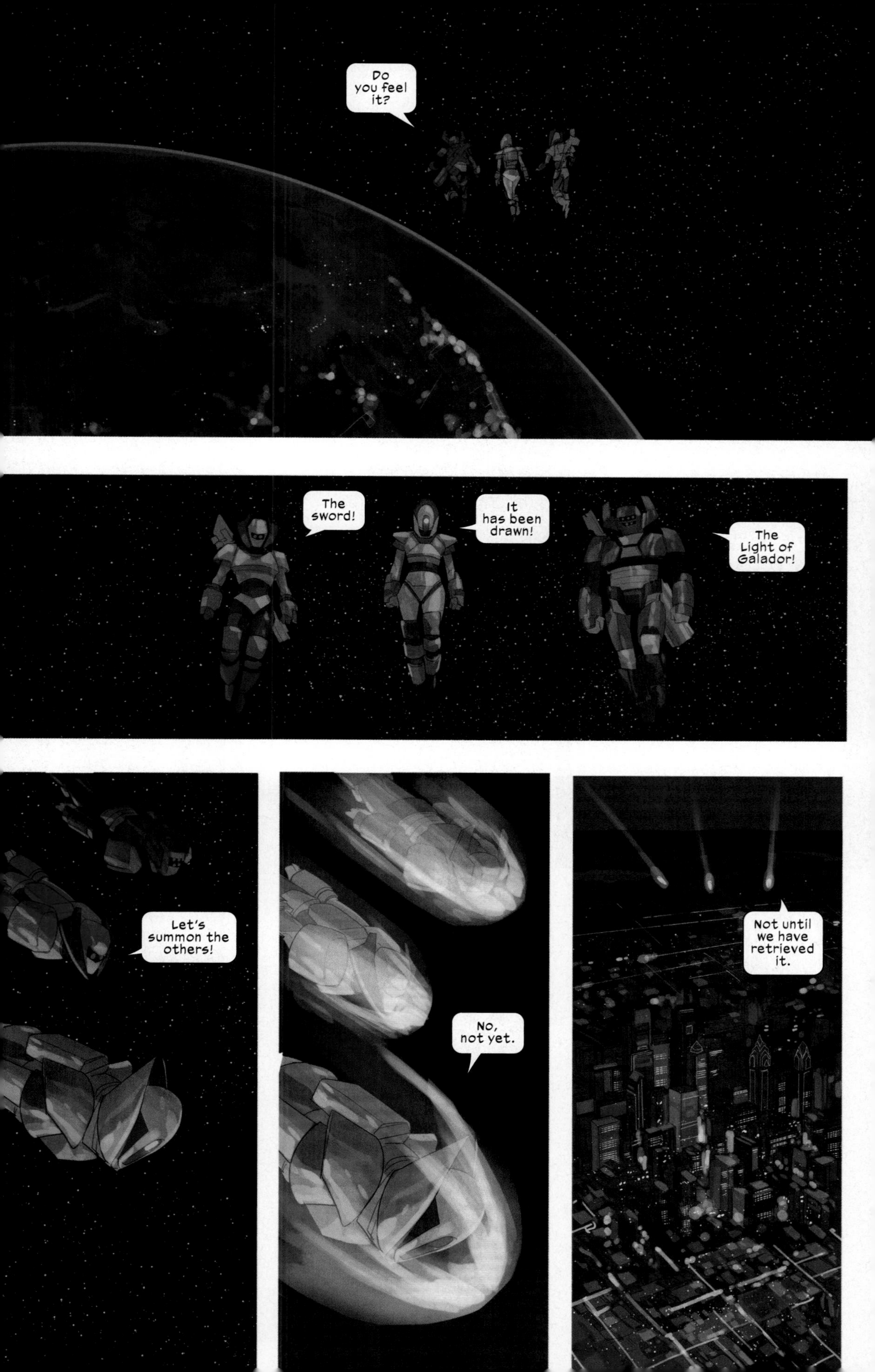
Do you feel it?
The sword!
It has been drawn!
The Light of Galador!
Let's summon the others!
No, not yet.
Not until we have retrieved it.

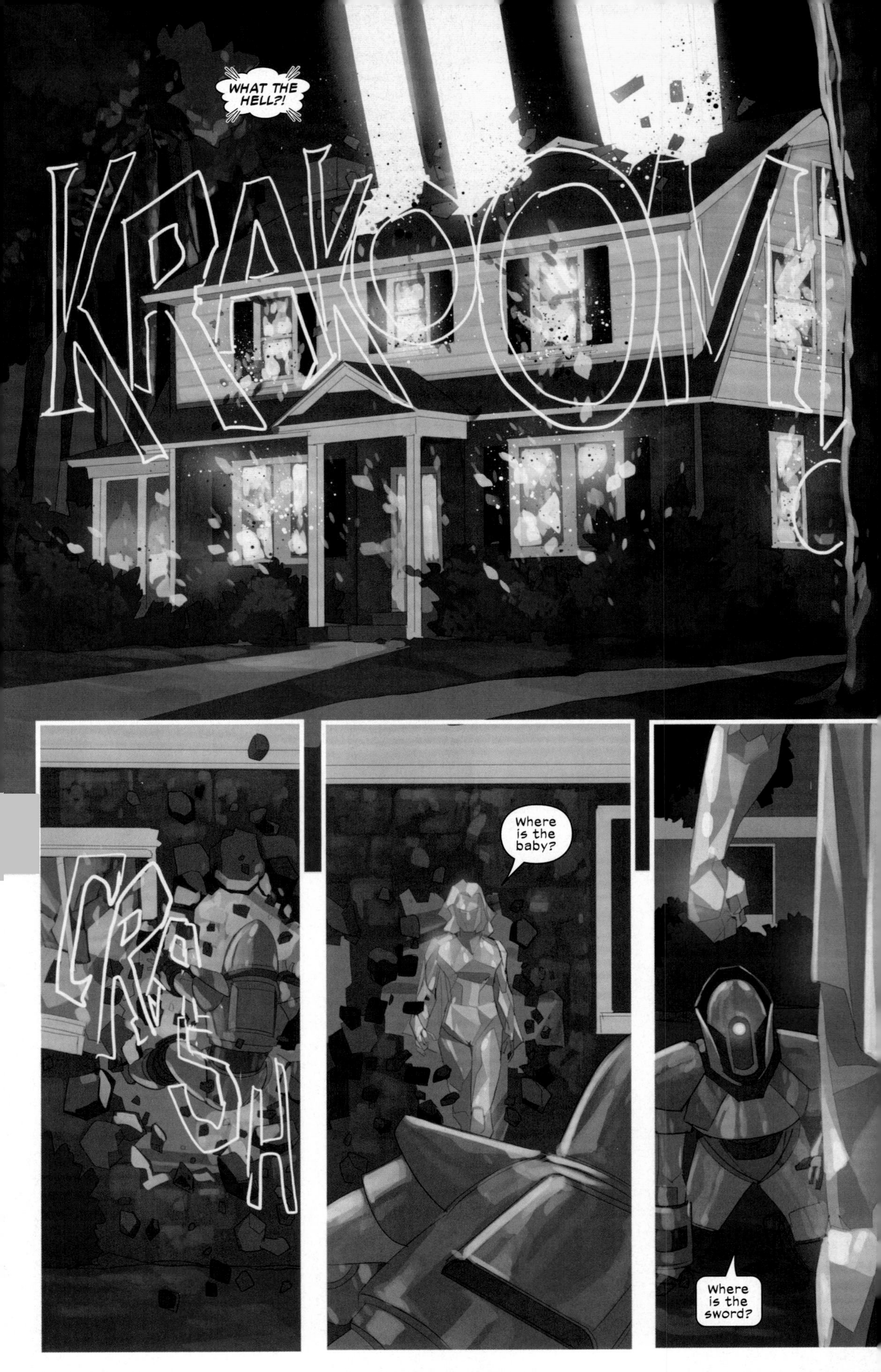
WHAT THE HELL?!
KRAKOOM
CRASH
Where is the baby?
Where is the sword?

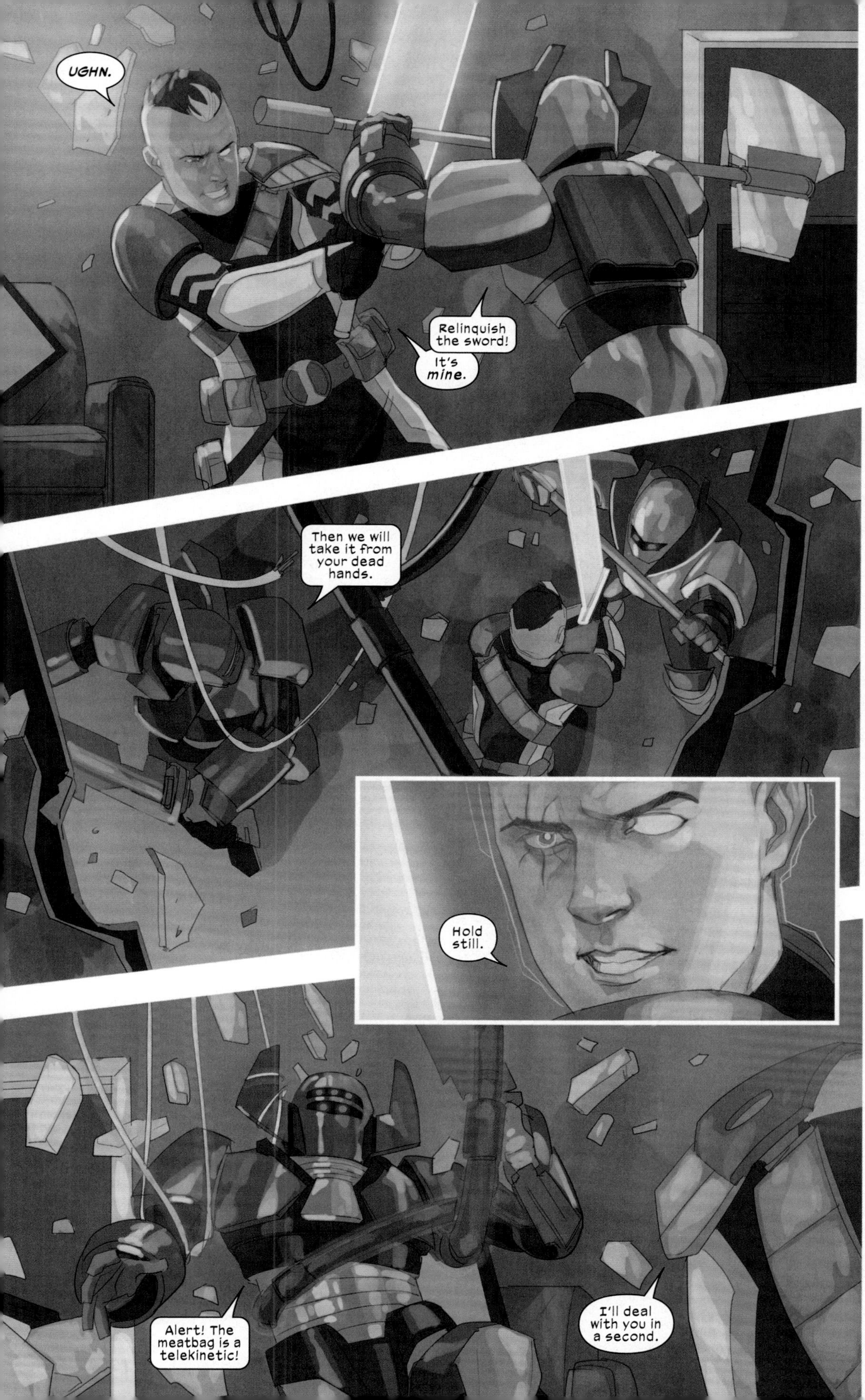
UGHN.
Relinquish the sword!
It's *mine*.
Then we will take it from your dead hands.
Hold still.
Alert! The meatbag is a telekinetic!
I'll deal with you in a second.

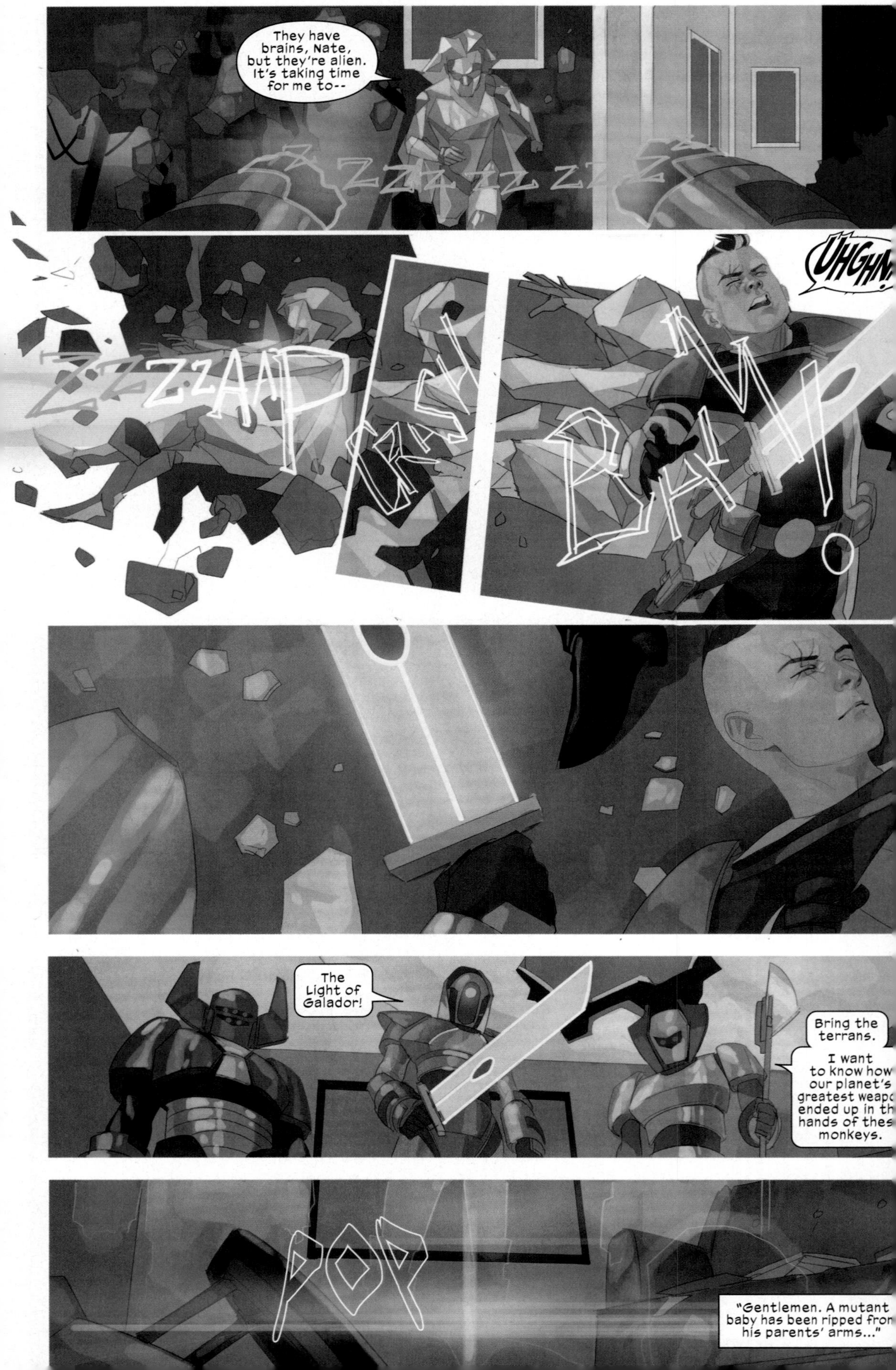

They have brains, Nate, but they're alien. It's taking time for me to--
ZZZZZZZZZ
ZZZZZAAP
CRASH
BRAM
UHGHN!
The Light of Galador!
Bring the terrans.
I want to know how our planet's greatest weapo ended up in th hands of thes monkeys.
POP
"Gentlemen. A mutant baby has been ripped fron his parents' arms..."

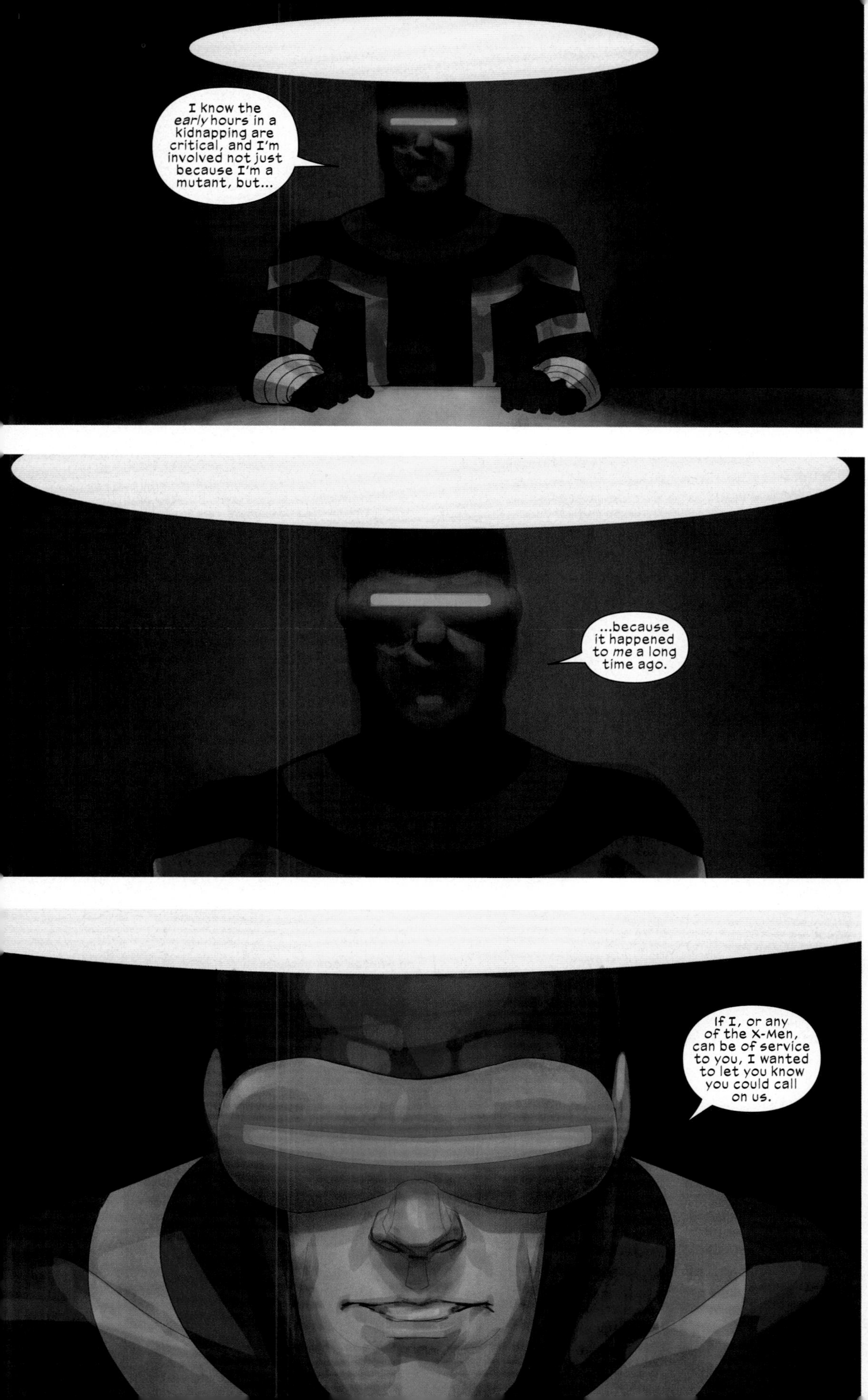
I know the *early* hours in a kidnapping are critical, and I'm involved not just because I'm a mutant, but...
...because it happened to *me* a long time ago.
If I, or any of the X-Men, can be of service to you, I wanted to let you know you could call on us.

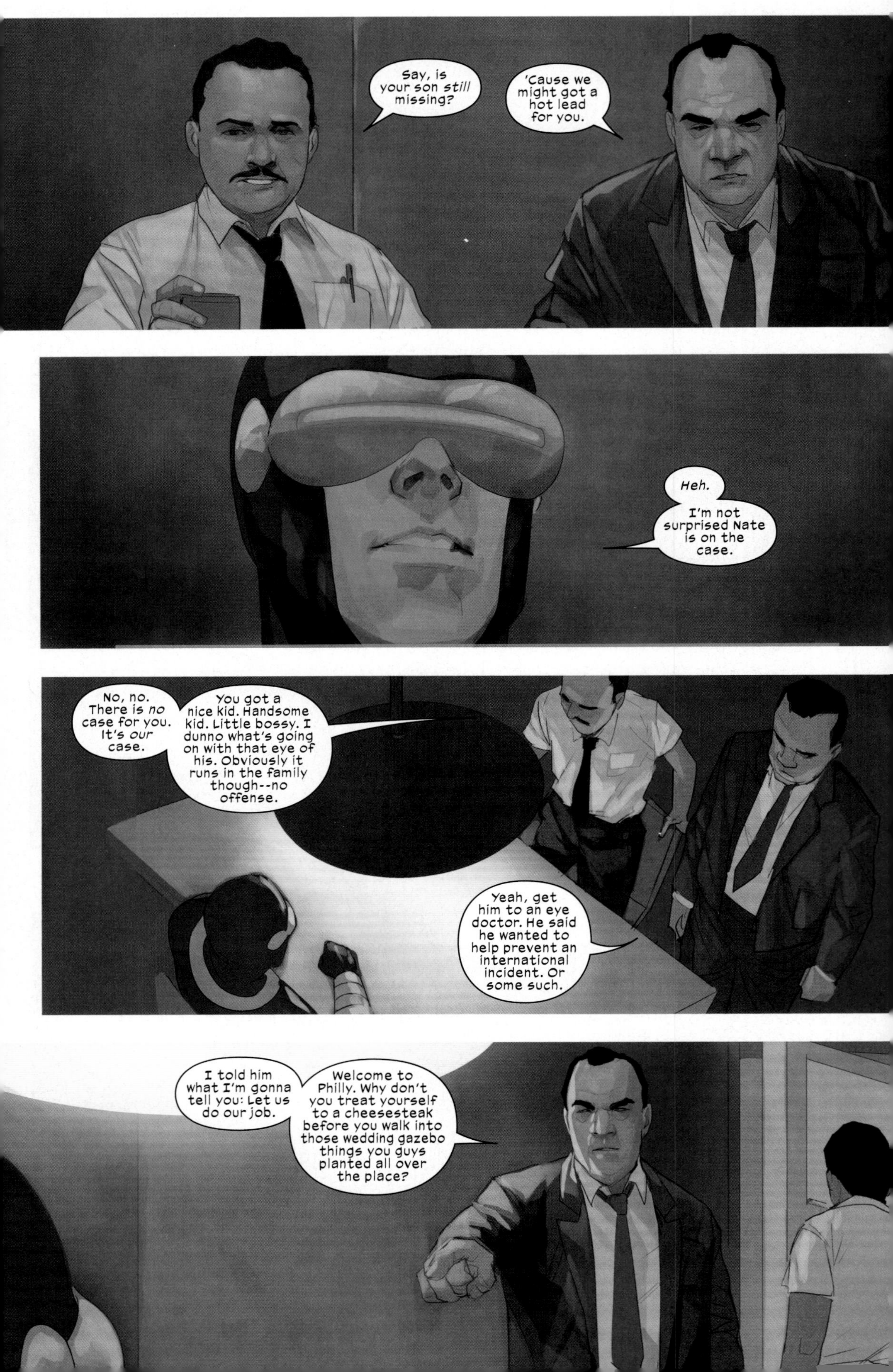
Say, is your son *still* missing?
'Cause we might got a hot lead for you.
Heh.
I'm not surprised Nate is on the case.
No, no. There is *no* case for you. It's *our* case.
You got a nice kid. Handsome kid. Little bossy. I dunno what's going on with that eye of his. Obviously it runs in the family though--no offense.
Yeah, get him to an eye doctor. He said he wanted to help prevent an international incident. Or some such.
I told him what I'm gonna tell you: Let us do our job.
Welcome to Philly. Why don't you treat yourself to a cheesesteak before you walk into those wedding gazebo things you guys planted all over the place?

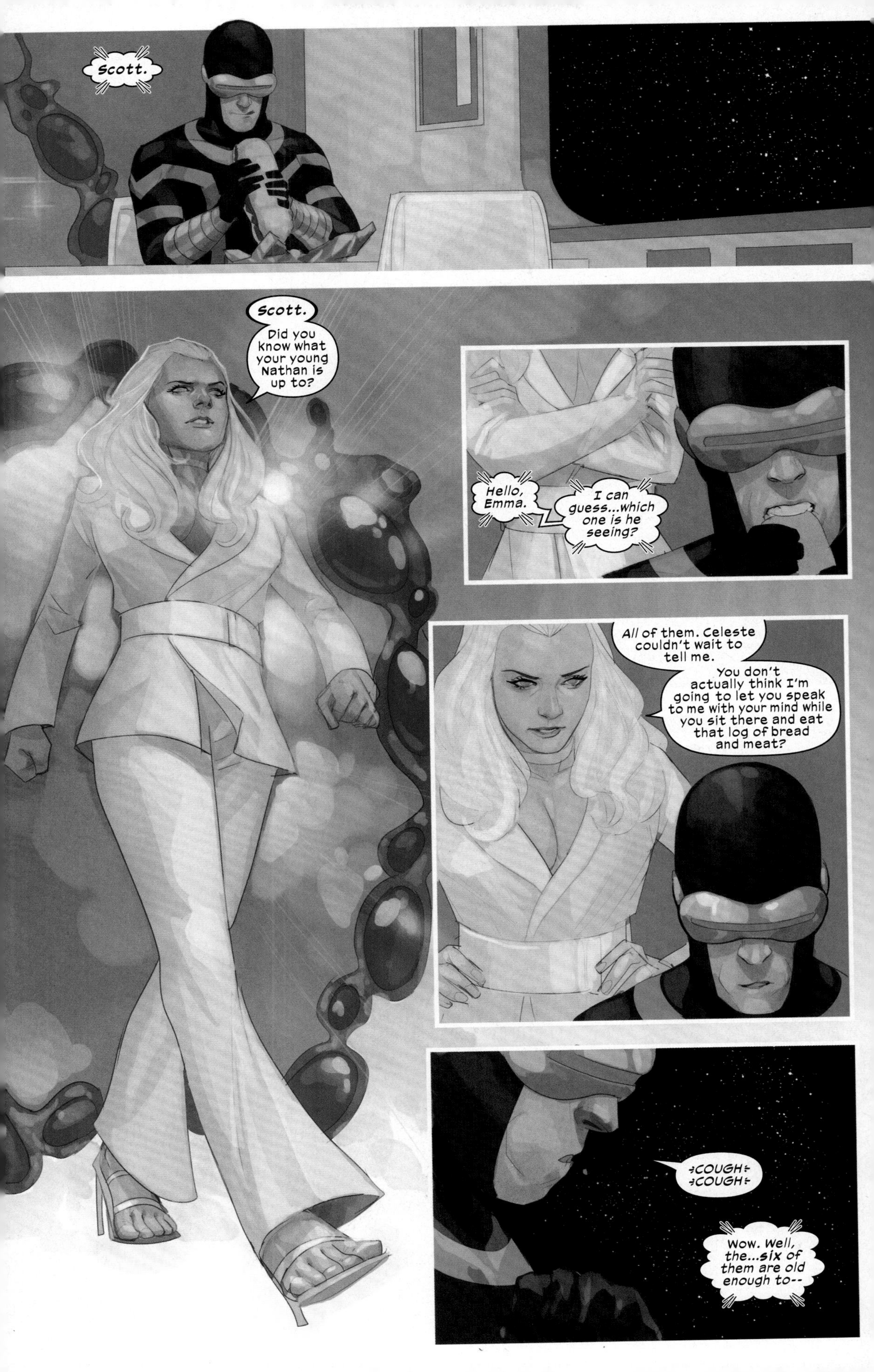
Scott.
Scott.
Did you know what your young Nathan is up to?
Hello, Emma.
I can guess...which one is he seeing?
All of them. Celeste couldn't wait to tell me.
You don't actually think I'm going to let you speak to me with your mind while you sit there and eat that log of bread and meat?
COUGH COUGH
Wow. Well, the...six of them are old enough to--

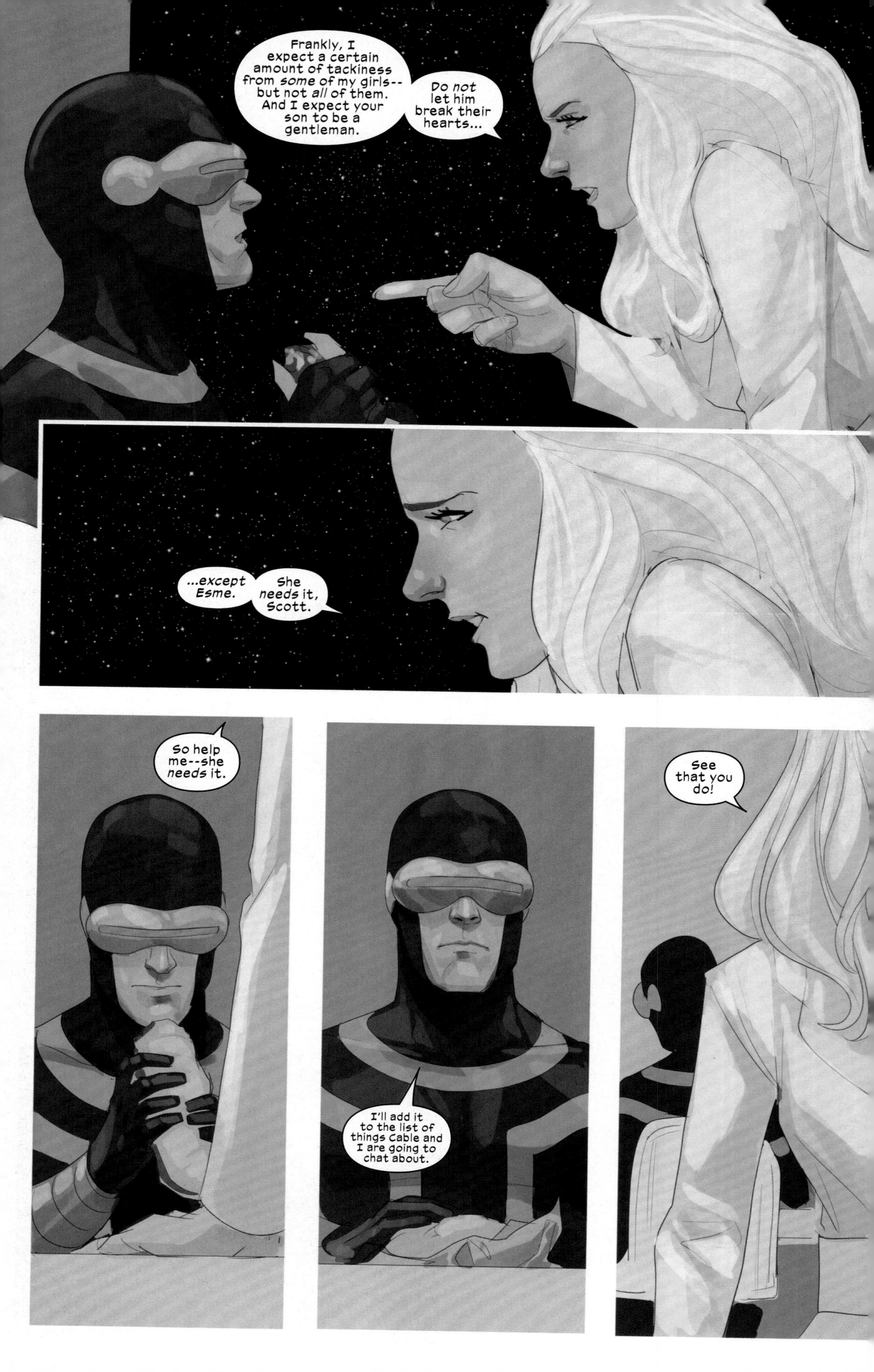
Frankly, I expect a certain amount of tackiness from *some* of my girls-- but not *all* of them. And I expect your son to be a gentleman.
Do *not* let him break their hearts...
...except Esme.
She *needs* it, Scott.
So help me--she *needs* it.
I'll add it to the list of things Cable and I are going to chat about.
See that you do!

EMAIL TRANSCRIPTS

FROM: Molina & DiStefano
RE: Baby Sherman kidnapping

Hey Boss,

Busy day. We got a visit from the mutants, and we were going over the enemies list of the parents. It's hilarious.

We canvassed the neighbors, most are long-term owners or renters. There was one house that the neighbors unanimously threw some side-eye at: turns out one of the houses within sight of the crime scene was rented to a guy who might've been in one of the new cults that sprung up. He was seen throwing pajama parties and the like, and now they're suddenly gone. We're gonna get a warrant and search that rental house tonight with the crime scene guys.

—

FROM: Molina & DiStefano
Update: RE: RE: Baby Sherman kidnapping

The house got blowed up. I guess we're gonna need to haul those Krakoans back. Any idea how to do that?

—

THE HUNT

Entry 002

The isolation is hard. If it weren't for the chronometer in my arm I wouldn't have the slightest notion of how long I've been locked away in this place. I know what I'm doing is vitally important and why I have to go it alone, but it's still difficult. Sometimes I talk to the dog. It never returns the favor.

I've cleared one hole after the other, and although I'm making progress breaking up the legion of demons, I remain frustratingly behind. The only good news is that I haven't found any evidence the hostages have been harmed.

I've kept up with the markers on the ground. If I go down and this book is found, then anyone following in my footsteps should continue in the direction of the Dog Star in the sky. The stars are backwards here, but you can make sense of them after your eyes adjust.

I have the bastard on the run, and I'm proceeding at best possible pace. My thoughts are loud in my head now, but I try to relax and breathe and think of the better times that are sure to follow after I manage to walk out of this quiet hell.

-C

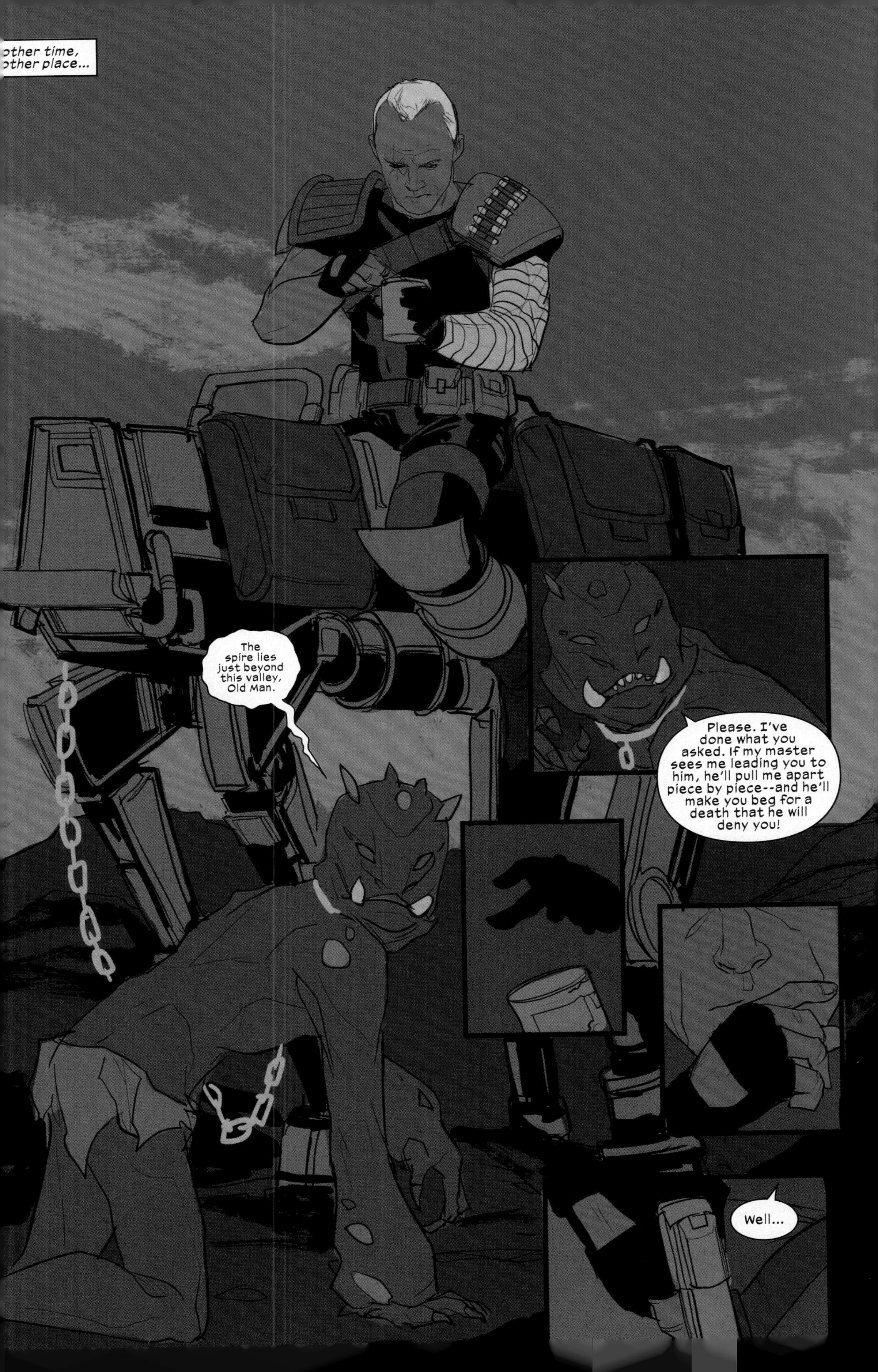

other time,
other place...
The spire lies just beyond this valley, Old Man.
Please. I've done what you asked. If my master sees me leading you to him, he'll pull me apart piece by piece--and he'll make you beg for a death that he will deny you!
Well...

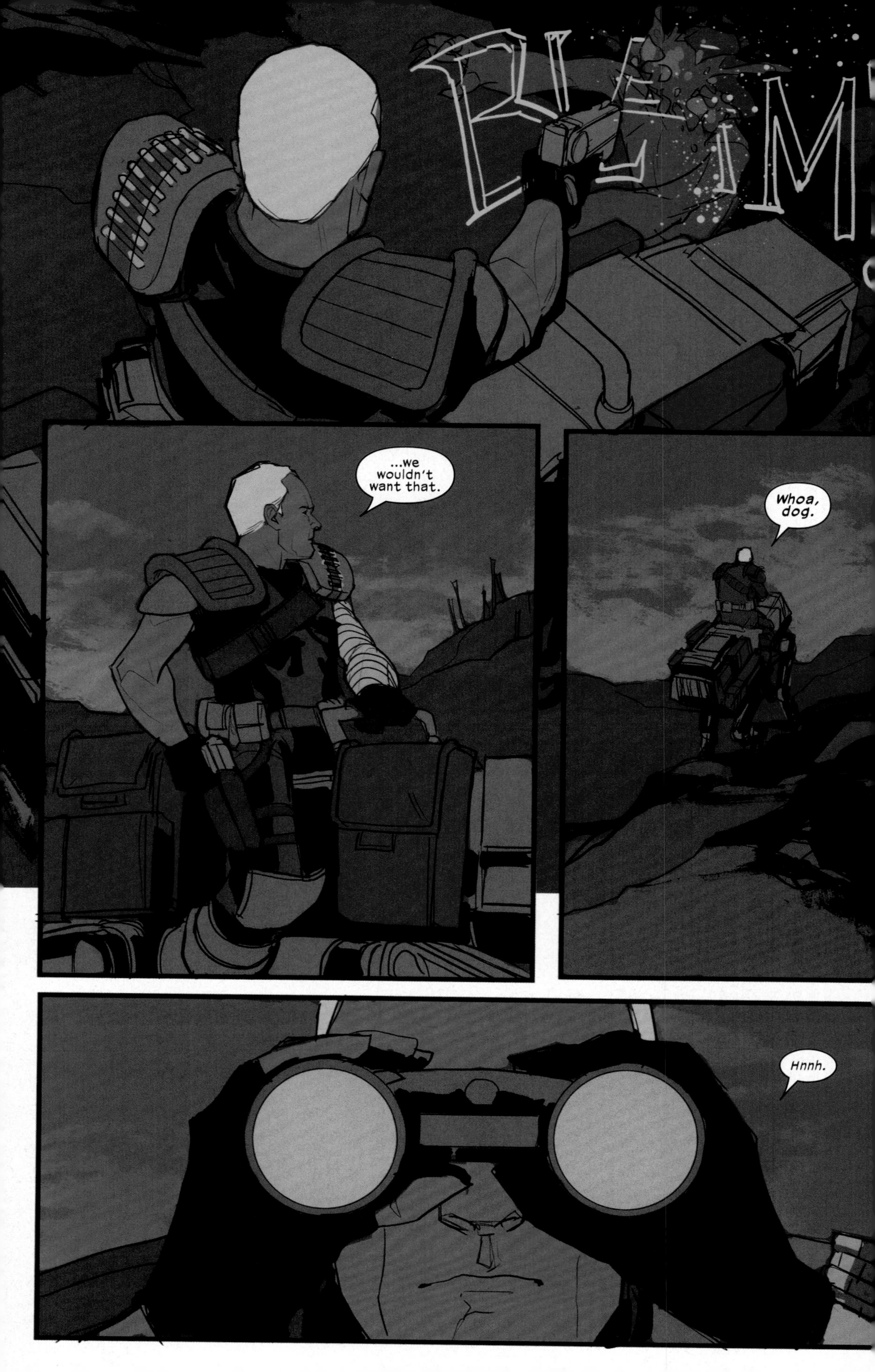
BLAM
...we wouldn't want that.
Whoa, dog.
Hnnh.

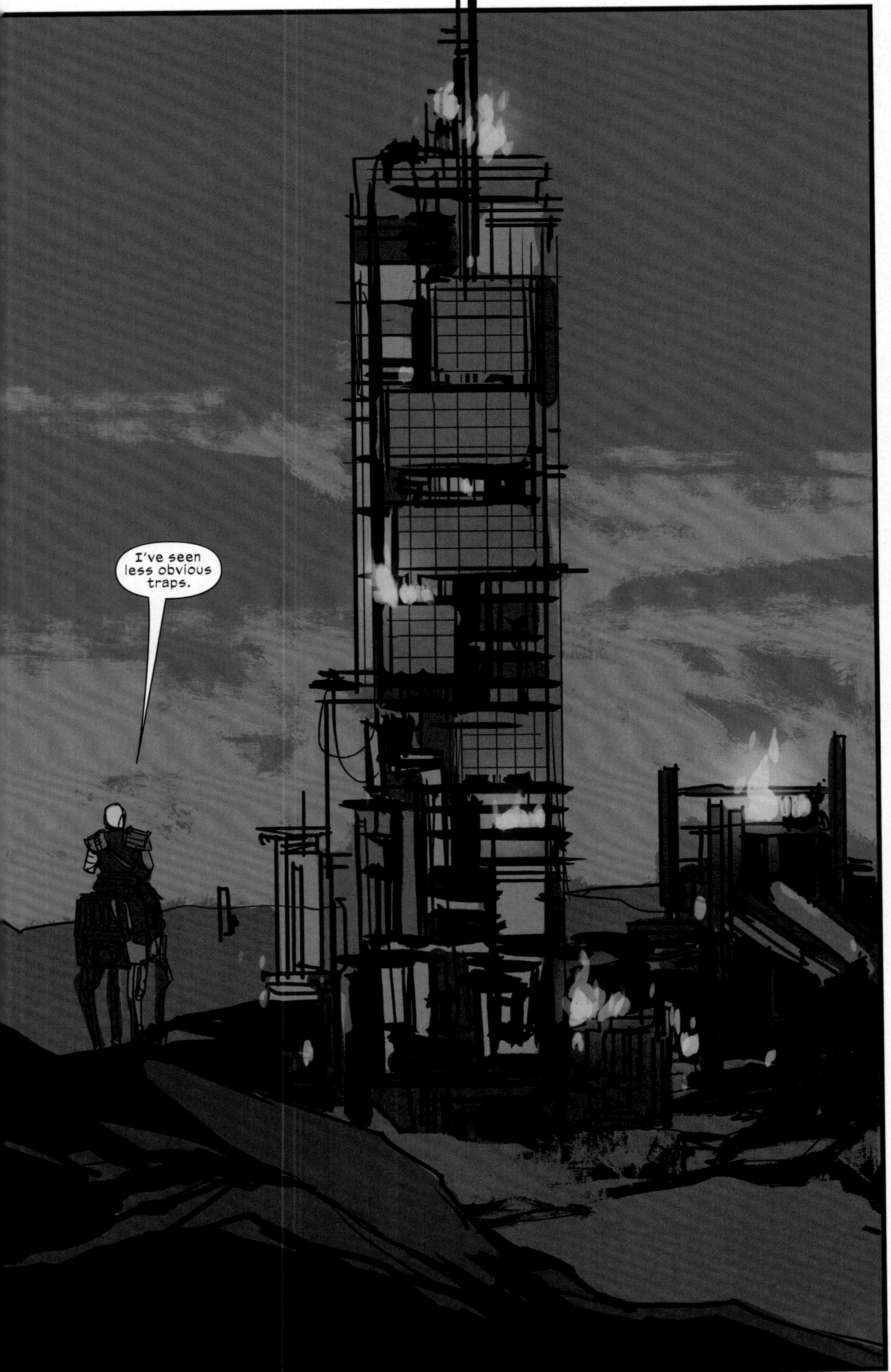
I've seen less obvious traps.

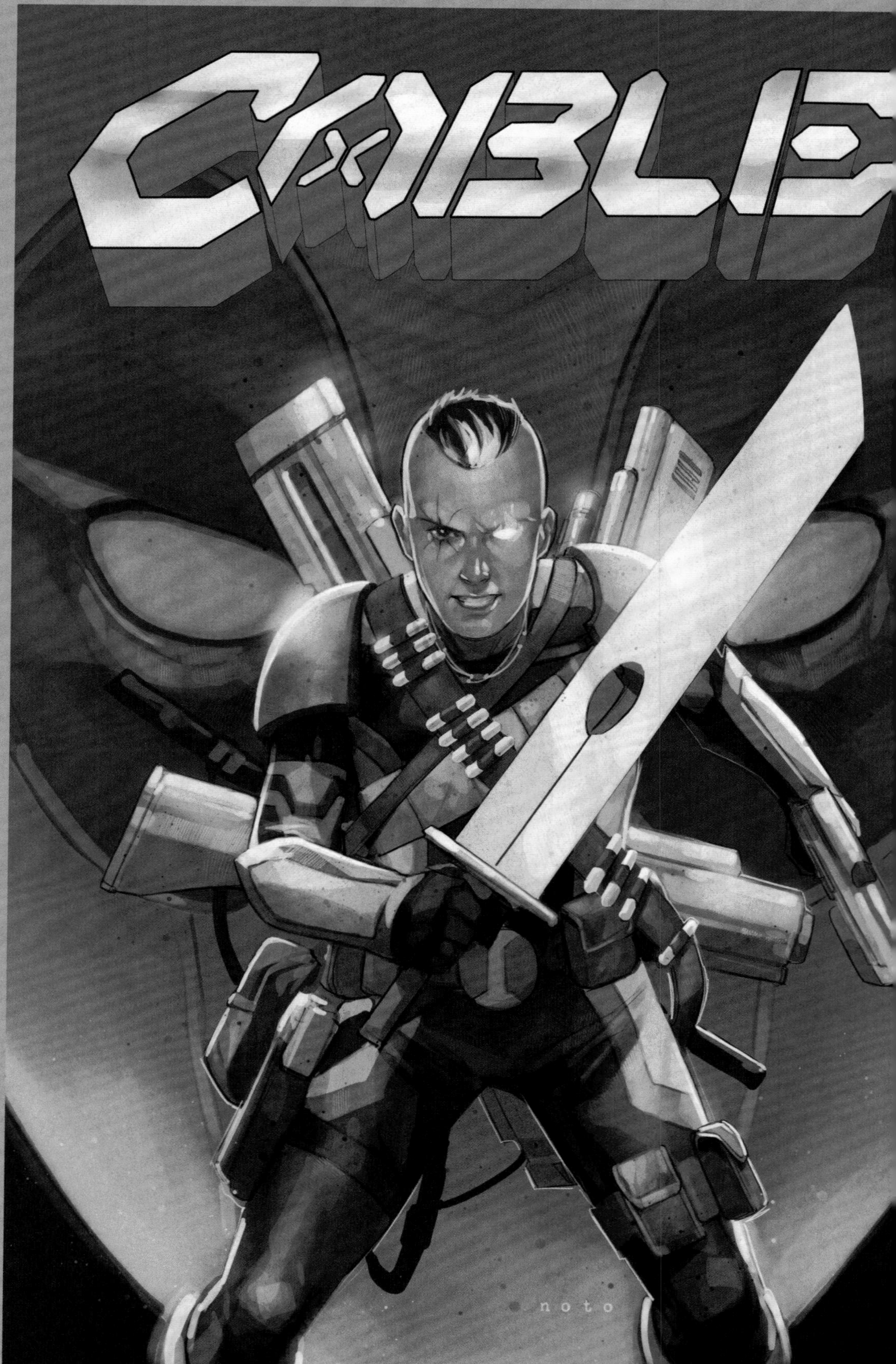
CABLE
noto

Ace in the Pouch

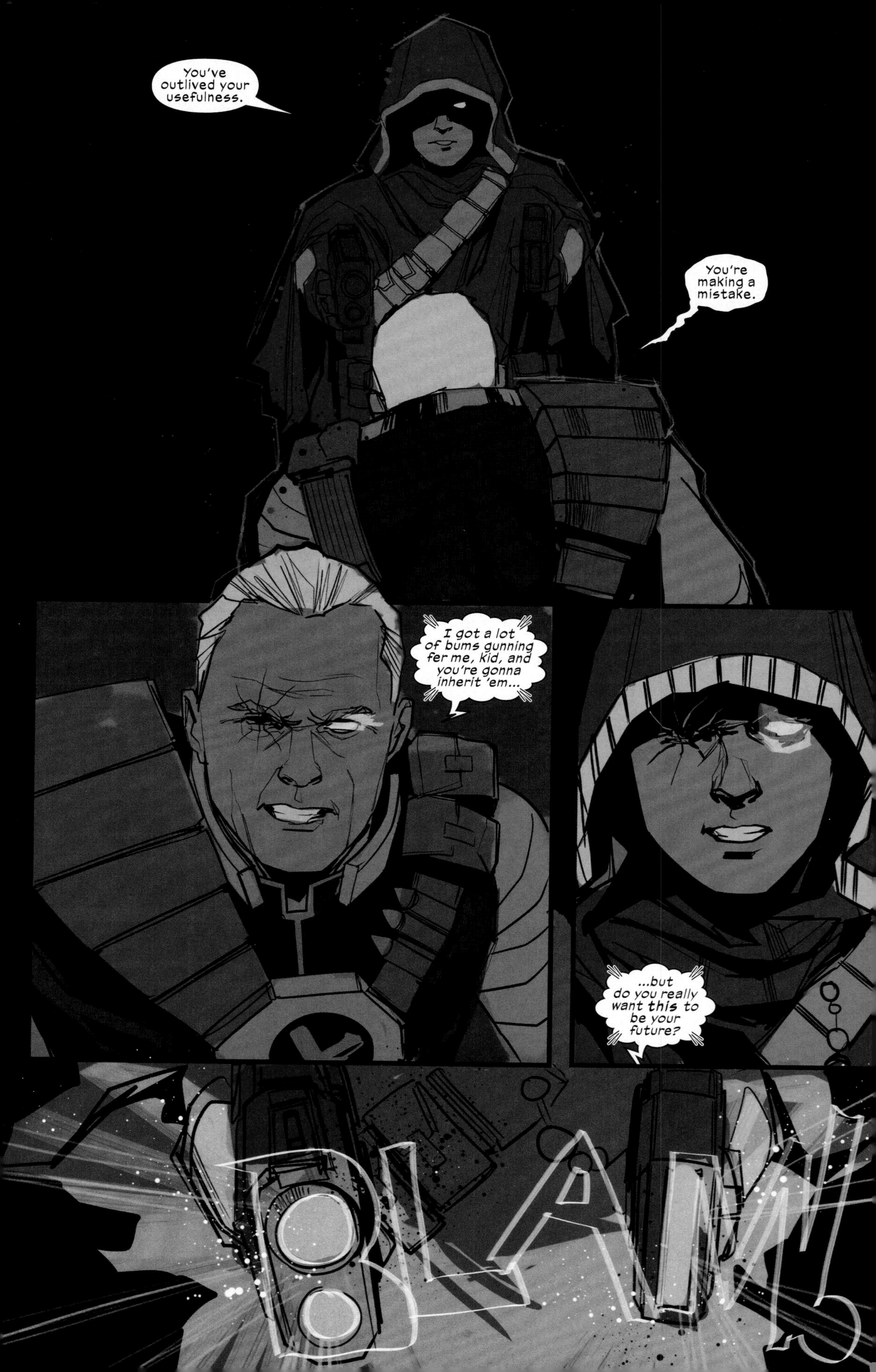
You've outlived your usefulness.
You're making a mistake.
I got a lot of bums gunning fer me, kid, and you're gonna inherit 'em...
...but do you really want this to be your future?
BLAM!

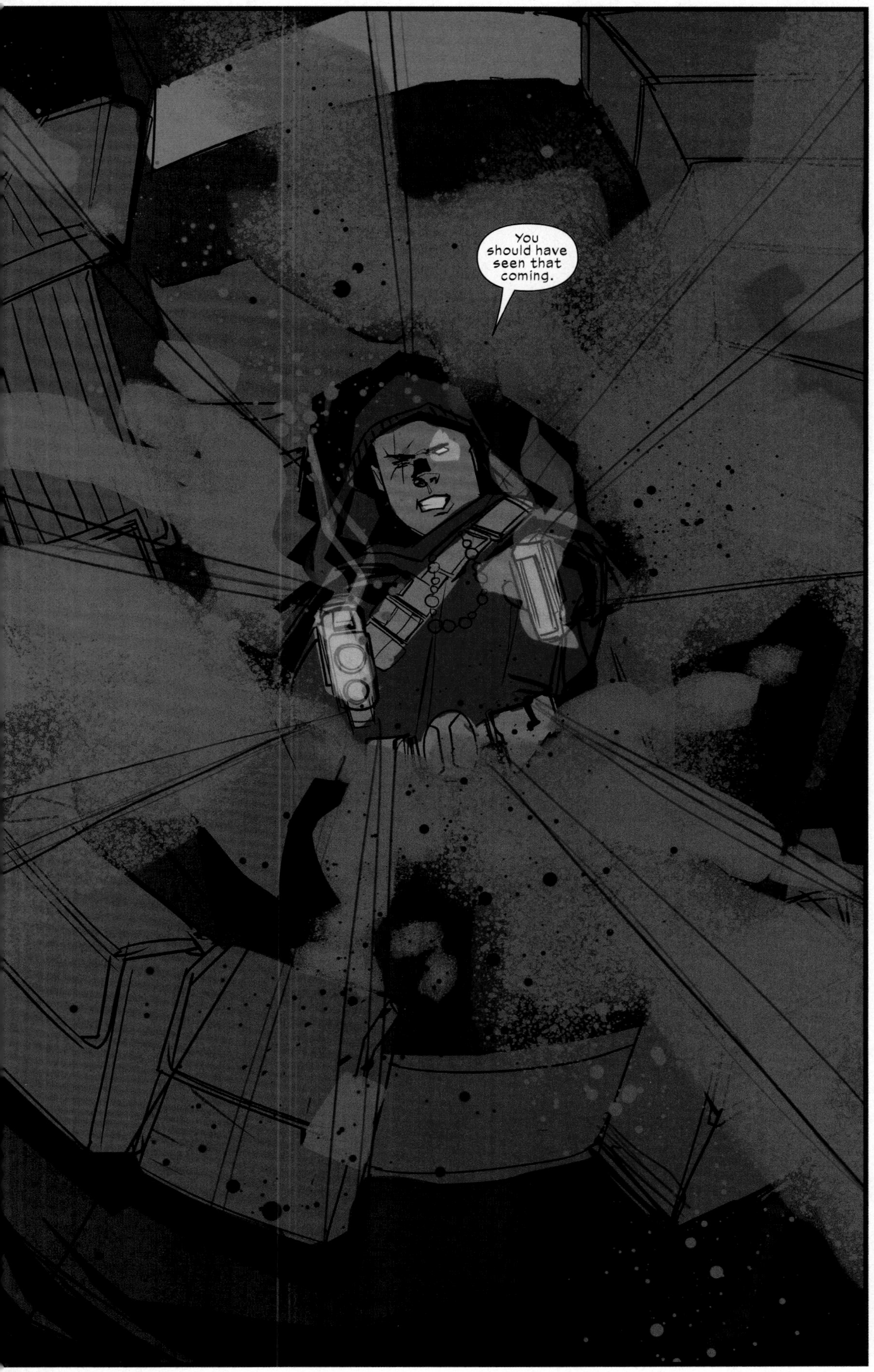
You should have seen that coming.

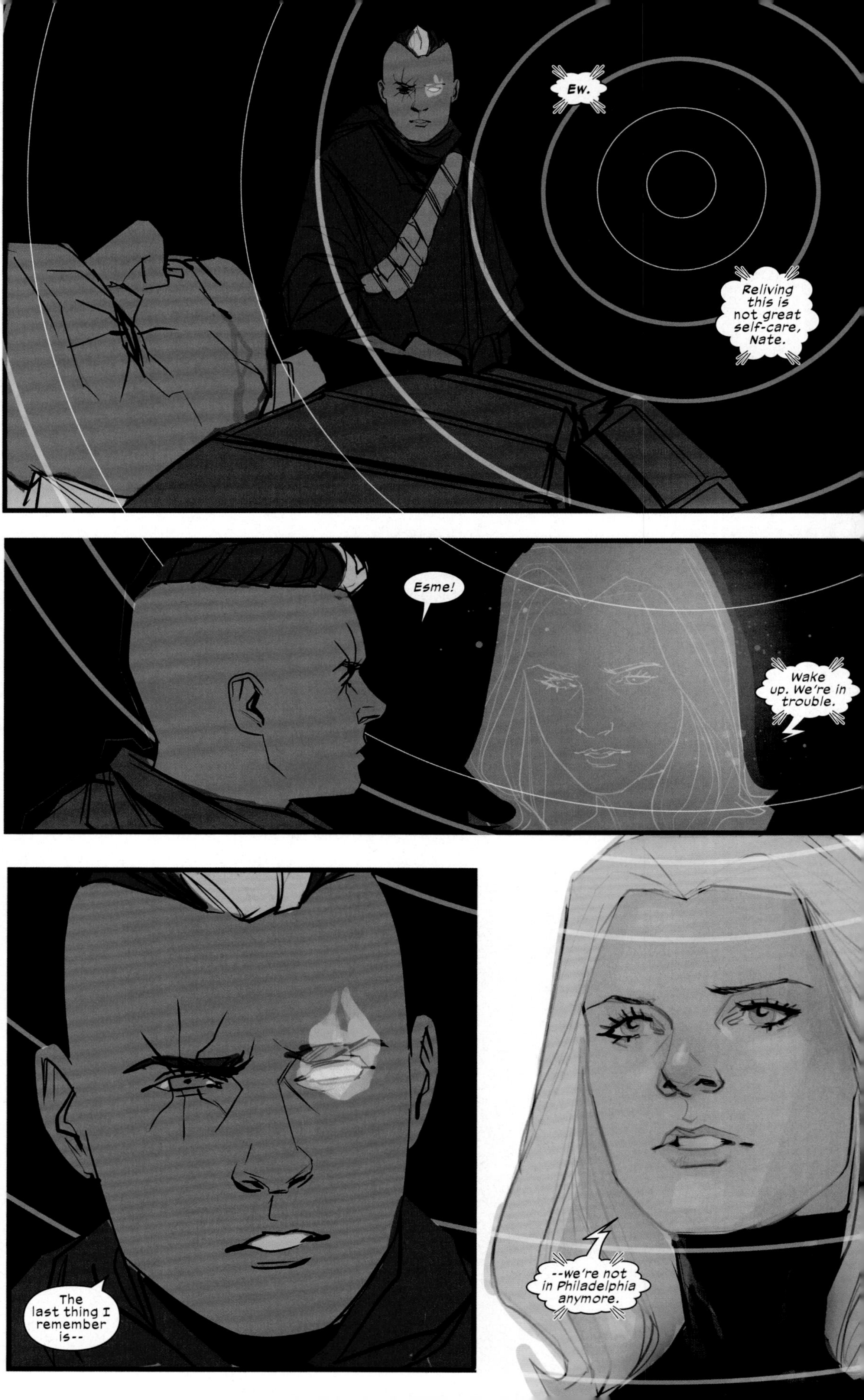
Ew.
Reliving this is not great self-care, Nate.
Esme!
Wake up. We're in trouble.
The last thing I remember is--
--we're not in Philadelphia anymore.

Welcome to the North Pole.

They aren't robots, Nathan. They're cyborgs with living brains...they're psi-shielded, but I can hear some of their communication.

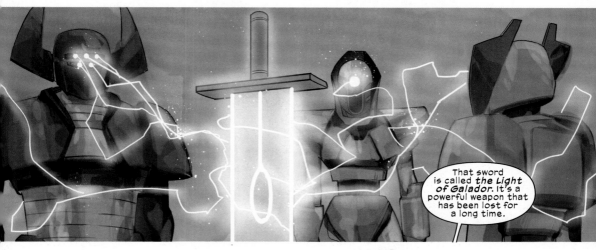

That sword is called *the Light of Galador*. It's a powerful weapon that has been lost for a long time.

They're arguing about what to do next. Evidently, they just discovered that their planet was destroyed while they were hibernating.

Their *"plan A"* was to use the sword to make their people restore their flesh bodies. The new *"plan B"* to beat is to transform Earth into their home planet with the power of the sword.

It can do that?! COOL!

They also don't understand how you were able to wield it.

Well, I am a cyborg.

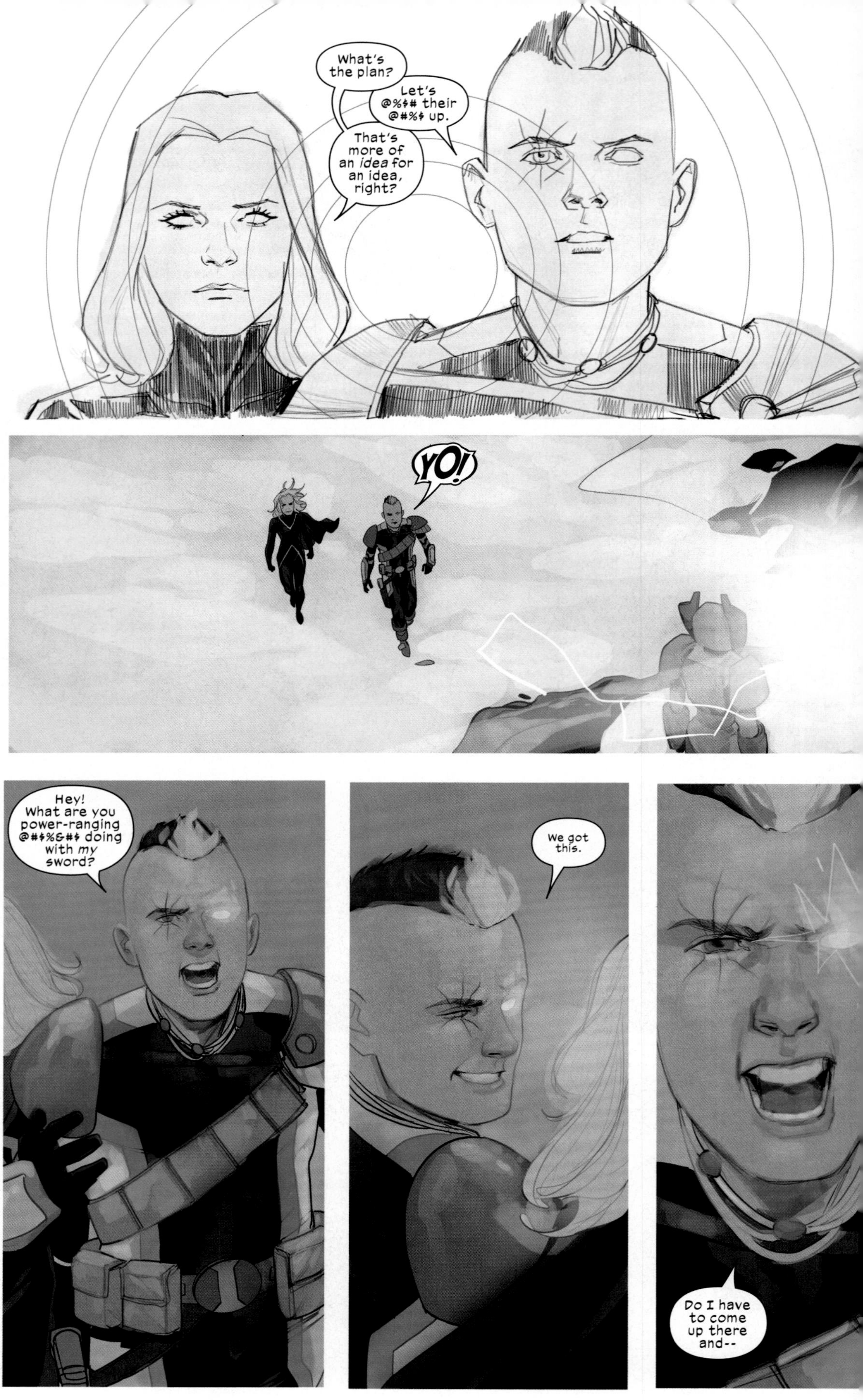
What's the plan?
Let's @%$# their @#%$ up.
That's more of an *idea* for an idea, right?
YO!
Hey! What are you power-ranging @#$%&#$ doing with *my* sword?
We got this.
Do I have to come up there and--

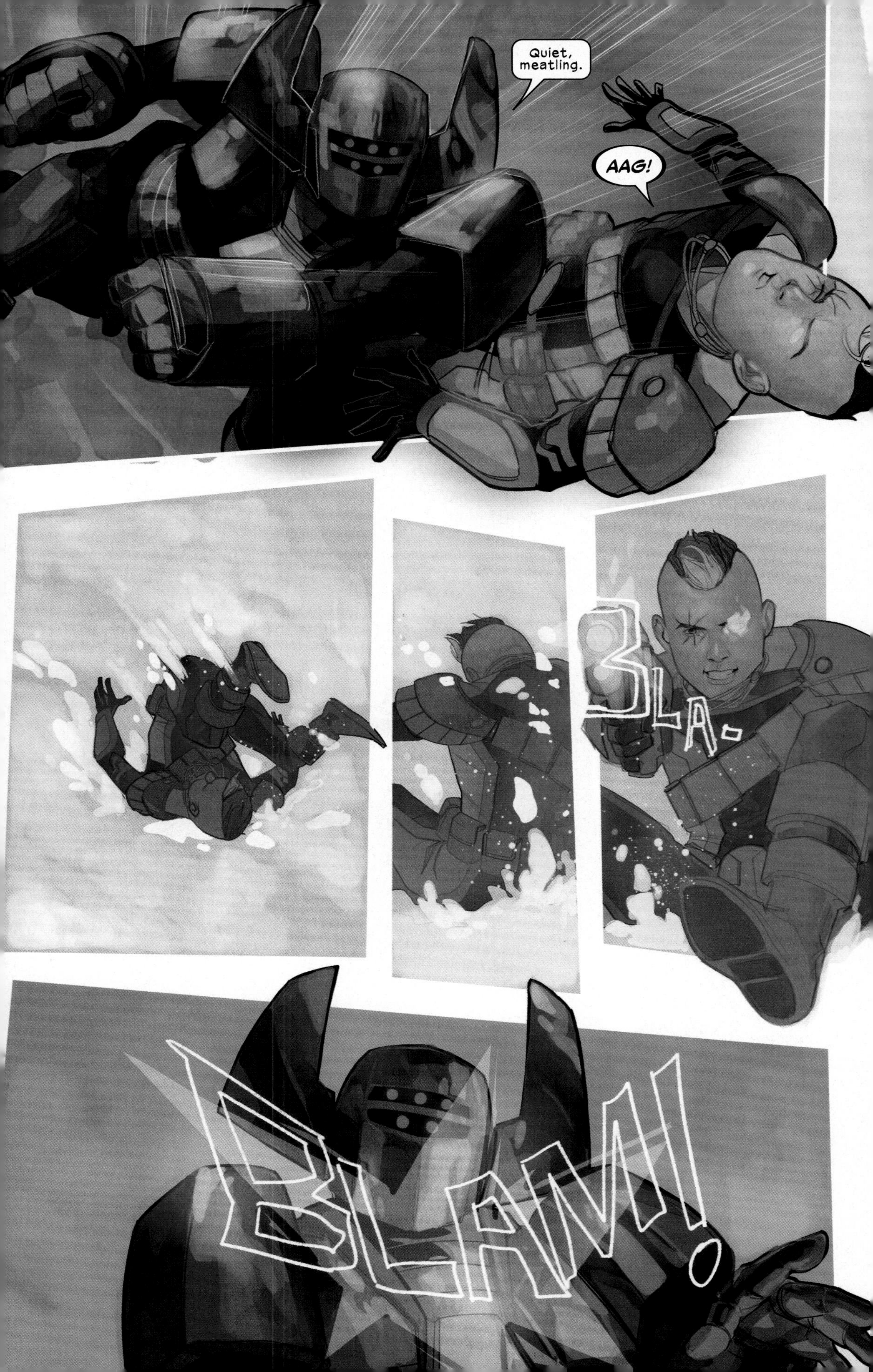
Quiet, meatling.
AAG!
BLA.
BLAM!

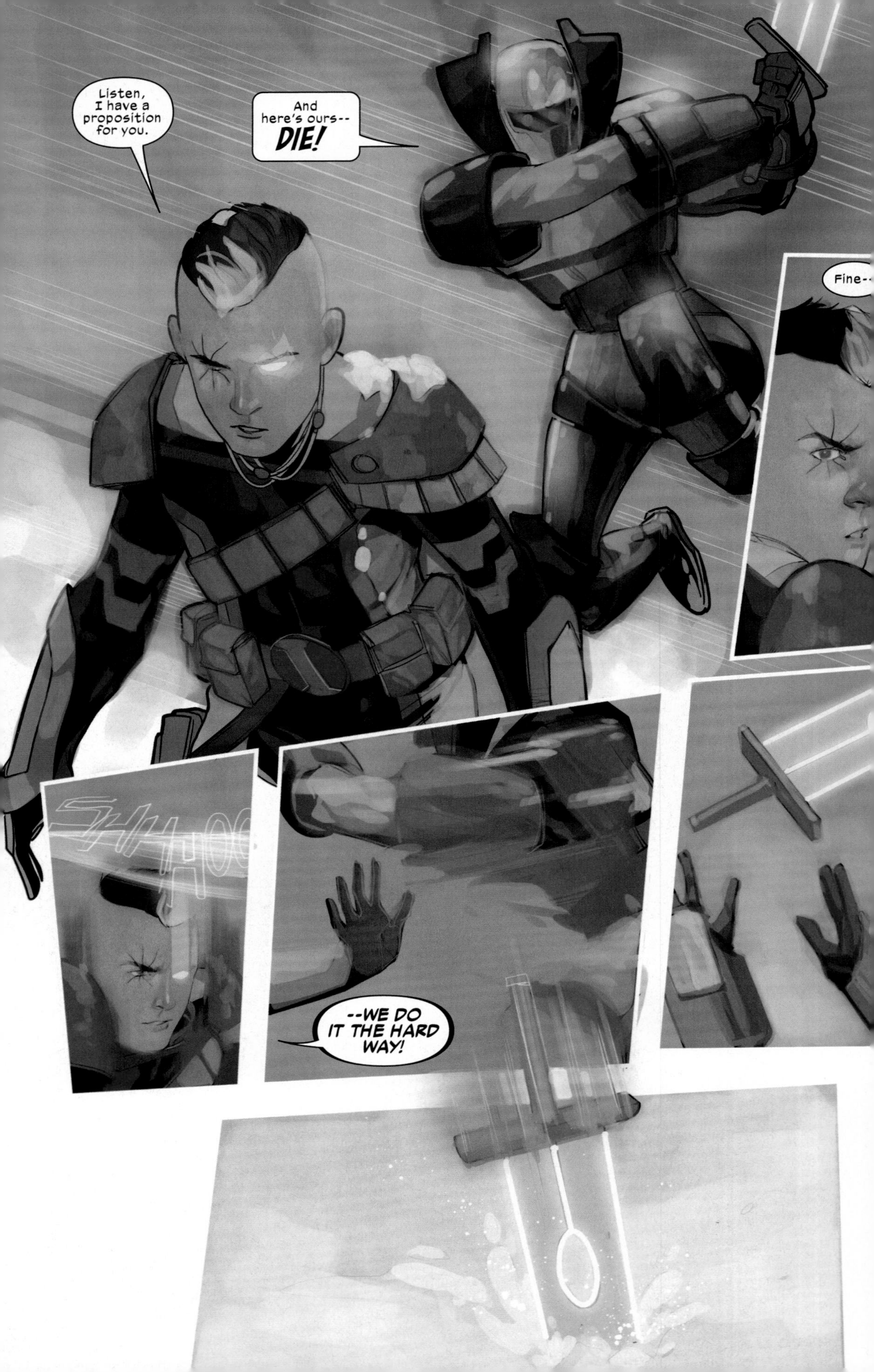

Listen, I have a proposition for you.
And here's ours-- DIE!
Fine--
SHHOOO
--WE DO IT THE HARD WAY!

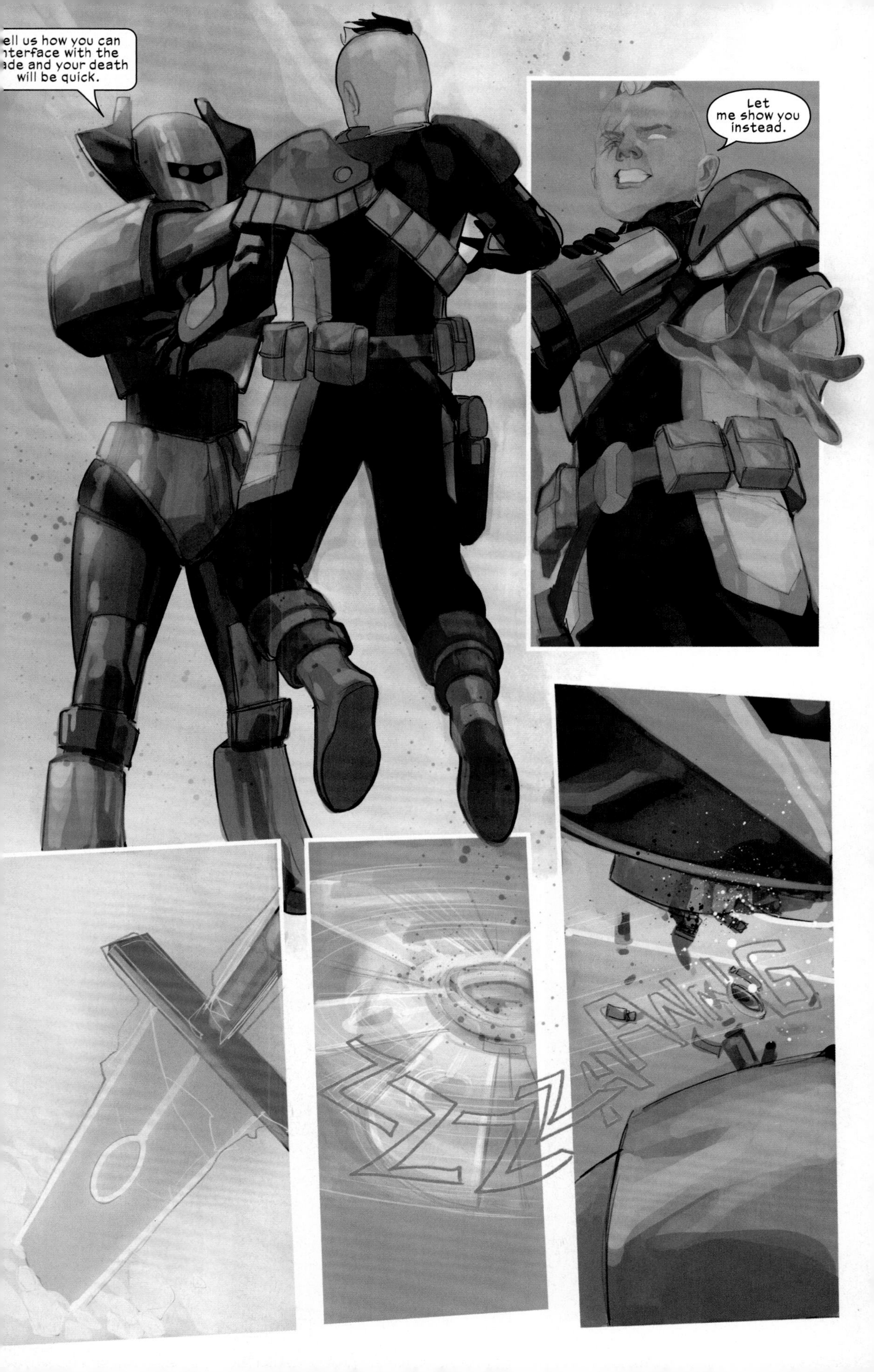
ell us how you can nterface with the ade and your death will be quick.
Let me show you instead.
ZZZAANNG

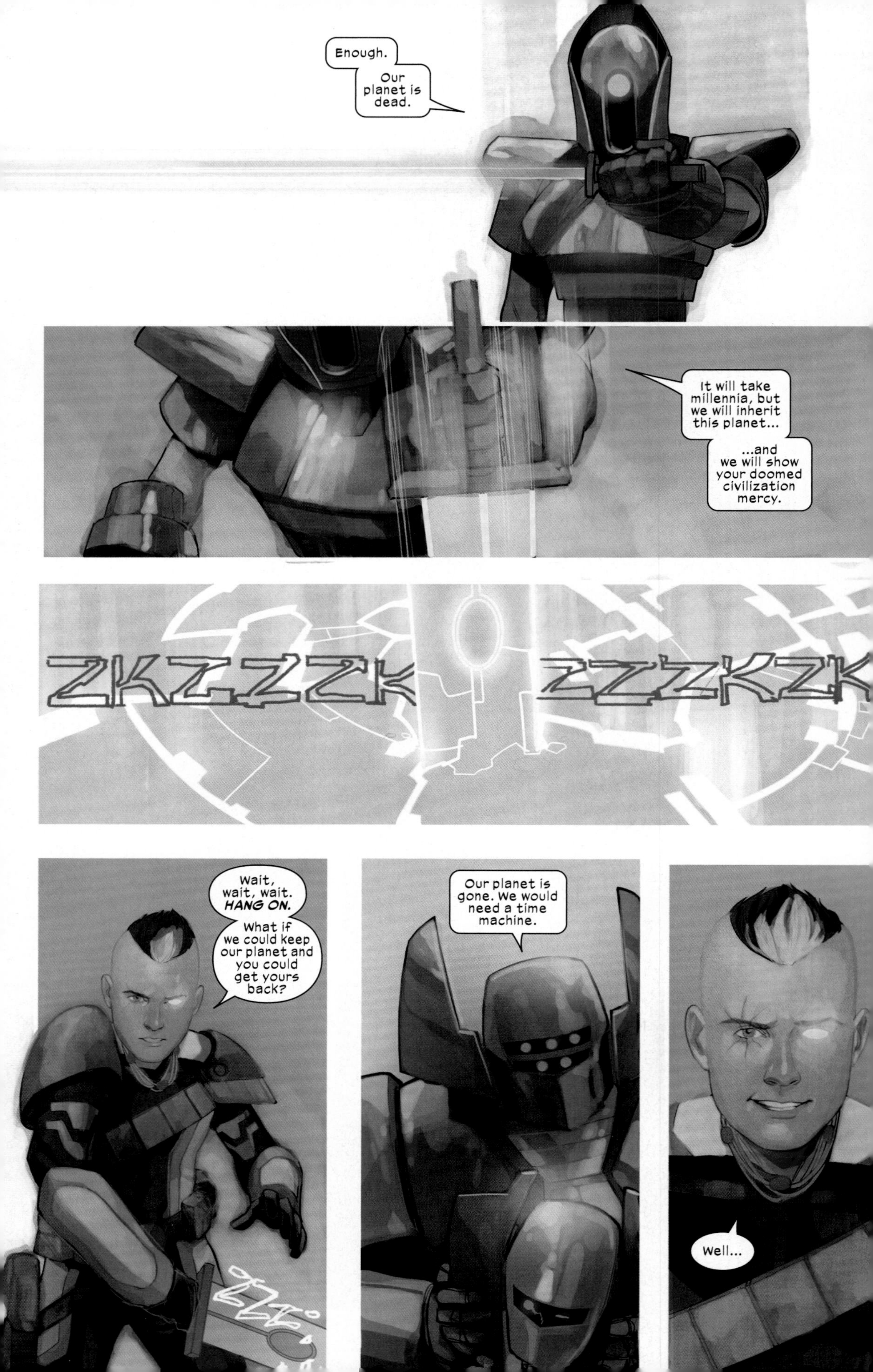
Enough.
Our planet is dead.
It will take millennia, but we will inherit this planet...
...and we will show your doomed civilization mercy.
ZKZZZK ZZZKZK
Wait, wait, wait. *HANG ON.*
What if we could keep our planet and you could get yours back?
Our planet is gone. We would need a time machine.
Well...

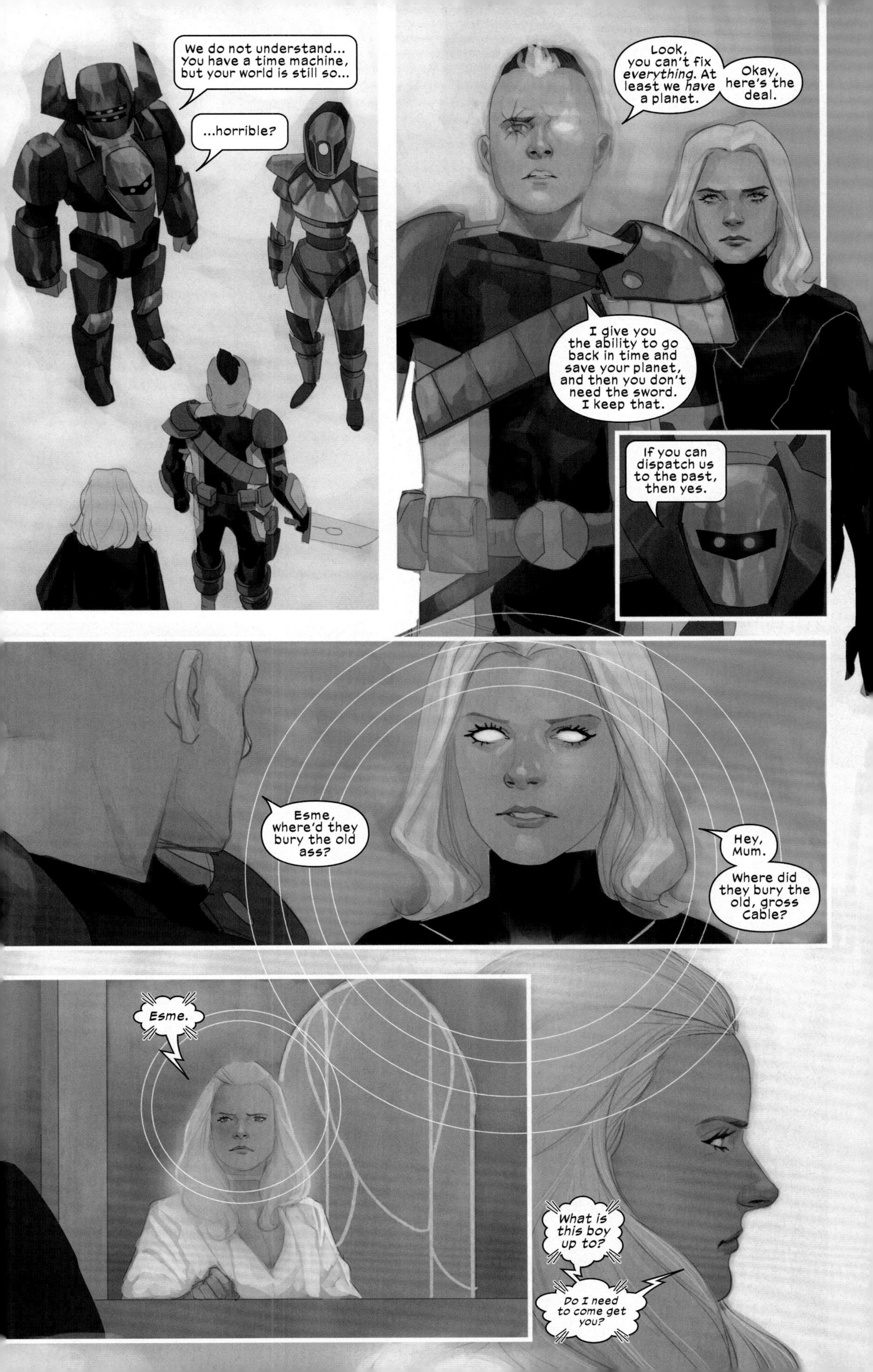
We do not understand... You have a time machine, but your world is still so...
...horrible?
Look, you can't fix *everything*. At least we *have* a planet.
Okay, here's the deal.
I give you the ability to go back in time and save your planet, and then you don't need the sword. I keep that.
If you can dispatch us to the past, then yes.
Esme, where'd they bury the old ass?
Hey, Mum.
Where did they bury the old, gross Cable?
Esme.
What is this boy up to?
Do I need to come get you?

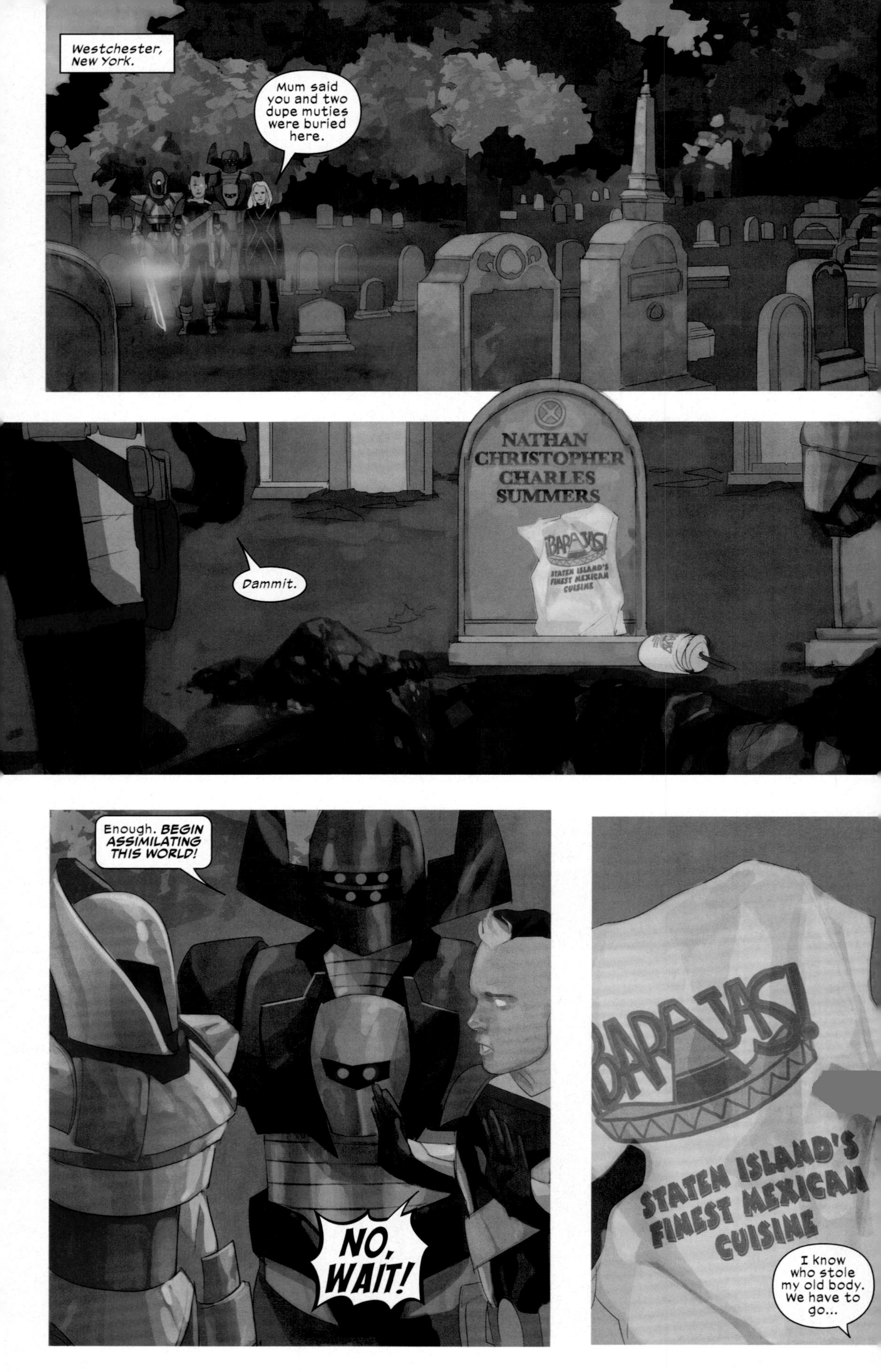
Westchester, New York.
Mum said you and two dupe muties were buried here.
NATHAN CHRISTOPHER CHARLES SUMMERS
¡BARAJAS!
STATEN ISLAND'S FINEST MEXICAN CUISINE
Dammit.
Enough. BEGIN ASSIMILATING THIS WORLD!
NO, WAIT!
¡BARAJAS!
STATEN ISLAND'S FINEST MEXICAN CUISINE
I know who stole my old body. We have to go...

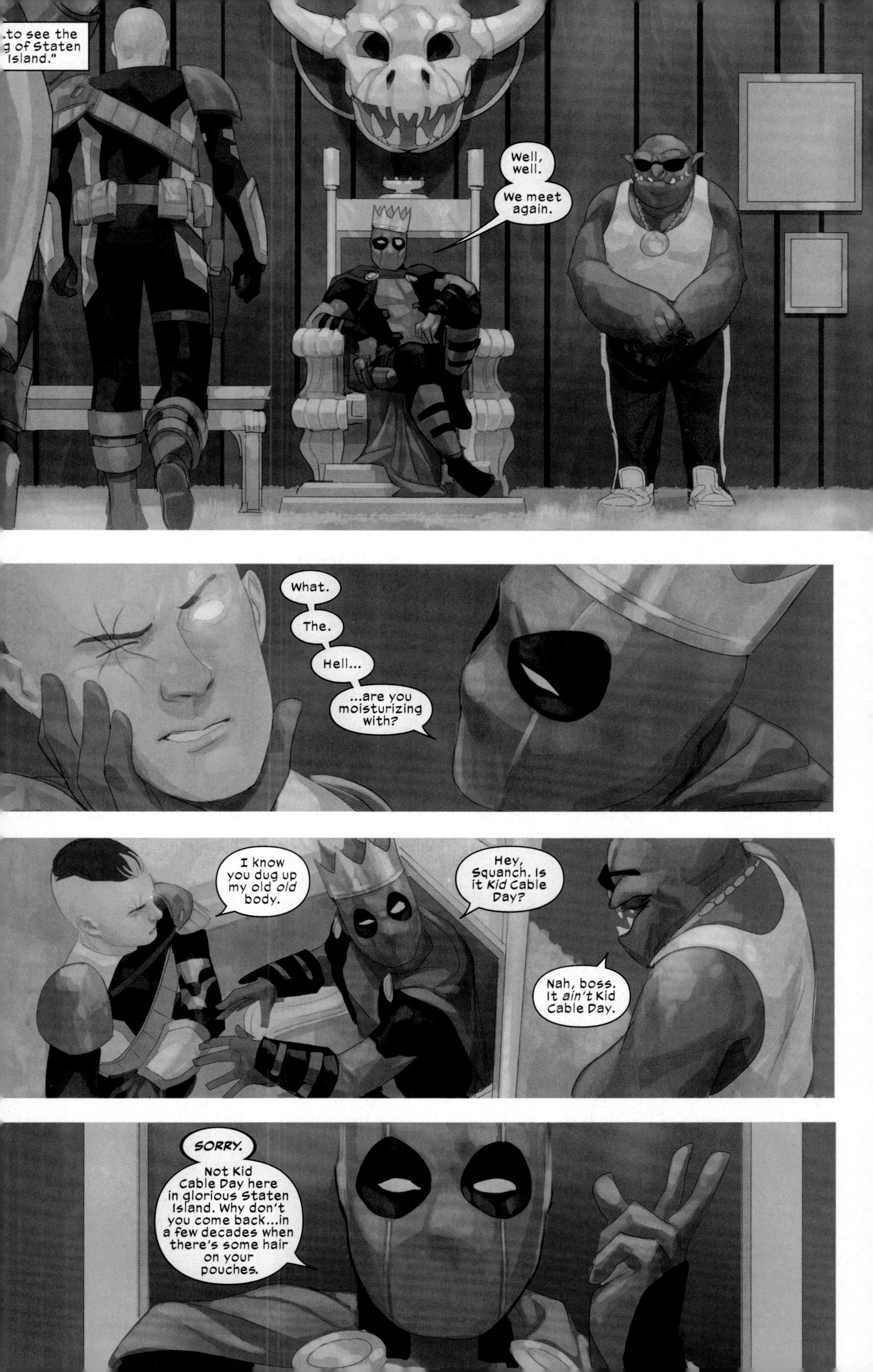

...to see the King of Staten Island."
Well, well.
We meet again.
What.
The.
Hell...
...are you moisturizing with?
I know you dug up my old *old* body.
Hey, Squanch. Is it *Kid* Cable Day?
Nah, boss. It *ain't* Kid Cable Day.
SORRY.
Not Kid Cable Day here in glorious Staten Island. Why don't you come back...in a few decades when there's some hair on your pouches.

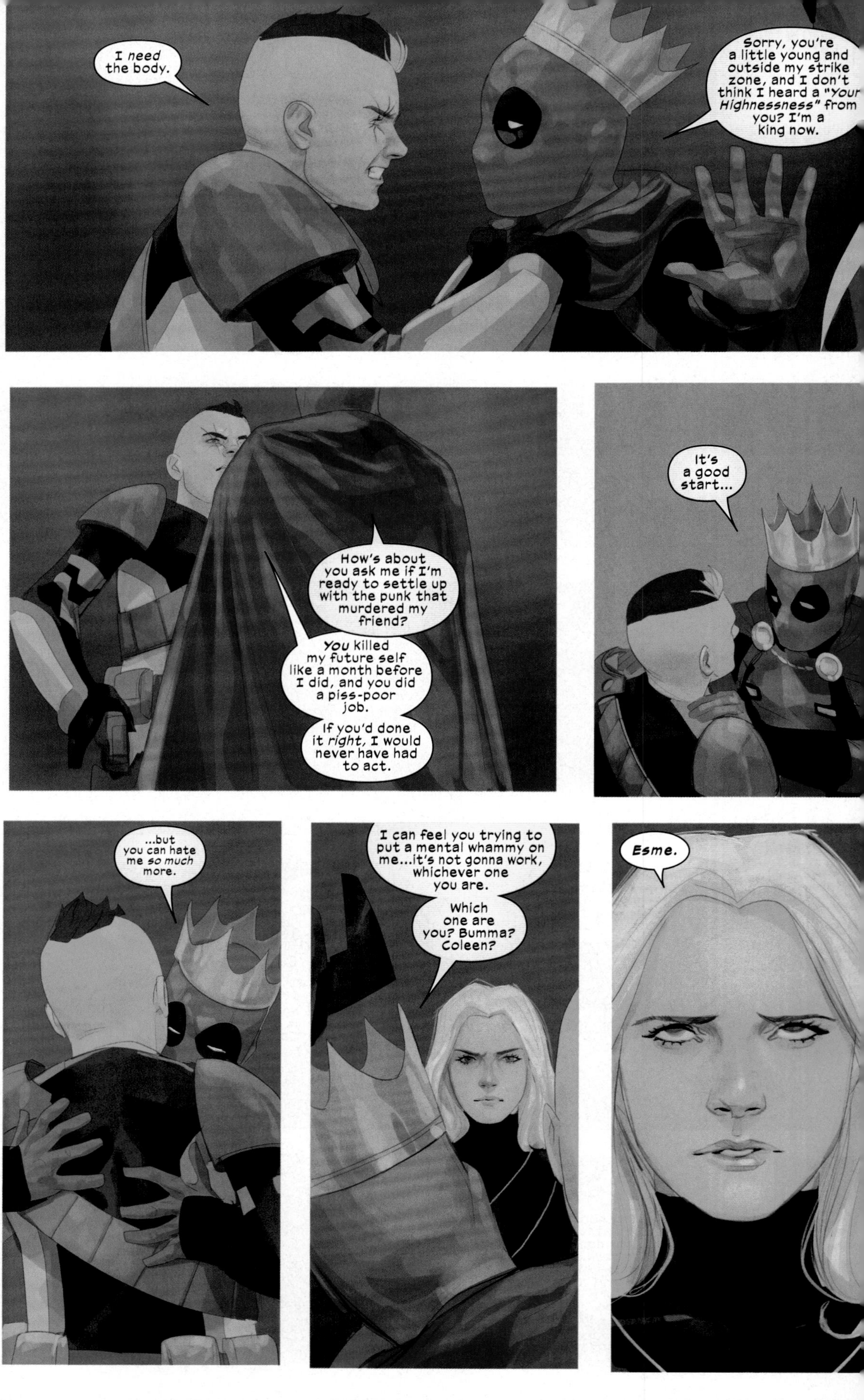
I *need* the body.
Sorry, you're a little young and outside my strike zone, and I don't think I heard a "*Your Highnessness*" from you? I'm a king now.
How's about you ask me if I'm ready to settle up with the punk that murdered my friend?
You killed my future self like a month before I did, and you did a piss-poor job.
If you'd done it *right,* I would never have had to act.
It's a good start...
...but you can hate me *so much* more.
I can feel you trying to put a mental whammy on me...it's not gonna work, whichever one you are.
Which one are you? Bumma? Coleen?
Esme.

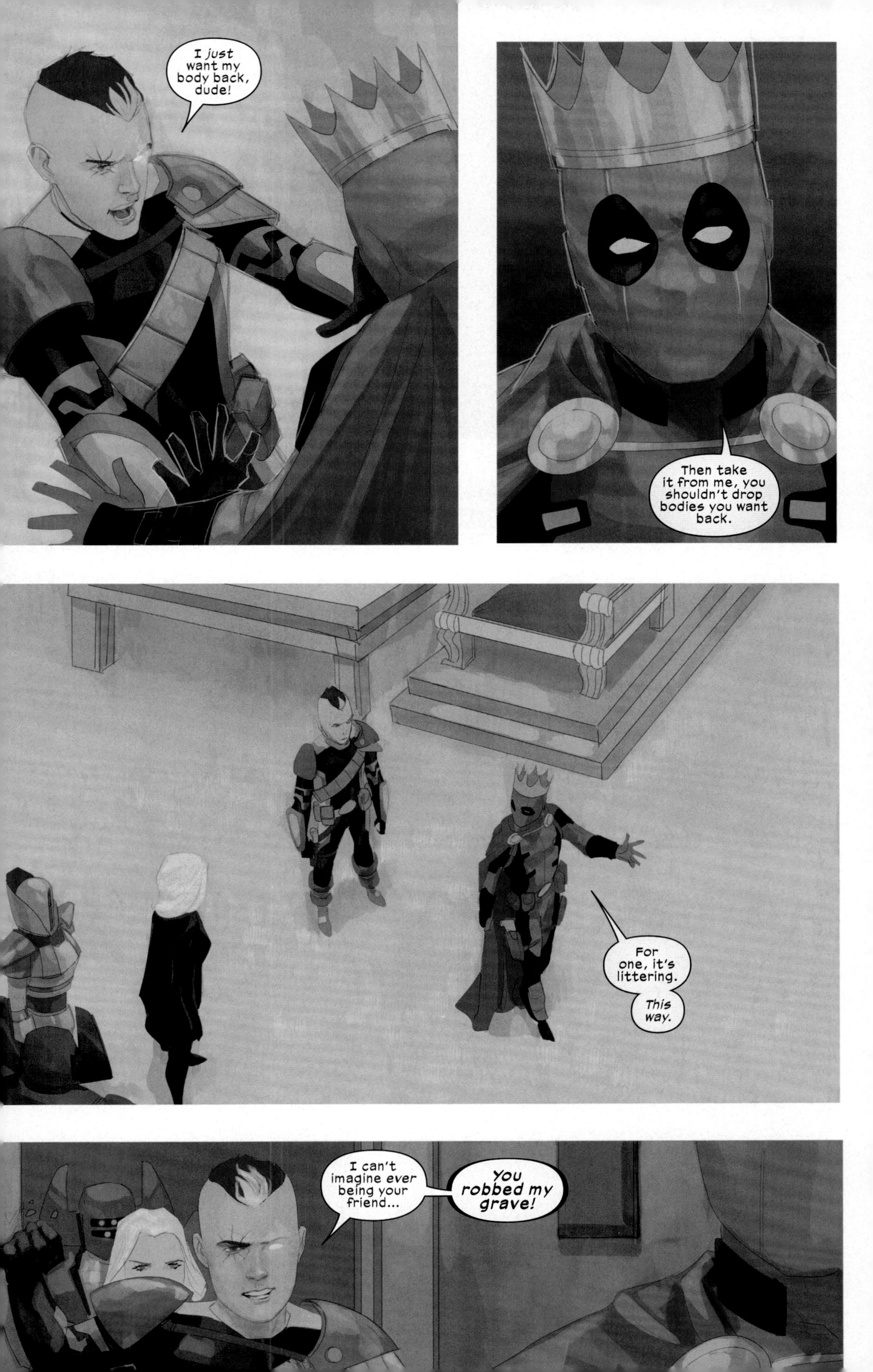
I just want my body back, dude!
Then take it from me, you shouldn't drop bodies you want back.
For one, it's littering.
This way.
I can't imagine ever being your friend...
You robbed my grave!

You know what?

Another one of my elderly heroes got grave-robbed too.

Benny Hill.

The Brits are *animals.* What is even happening over there?

I don't know who that is!

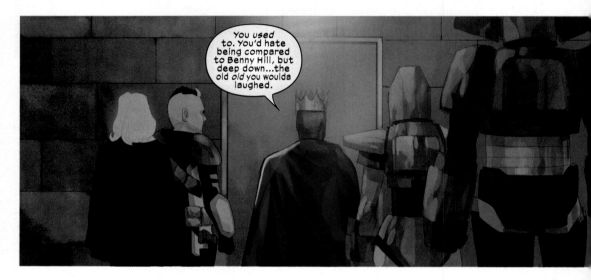

You *used* to. You'd hate being compared to Benny Hill, but deep down...the old *old* you woulda laughed.

Bable. Your crypt is on the other side of this door.

Are you... *sure* you want to enter?

I *need* to do this.

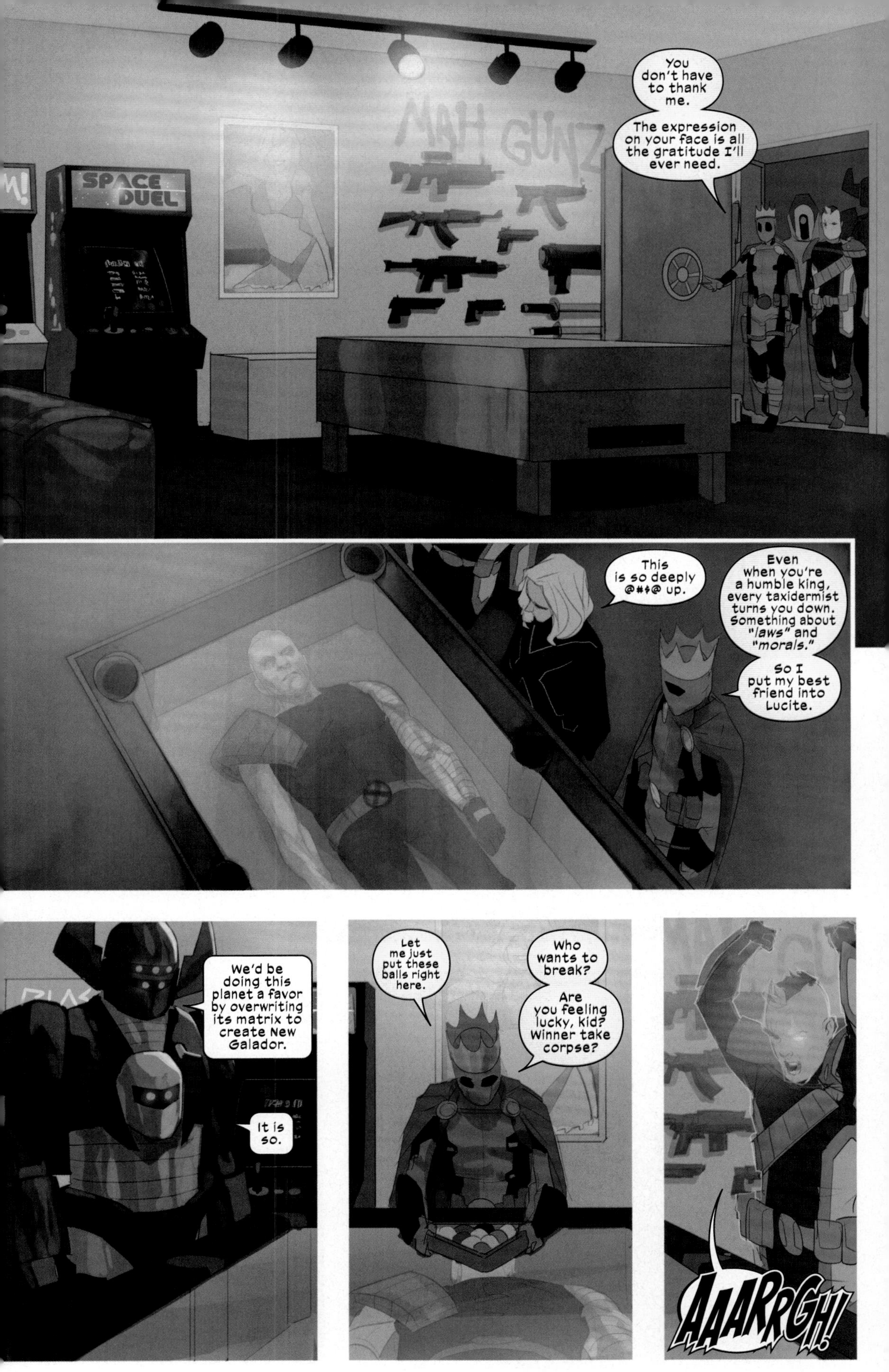
SPACE DUEL
MAH GUNZ
You don't have to thank me.
The expression on your face is all the gratitude I'll ever need.
This is so deeply @#$@ up.
Even when you're a humble king, every taxidermist turns you down. Something about "*laws*" and "*morals*."
So I put my best friend into Lucite.
We'd be doing this planet a favor by overwriting its matrix to create New Galador.
It is so.
Let me just put these balls right here.
Who wants to break?
Are you feeling lucky, kid? Winner take corpse?
AAARRGH!

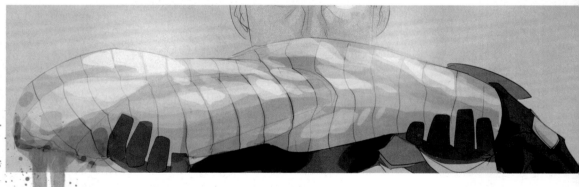

Oh god, old man. You've made some bad smells over the years, but this is the WORST.

Wade -

It pains me to ask this, but I need a favor.

After Stryfe nearly killed me the last time, I decided to reorganize my defense. My enemy is my equal, but he does not have the same resources I bring to the fight.

He does not have my allies. The people I call my friends...my family. Or you.

In the unlikely event that I die, assume that he was behind it regardless of what it looks like and do not let my body, the prosthetic arm or any ordnance fall into his possession.

If friendlies bury the body, intervene when you can move safely. I'll find you later.

Thanks,
Cable

My Dearest Nathan,

I have received your distressing missive, and I now take my quill
in hand to let you know that I am well and hope my
correspondence finds you similarly also...well.

I can think of no greater responsibility than to collect your
earthly remains after the other side of a heinous attack. I shall
keep a snow shovel and some garbage bags with me at all times, in
anticipation of the dreadful news reaching me that something has
happened to your old ass. As you know, I have been something of
an amateur funeral director for many years and knowing that my
work has caught your eye means the world to me.

I will of course keep a full accounting of expenses incurred should
it become necessary for me to clean up.

I have enclosed a daguerreotype of me to keep with you in the pouch
closest to your heart.

Sincerest sincerities,

D. Pool

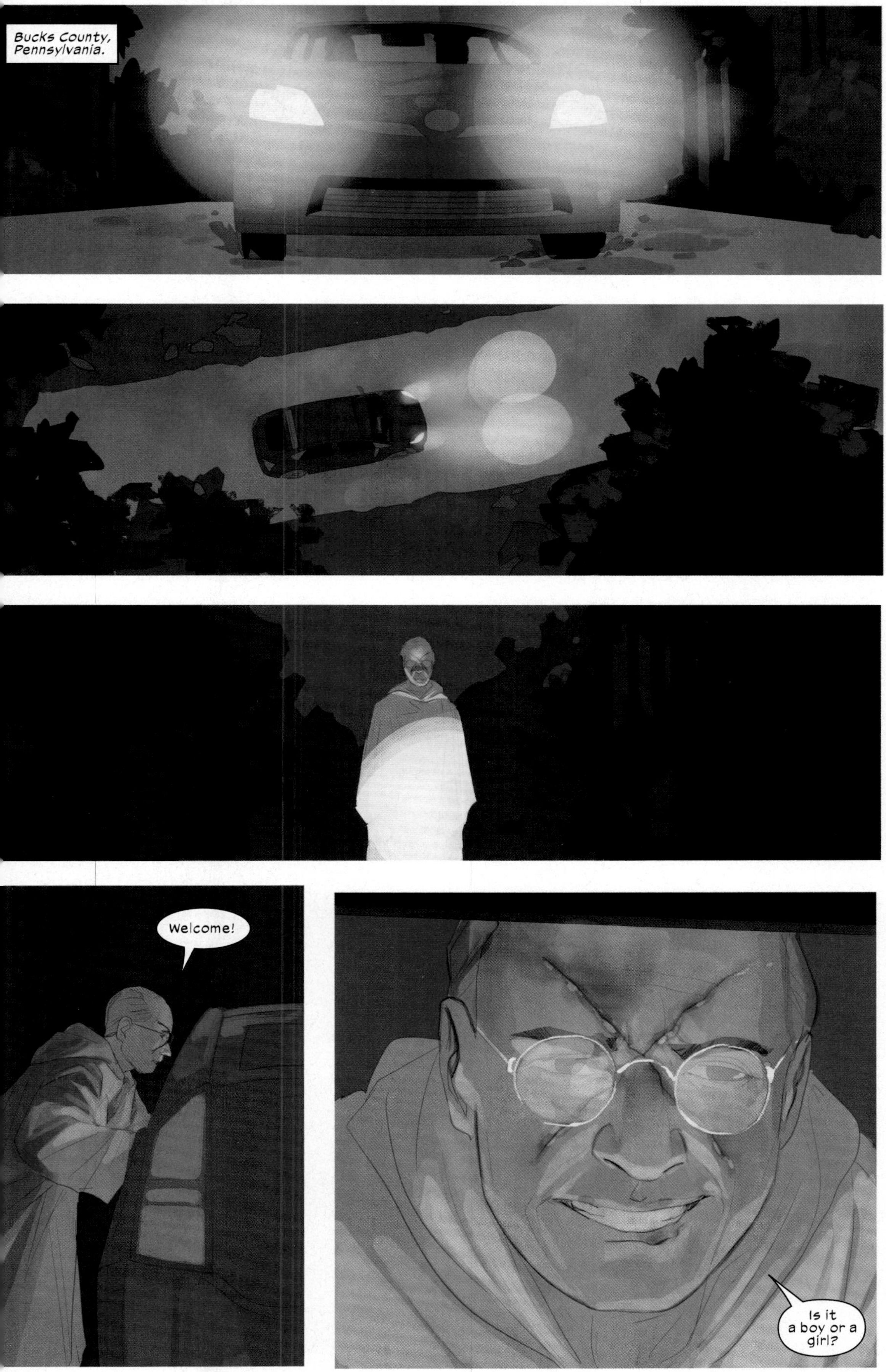
Bucks County, Pennsylvania.
Welcome!
Is it a boy or a girl?

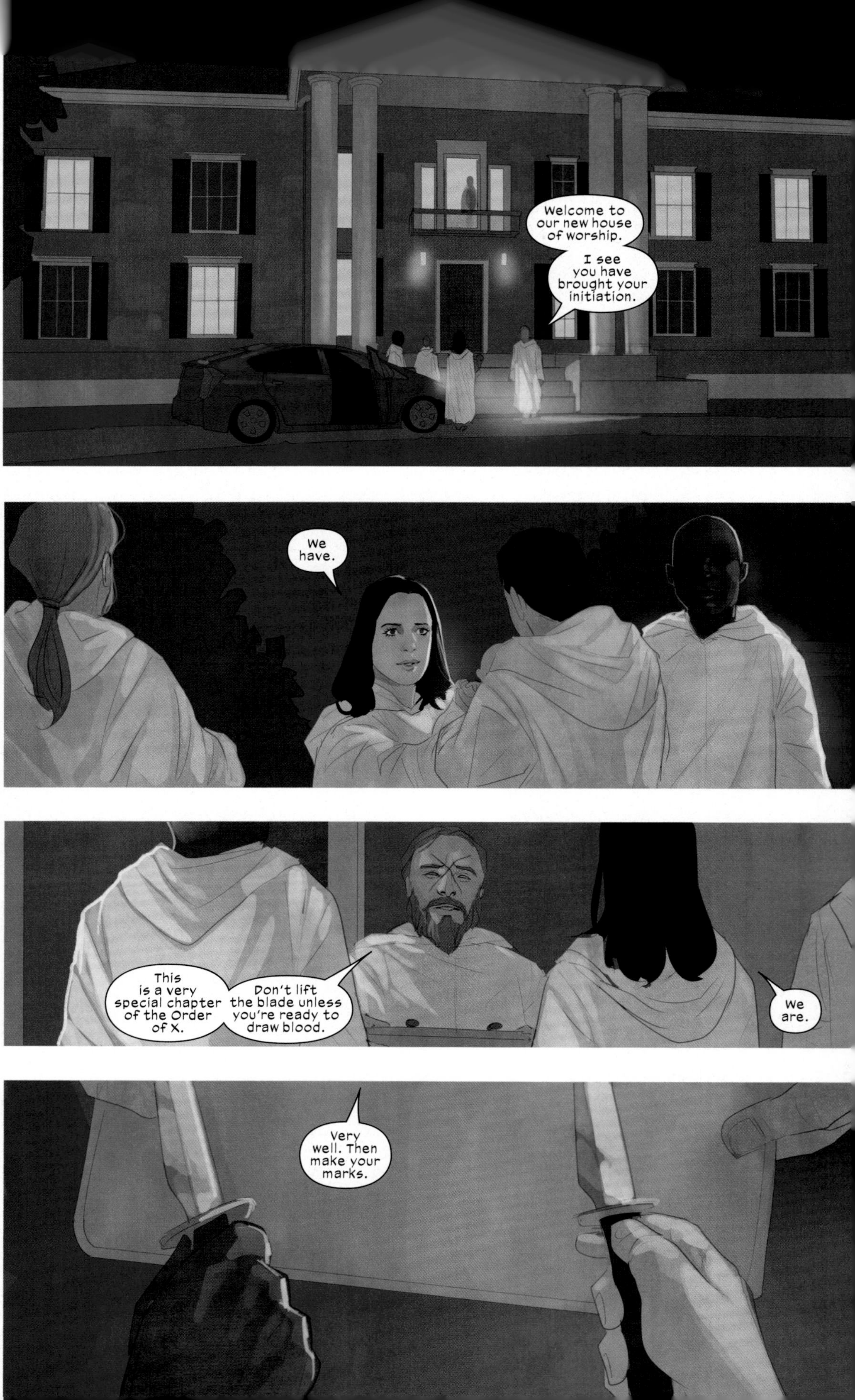
Welcome to our new house of worship.
I see you have brought your initiation.
We have.
This is a very special chapter of the Order of X.
Don't lift the blade unless you're ready to draw blood.
We are.
Very well. Then make your marks.

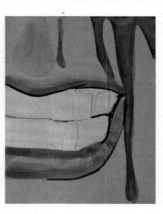
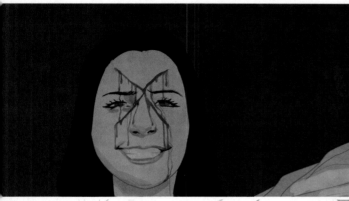

Behold, Monsignor! A mutant girl!

Glorious.

Put the little angel with the others.

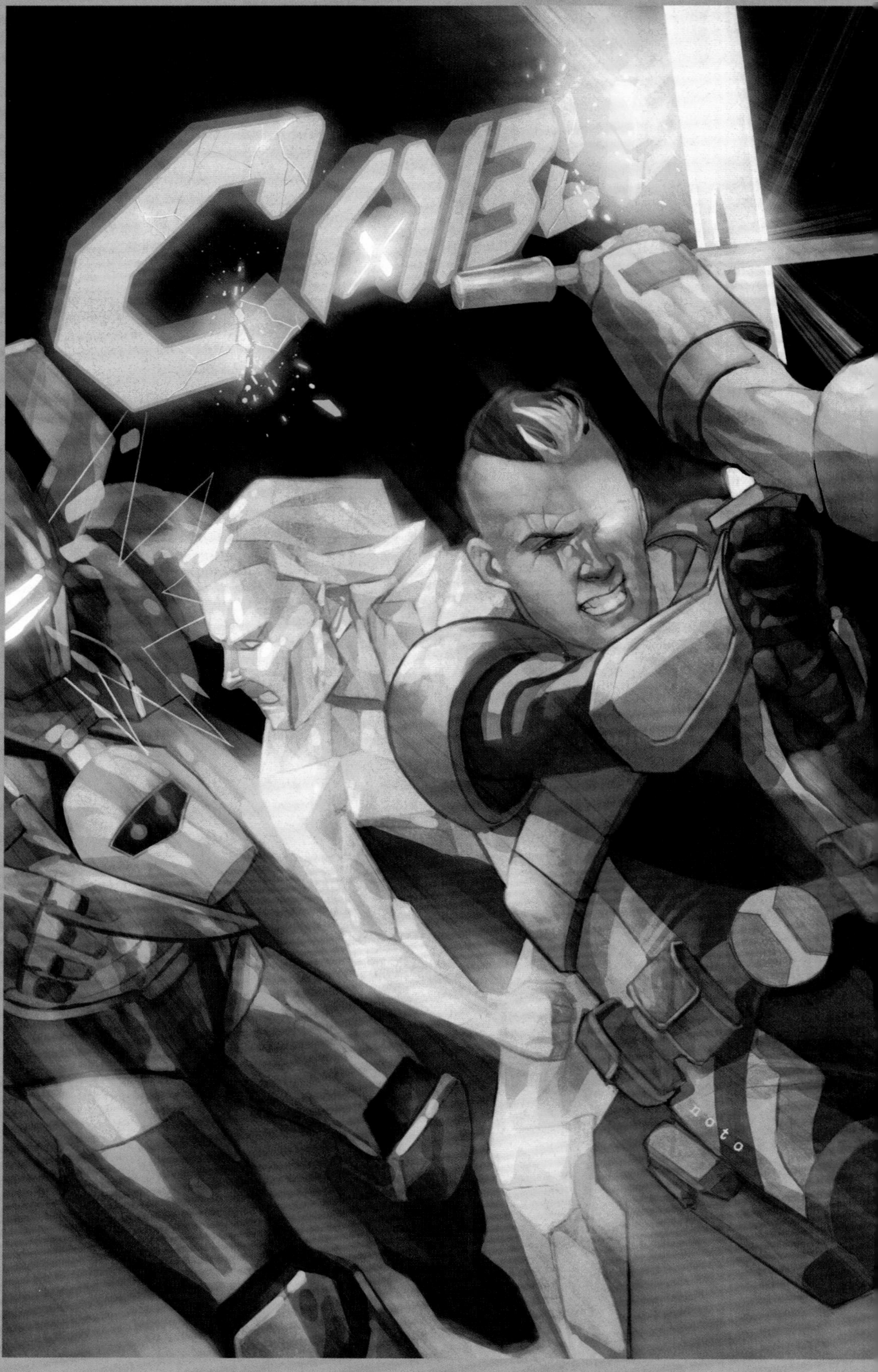
noto

The Big Bang

"Cable, have you ever heard of the planet *Galador?*

"Personally, I'd never even heard of the place or any of its heroes...

"...and certainly not its *villains.* Like the Galadorians who experimented on their own people.

"Political prisoners and petty thieves had every thing they would ever be stolen from them...

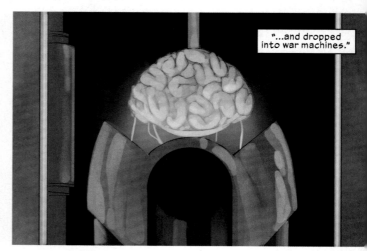

"...and dropped into war machines."

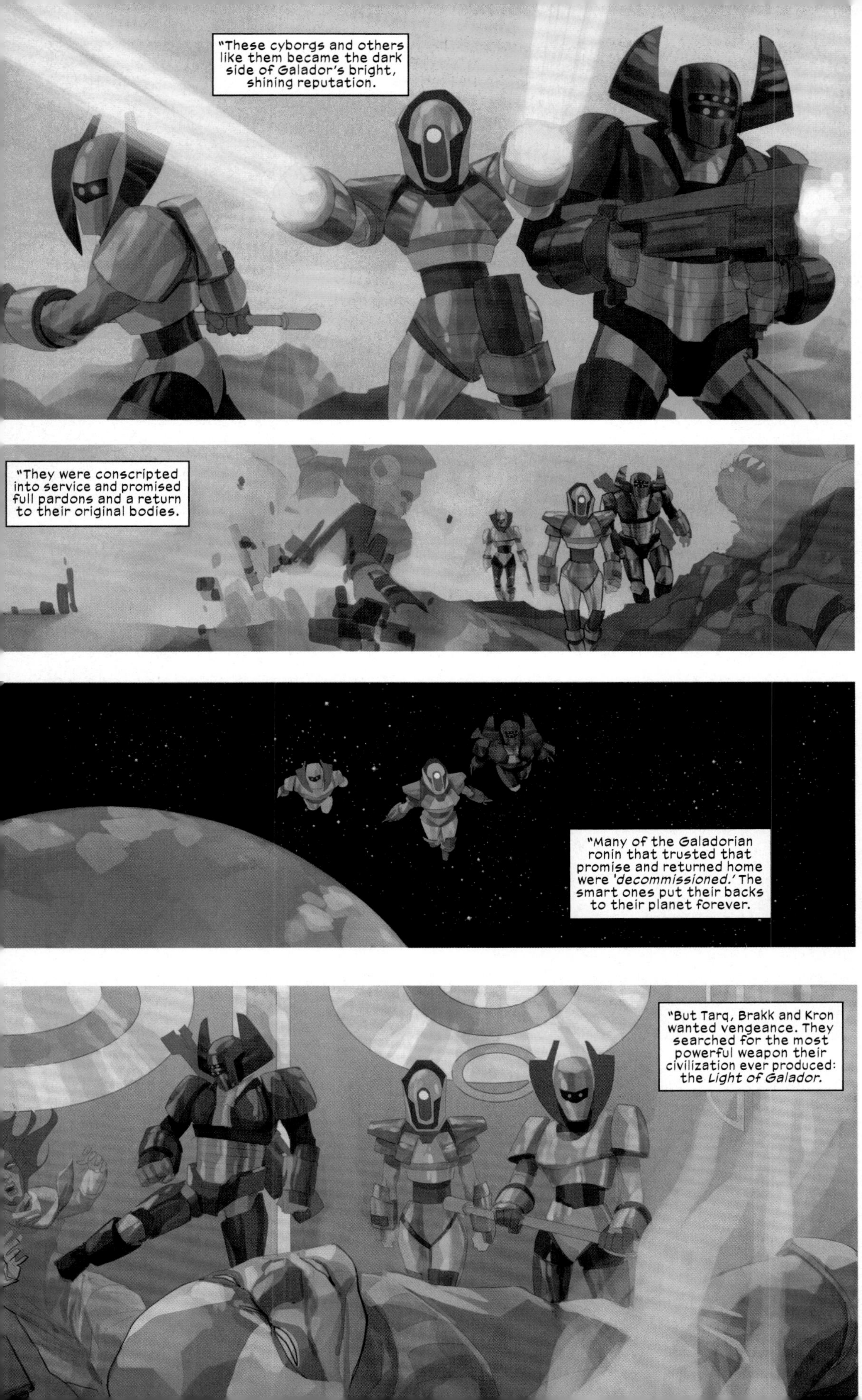
"These cyborgs and others like them became the dark side of Galador's bright, shining reputation.
"They were conscripted into service and promised full pardons and a return to their original bodies.
"Many of the Galadorian ronin that trusted that promise and returned home were *'decommissioned.'* The smart ones put their backs to their planet forever.
"But Tarq, Brakk and Kron wanted vengeance. They searched for the most powerful weapon their civilization ever produced: the *Light of Galador.*

"They lost track of the sword in our galaxy, and to conserve their ancient robot bodies they hibernated on a desolate world..."

"...but while they slept, Galador was destroyed."

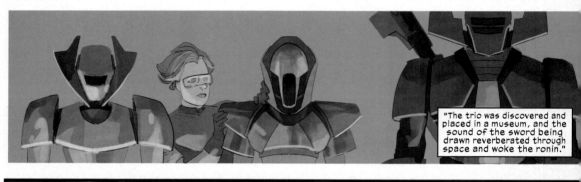

"The trio was discovered and placed in a museum, and the sound of the sword being drawn reverberated through space and woke the ronin."

Now they're stuck as robots AND they're homeless.

They were intent on killing us, until you offered them a time machine, so now they're winging it.

I know I've made a mistake.

We can't possibly give them a time machine. Luckily there are only three of them, and we can--

No, Nathan...

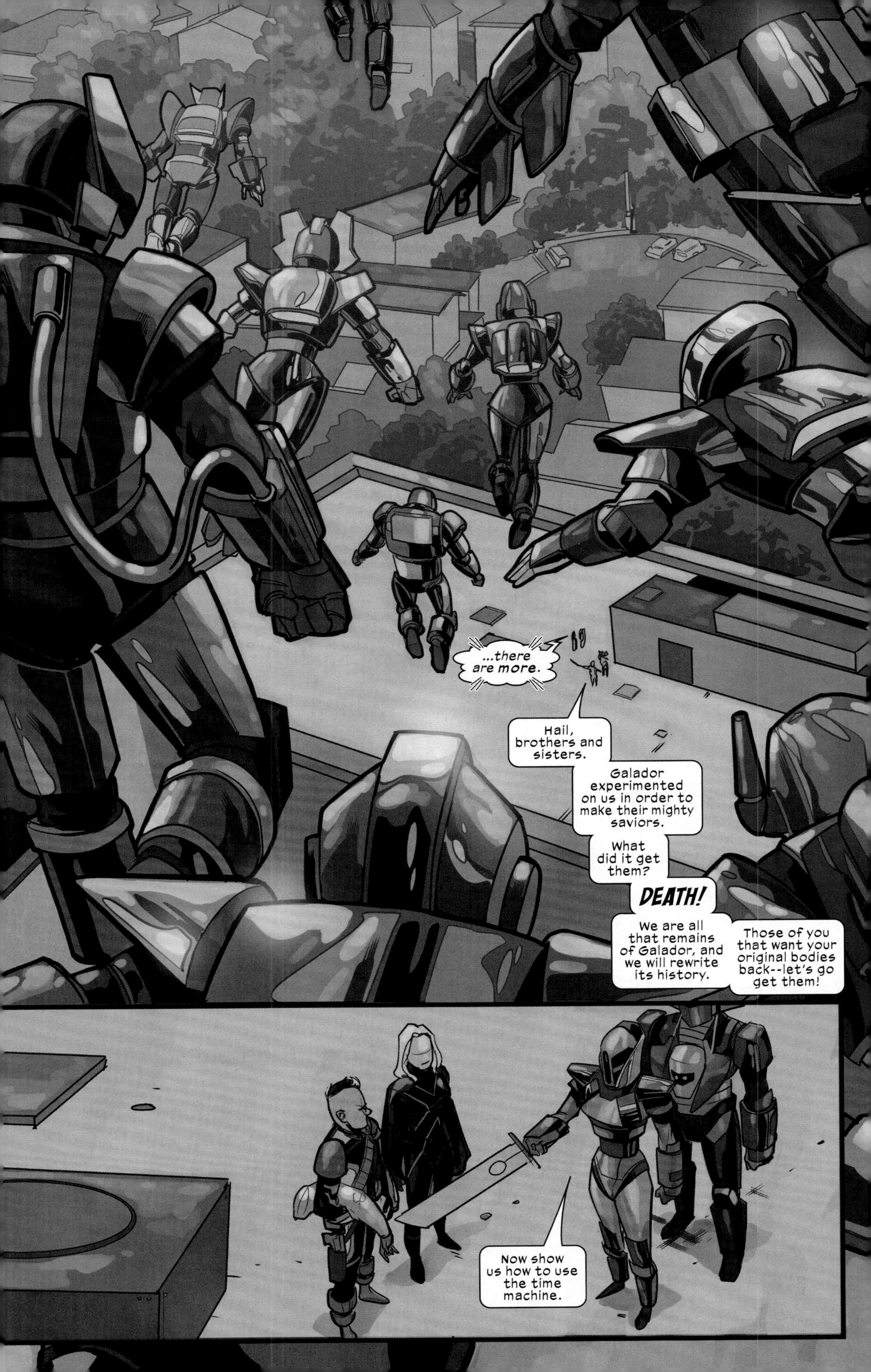
...there are more.
Hail, brothers and sisters.
Galador experimented on us in order to make their mighty saviors.
What did it get them?
DEATH!
We are all that remains of Galador, and we will rewrite its history.
Those of you that want your original bodies back--let's go get them!
Now show us how to use the time machine.

If I end up in resurrection protocols Emma may kill you and put you at the back of the line.

I know, I know. Lemme think.

Ironically, I don't have time enough to sabotage the time machine...

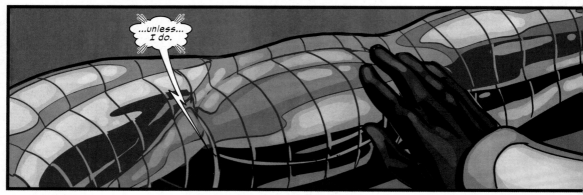

...unless... I do.

What if I have all the time in the world?

Heh.

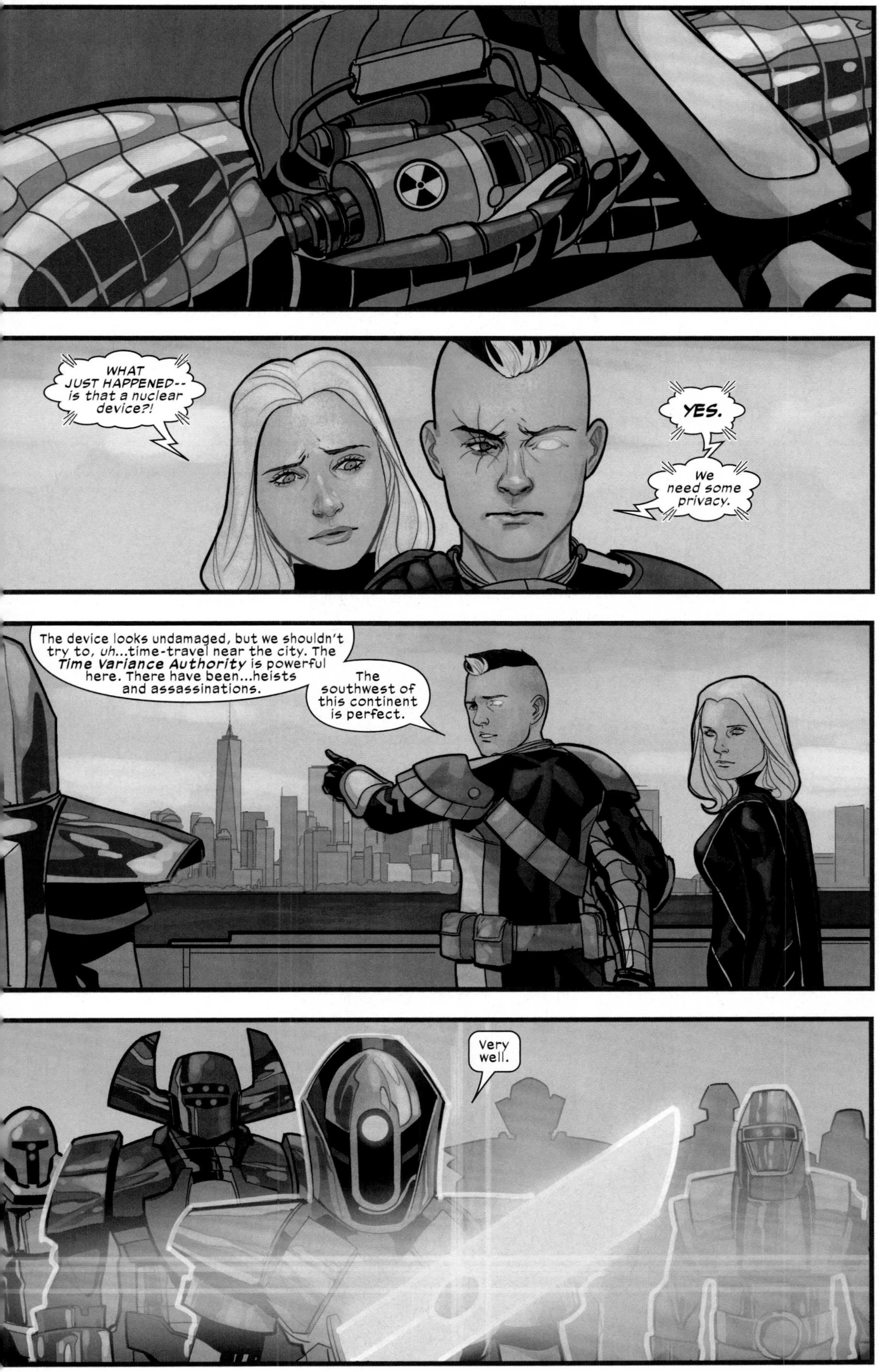
WHAT JUST HAPPENED-- is that a nuclear device?!
YES.
We need some privacy.
The device looks undamaged, but we shouldn't try to, uh...time-travel near the city. The Time Variance Authority is powerful here. There have been...heists and assassinations.
The southwest of this continent is perfect.
Very well.

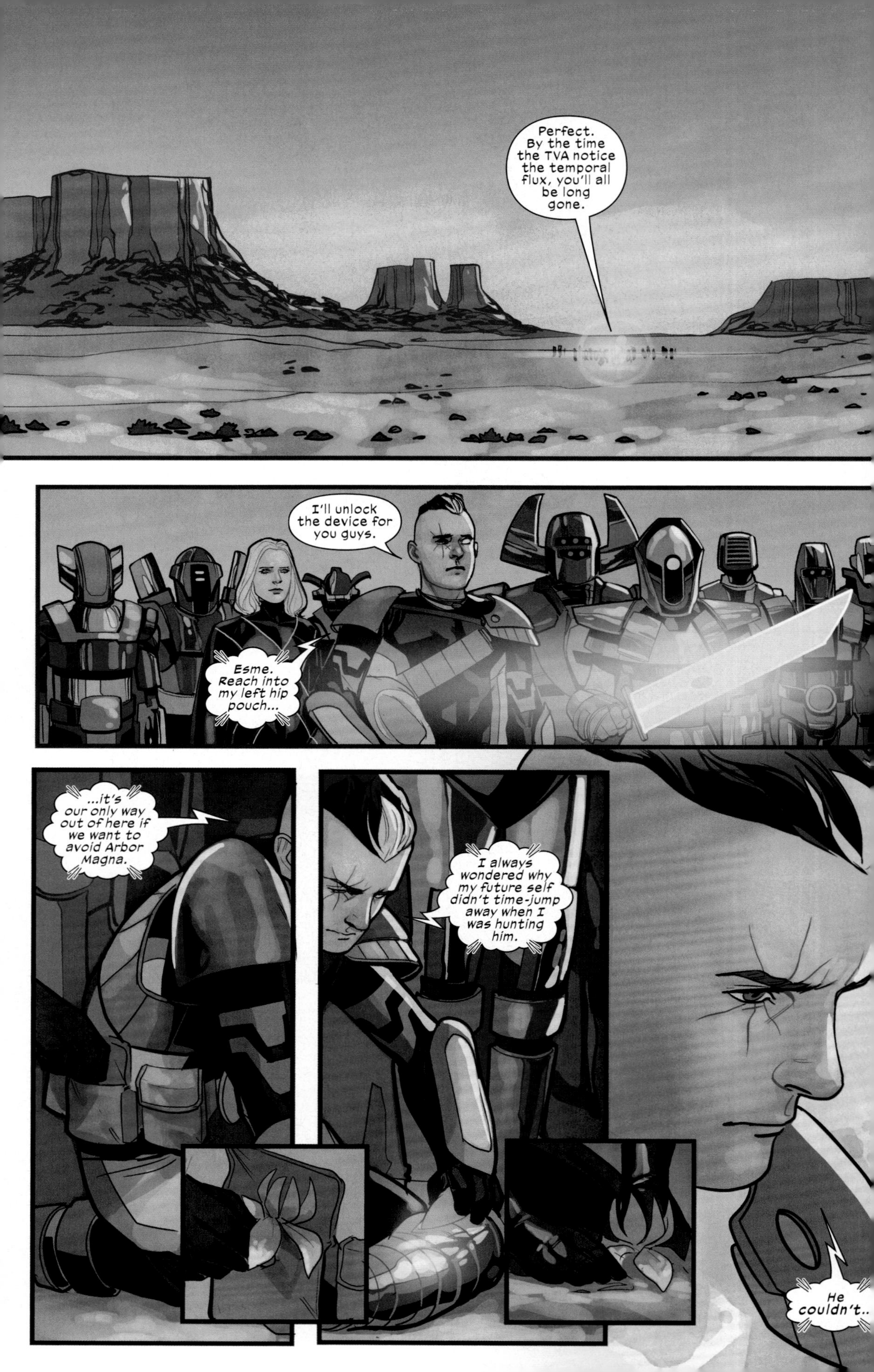
Perfect. By the time the TVA notice the temporal flux, you'll all be long gone.
I'll unlock the device for you guys.
Esme. Reach into my left hip pouch...
...it's our only way out of here if we want to avoid Arbor Magna.
I always wondered why my future self didn't time-jump away when I was hunting him.
He couldn't..

"...not without a time machine in his arm.

Stupid little #@‡%.

"The old bastard *knew* we'd need a bomb for today."

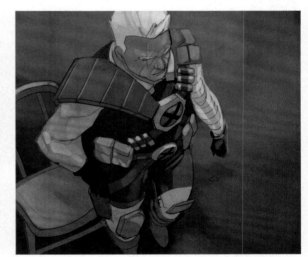

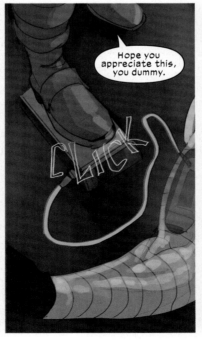

Hope you appreciate this, you dummy.

CLICK

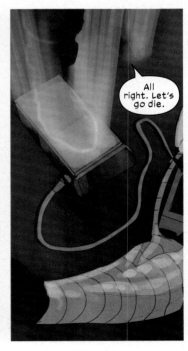

All right. Let's go die.

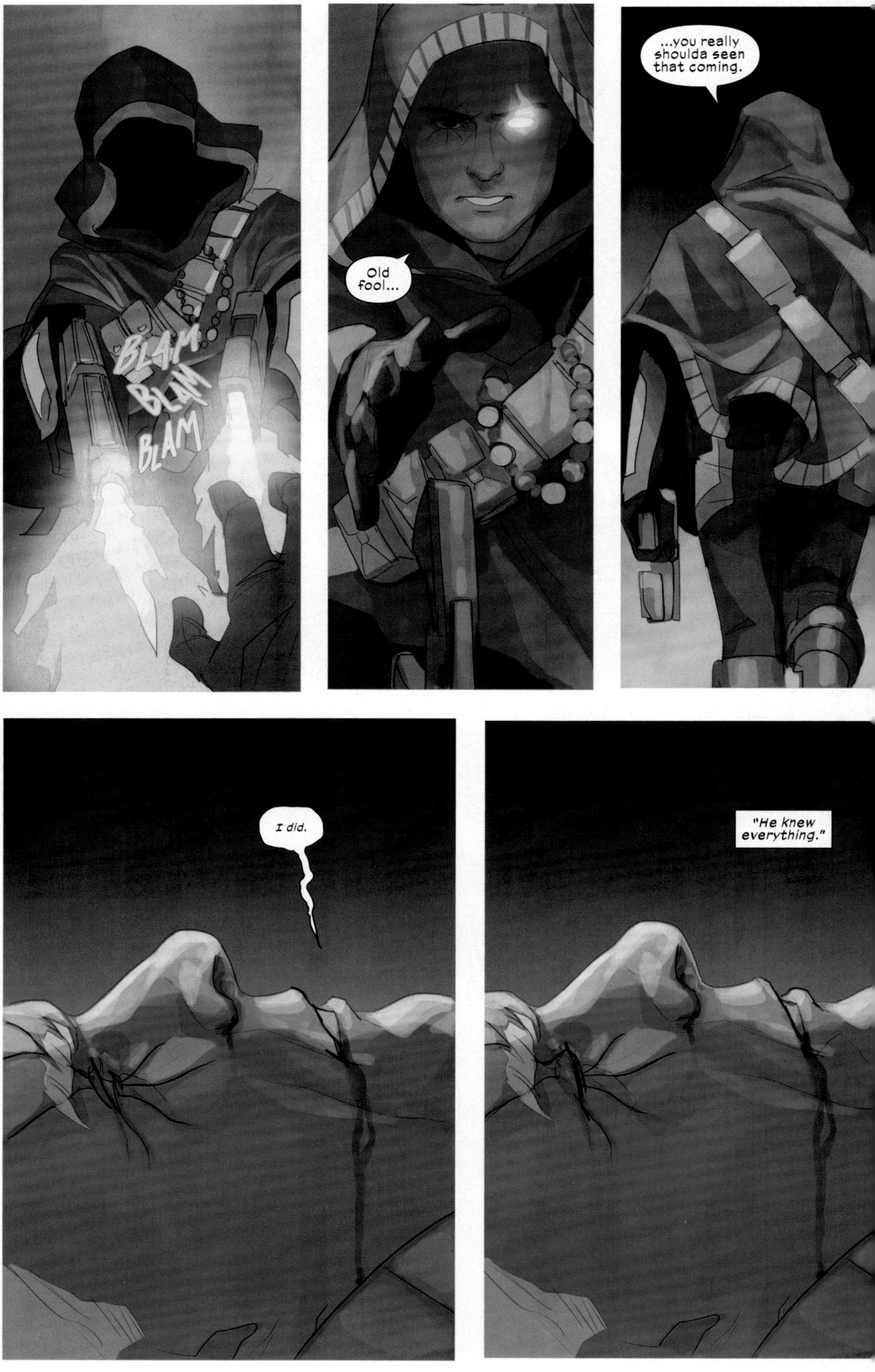
BLAM
BLAM
BLAM
Old fool...
...you really shoulda seen that coming.
I did.
"He knew everything."

Door's planted. You okay?
Yes. I was just remembering something Xavier said: We all have something to give for Krakoa.
You had better *not* be stalling, Terran.
Not at all. You're good to go.
Time machine activated. Please say or enter your intended chronal coordinates.

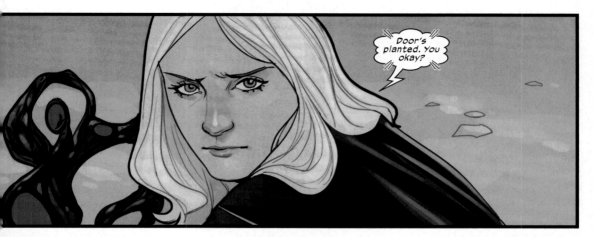

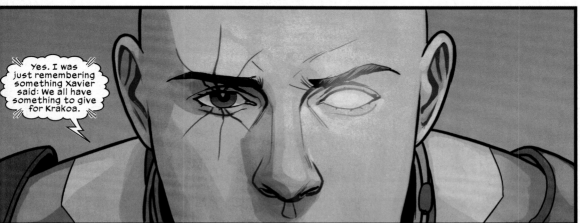

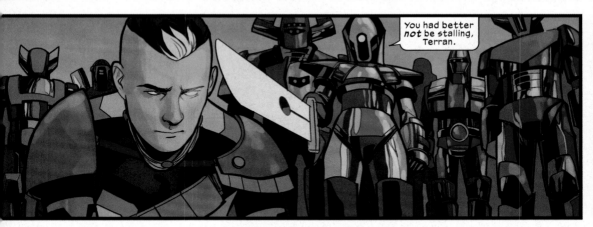

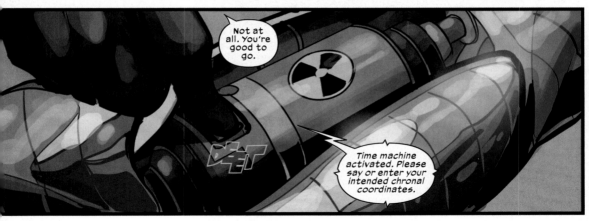

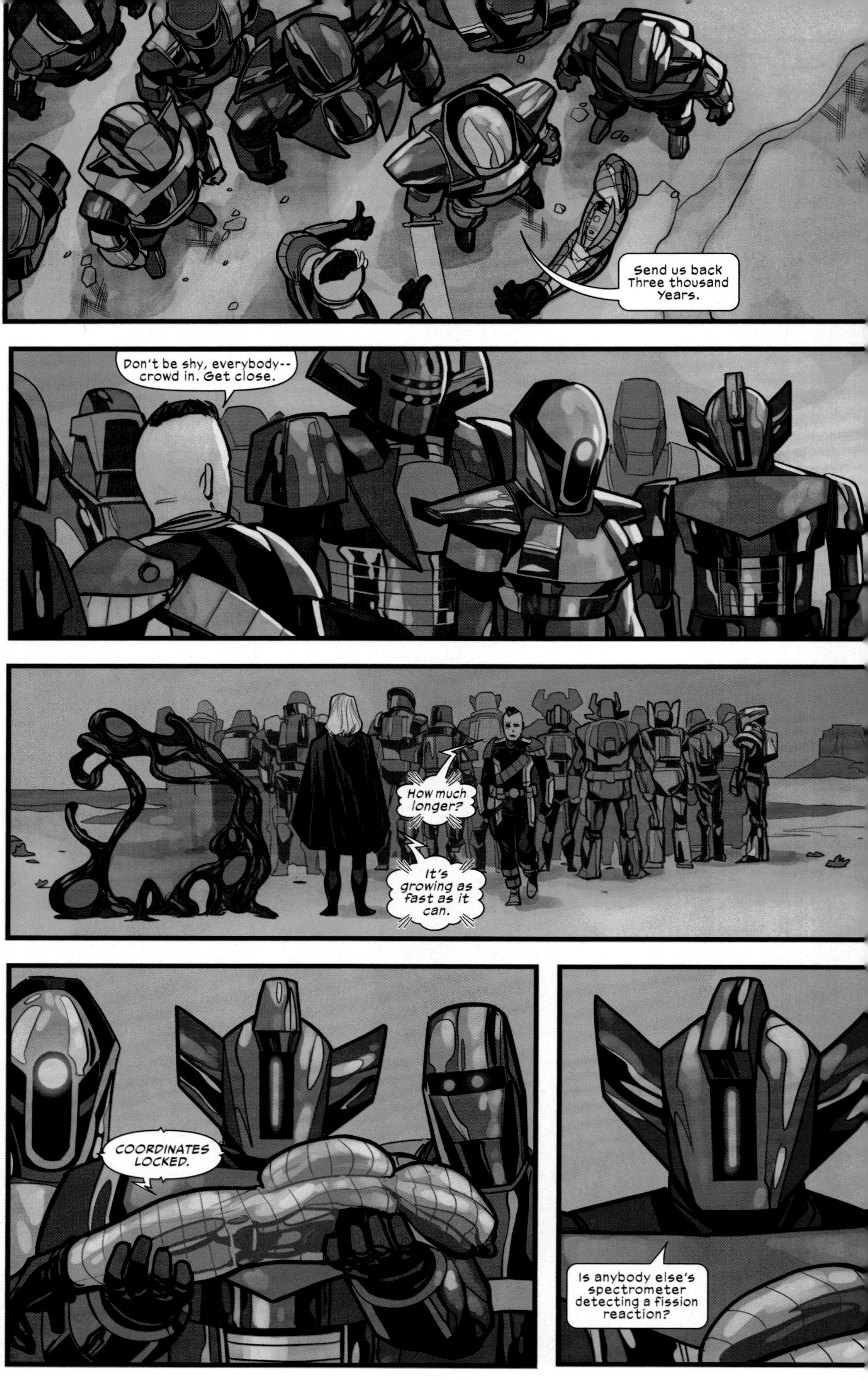

Send us back Three thousand Years.
Don't be shy, everybody-- crowd in. Get close.
How much longer?
It's growing as fast as it can.
COORDINATES LOCKED.
Is anybody else's spectrometer detecting a fission reaction?

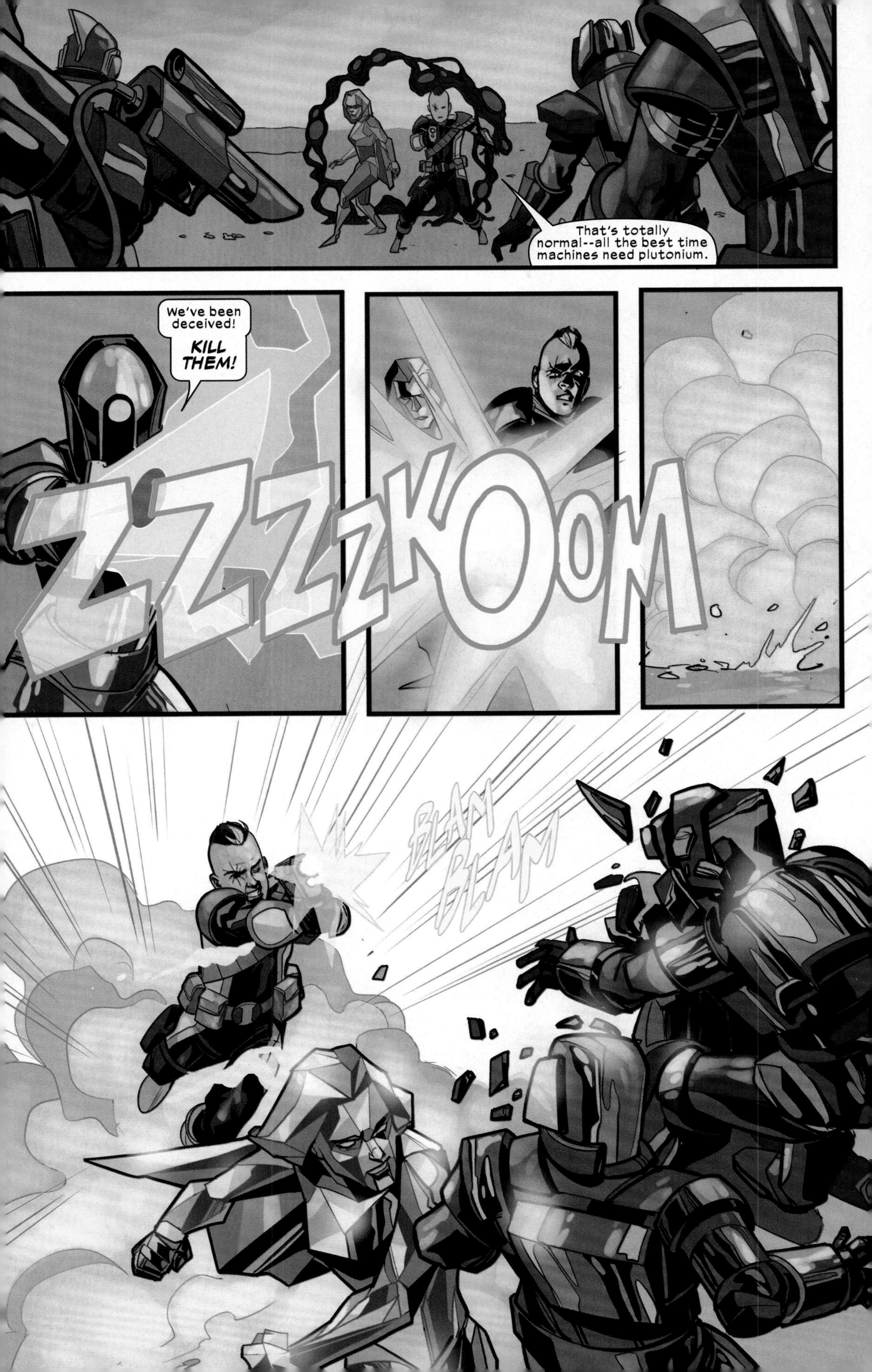
That's totally normal--all the best time machines need plutonium.
We've been deceived! KILL THEM!
ZZZZKOOM
BLAM
BLAM

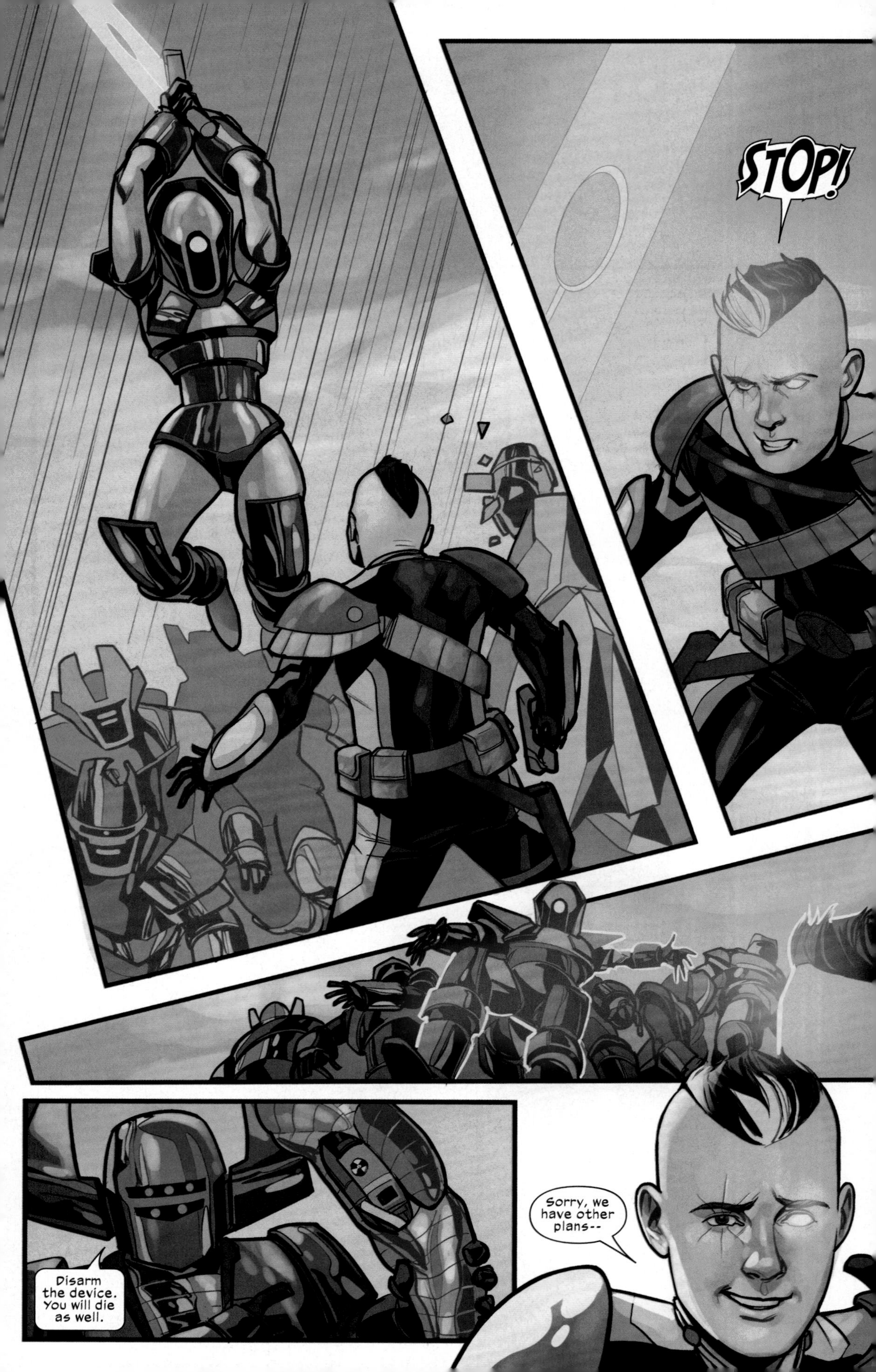
STOP!
Disarm the device. You will die as well.
Sorry, we have other plans--

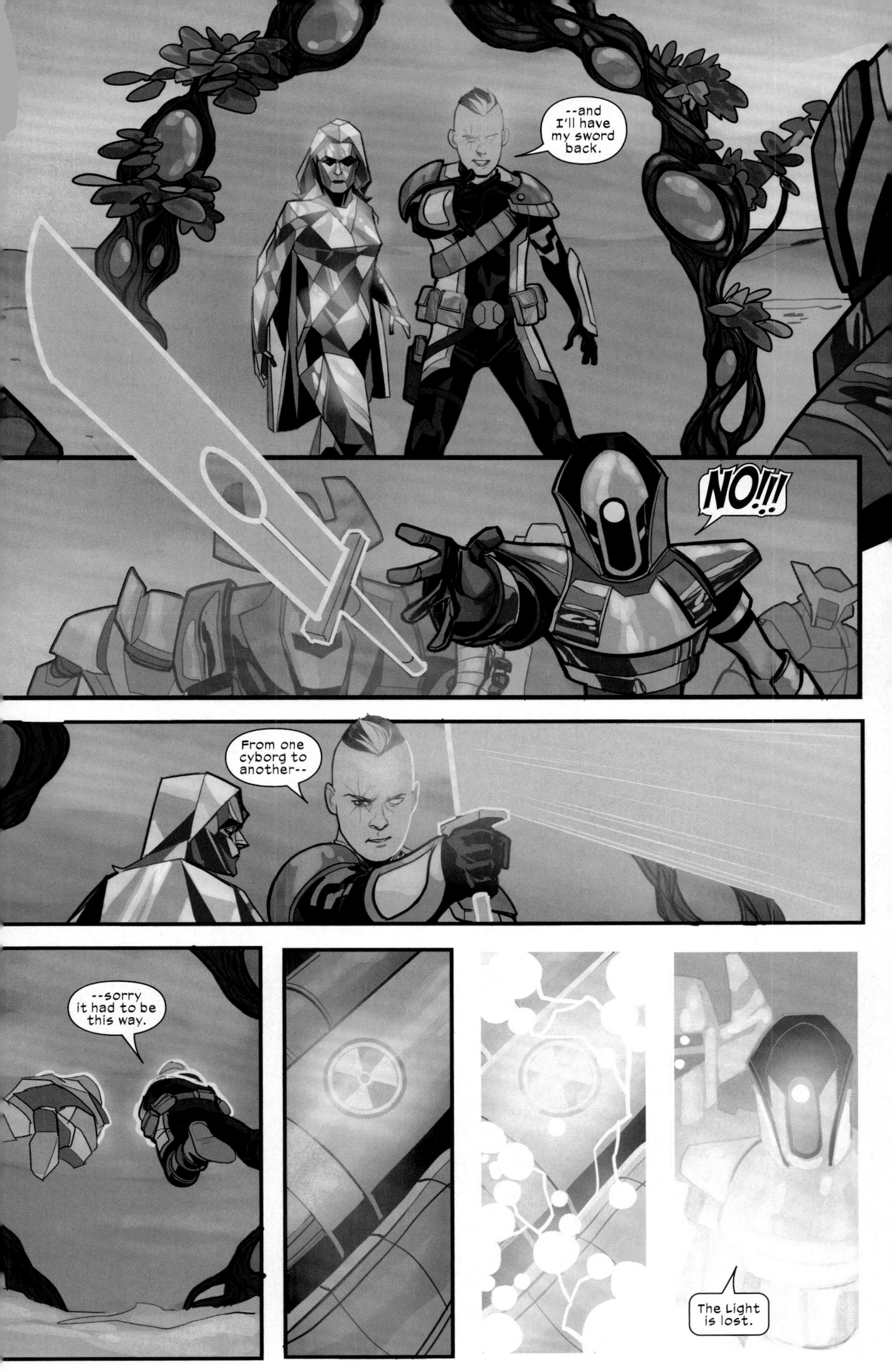
--and I'll have my sword back.
NO!!!
From one cyborg to another--
--sorry it had to be this way.
The Light is lost.

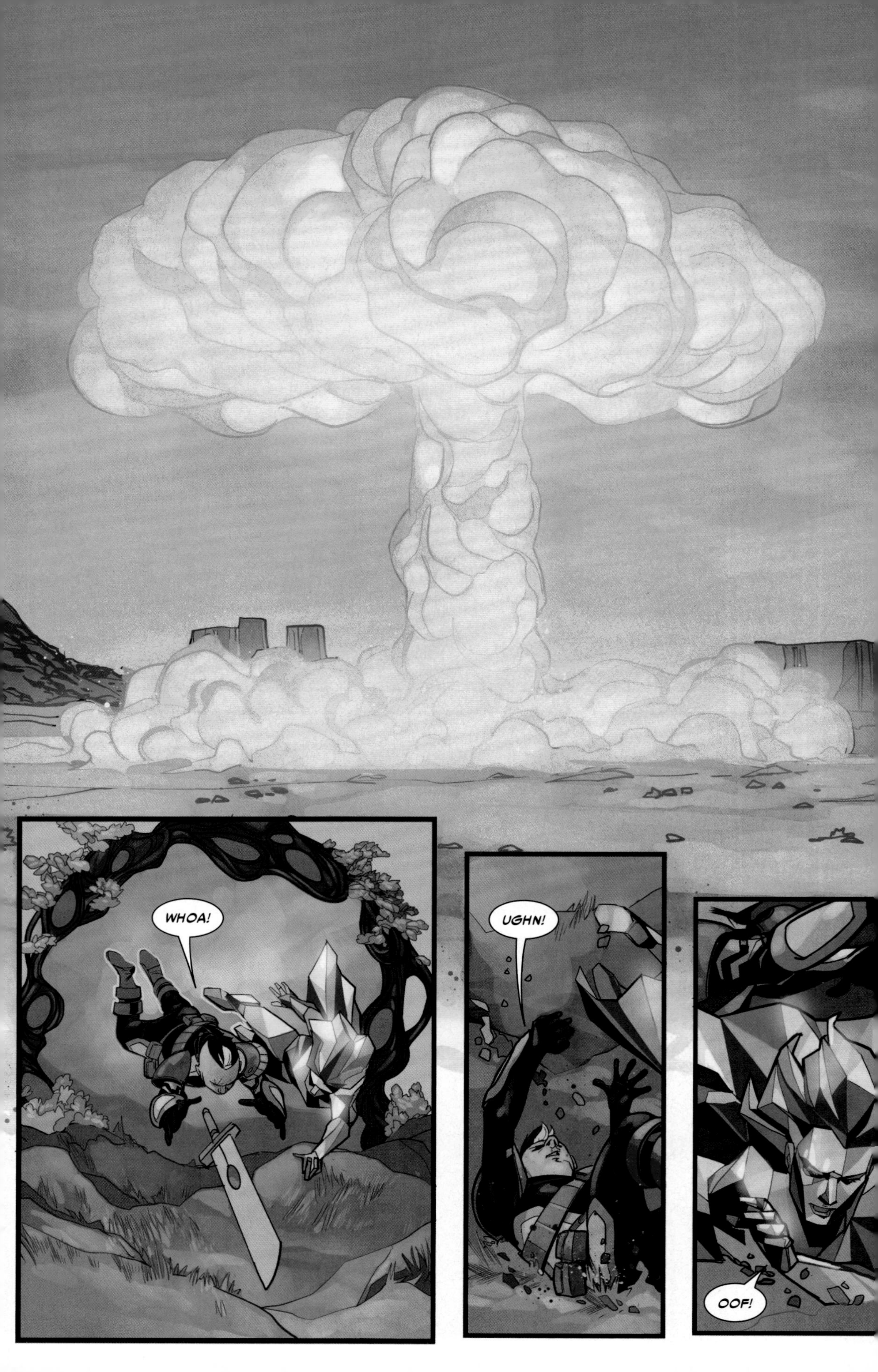
WHOA!
UGHN!
OOF!

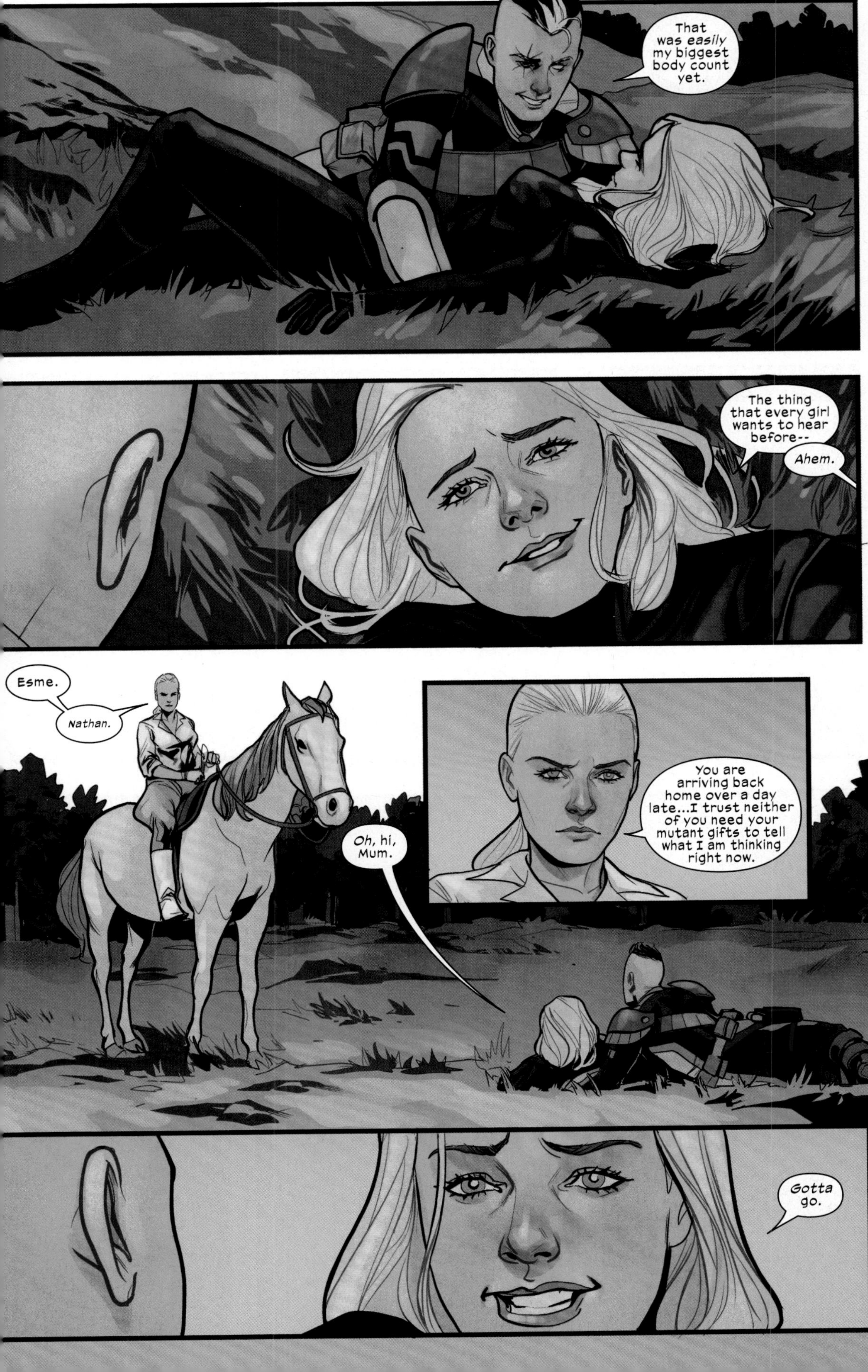
That was easily my biggest body count yet.
The thing that every girl wants to hear before--
Ahem.
Esme.
Nathan.
Oh, hi, Mum.
You are arriving back home over a day late...I trust neither of you need your mutant gifts to tell what I am thinking right now.
Gotta go.

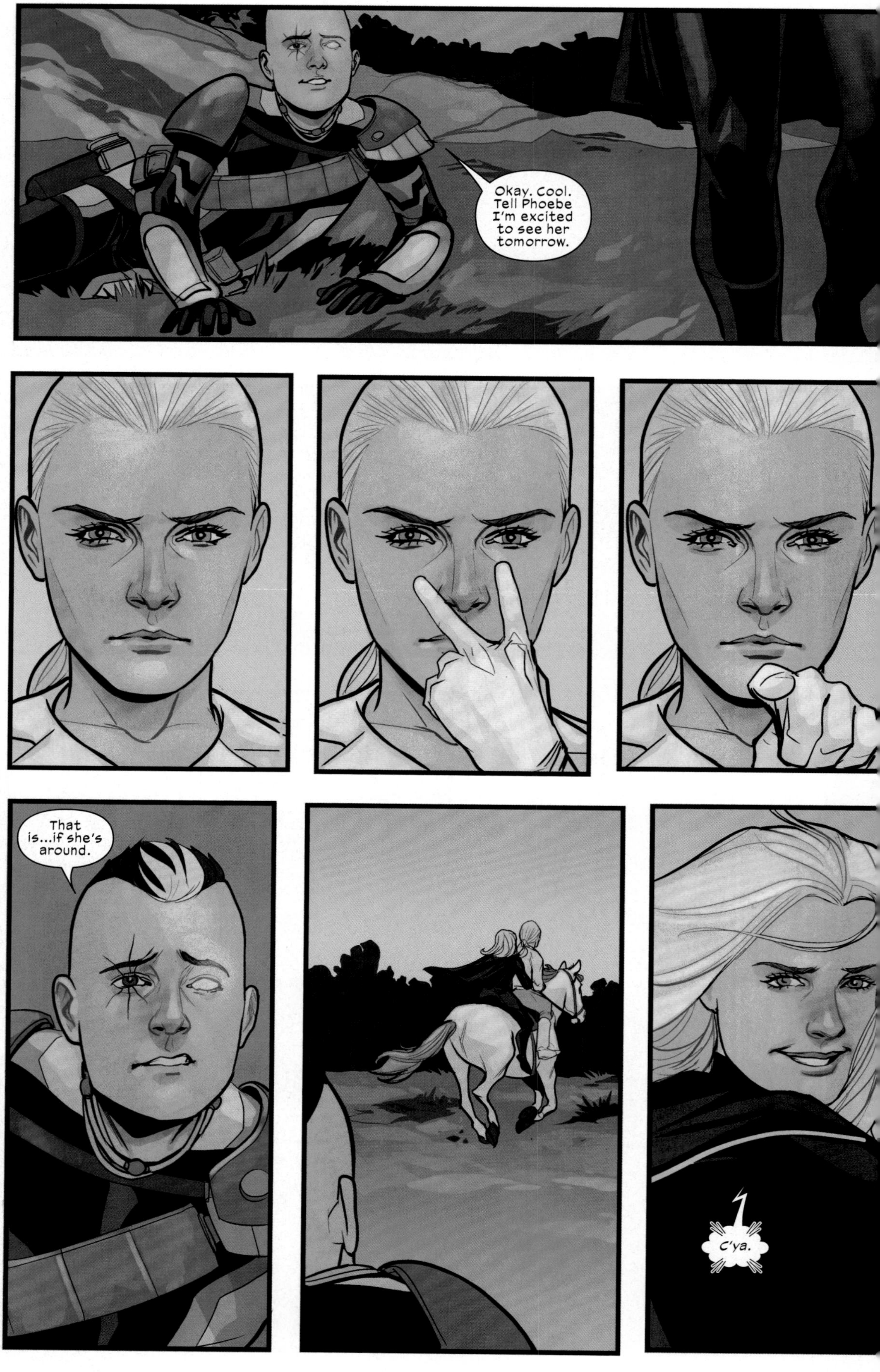
Okay. Cool. Tell Phoebe I'm excited to see her tomorrow.
That is...if she's around.
C'ya.

[ULTRA LOW-FREQUENCY DATA BURST]

Xerek, the Light of Galador is currently on Earth. It is in the hands
of a young Terran cyborg named Nathan Summers, A.K.A. "Cable."
All pertinent information is being uploaded to you now. In 1.5
seconds I, along with the remaining ronin of Galador, will meet a
fiery end in a crude atomic detonation. We underestimated the
Terrans -- and the ruling class of mutants in particular.

Suggest extended observation before striking. The subject has
exhibited telekinesis and weapons training, and only too late did we
understand they are also telepathic. We became greedy and
diverted from the plan to try to acquire a time machine.

The planet is largely still dependent on carbon, but not the
subject's clan. They display a high degree of technological prowess
and likely nonlinear dimensional travel.

Someday in the future, you will wake up to this grim news. Perhaps
you are not the last Galadorian Knight, but we know of no other.

Let it be known that at the moment of the fission blast there are:
Brakka
Tarq
Kron
Kron II
Blackstar
VeaV
00010011
Sorn
Vorn
S101000101110110111101001001 [END COMMS]

FROM THE X-DESK

To: Molina, Philadelphia PD
cc: DiStefano, Philadelphia PD

Saw your report about mutant contact. Let me know how this plays out. In return for sharing what you find, here's a down payment: Look at the Order of X. See attached files and a transcript of chats between burners we found in the phone of a detainee.

You're welcome from your friends on the X-Desk.

**

BLOCKED PHILLY NUMBER:
M--
I know you said to only write in an emergency, but after we exfiltrated the last arrival to you we returned to find that our safe house was destroyed in a battle involving mutants. There is nothing for anyone to find to connect the Order to the location.

BLOCKED BUCKS COUNTY, PA, NUMBER:
You killed the dog?

BLOCKED PHILLY NUMBER:
There was no time. Stinger noticed the baby missing much quicker than anticipated. I was going to kill the dog now, but it's been recovered. Are you sure that is...a priority?

BLOCKED BUCKS COUNTY, PA, NUMBER:
Kill the dog and then yourself. If you fail in either task then your sins will be inherited by your family, and they will pay heavy interest. Do not write back. Acknowledge receipt of fate by simply giving me a thumbs-up on this message.

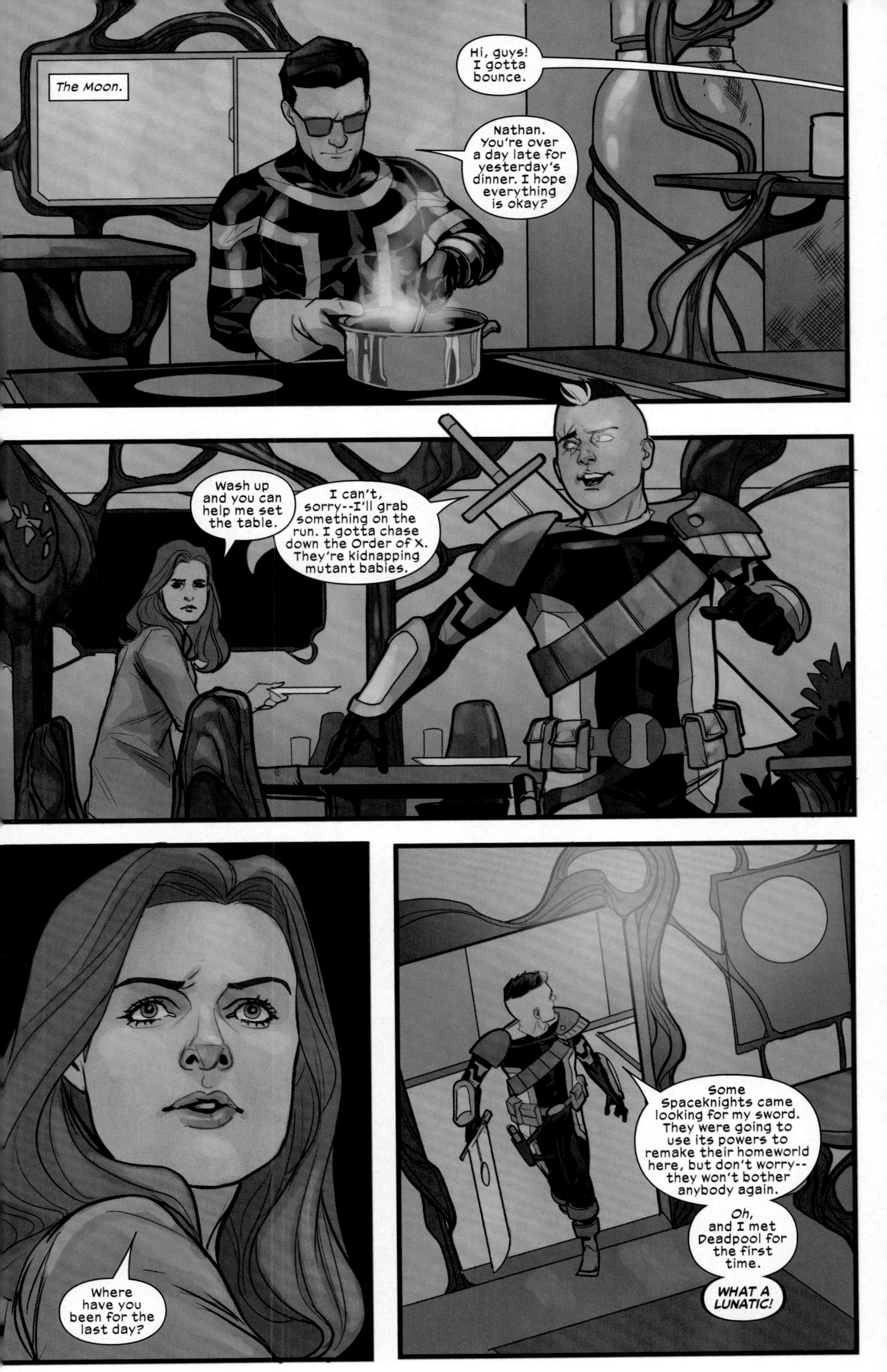
The Moon.
Hi, guys! I gotta bounce.
Nathan. You're over a day late for yesterday's dinner. I hope everything is okay?
Wash up and you can help me set the table.
I can't, sorry--I'll grab something on the run. I gotta chase down the Order of X. They're kidnapping mutant babies.
Where have you been for the last day?
Some SpaceKnights came looking for my sword. They were going to use its powers to remake their homeworld here, but don't worry-- they won't bother anybody again.
Oh, and I met Deadpool for the first time.
WHAT A LUNATIC!

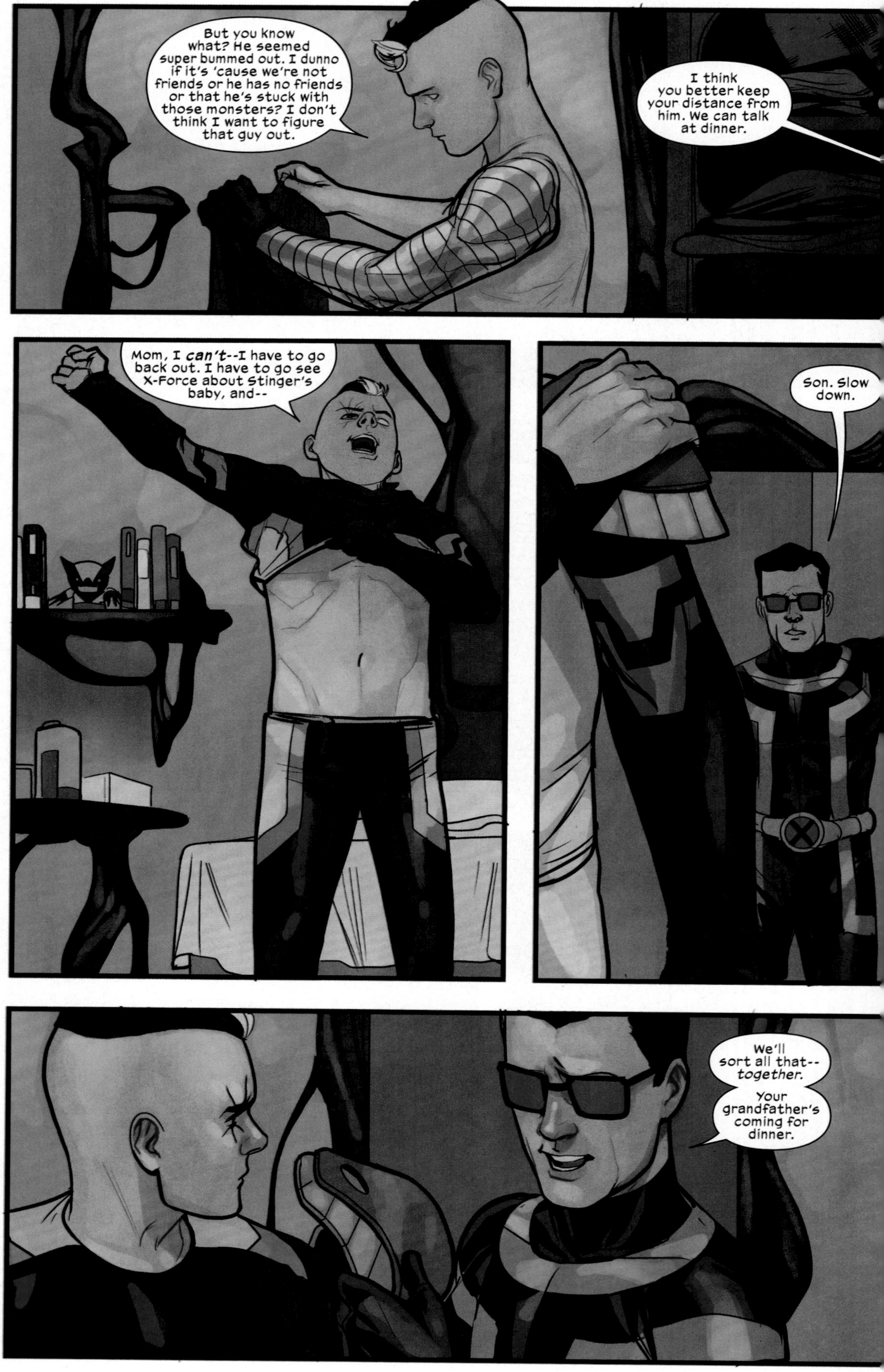
But you know what? He seemed super bummed out. I dunno if it's 'cause we're not friends or he has no friends or that he's stuck with those monsters? I don't think I want to figure that guy out.
I think you better keep your distance from him. We can talk at dinner.
Mom, I *can't*--I have to go back out. I have to go see X-Force about Stinger's baby, and--
Son. Slow down.
We'll sort all that-- *together.*
Your grandfather's coming for dinner.

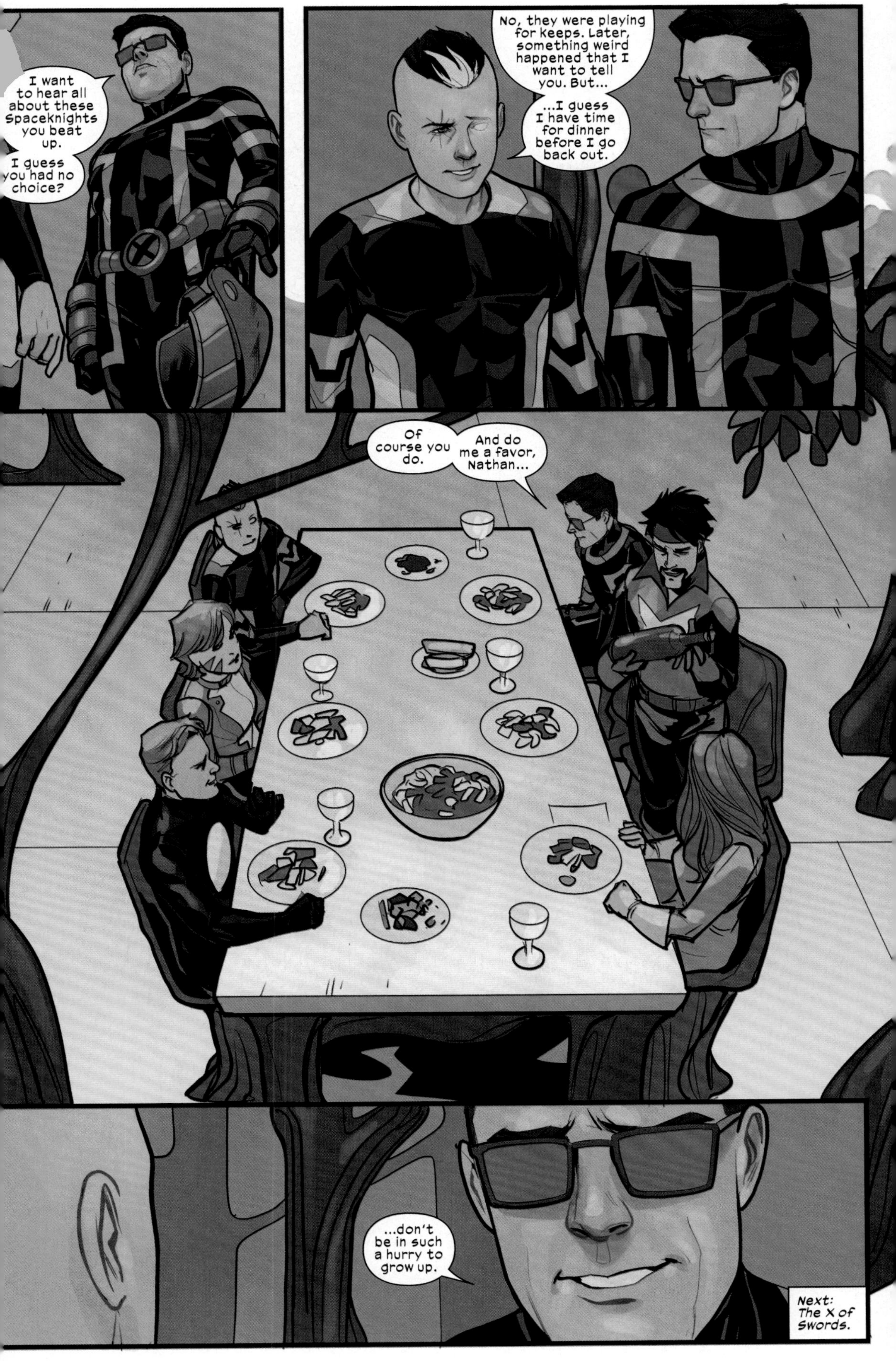
I want to hear all about these Spaceknights you beat up.
I guess you had no choice?
No, they were playing for keeps. Later, something weird happened that I want to tell you. But...
...I guess I have time for dinner before I go back out.
Of course you do.
And do me a favor, Nathan...
...don't be in such a hurry to grow up.
Next: The X of Swords.

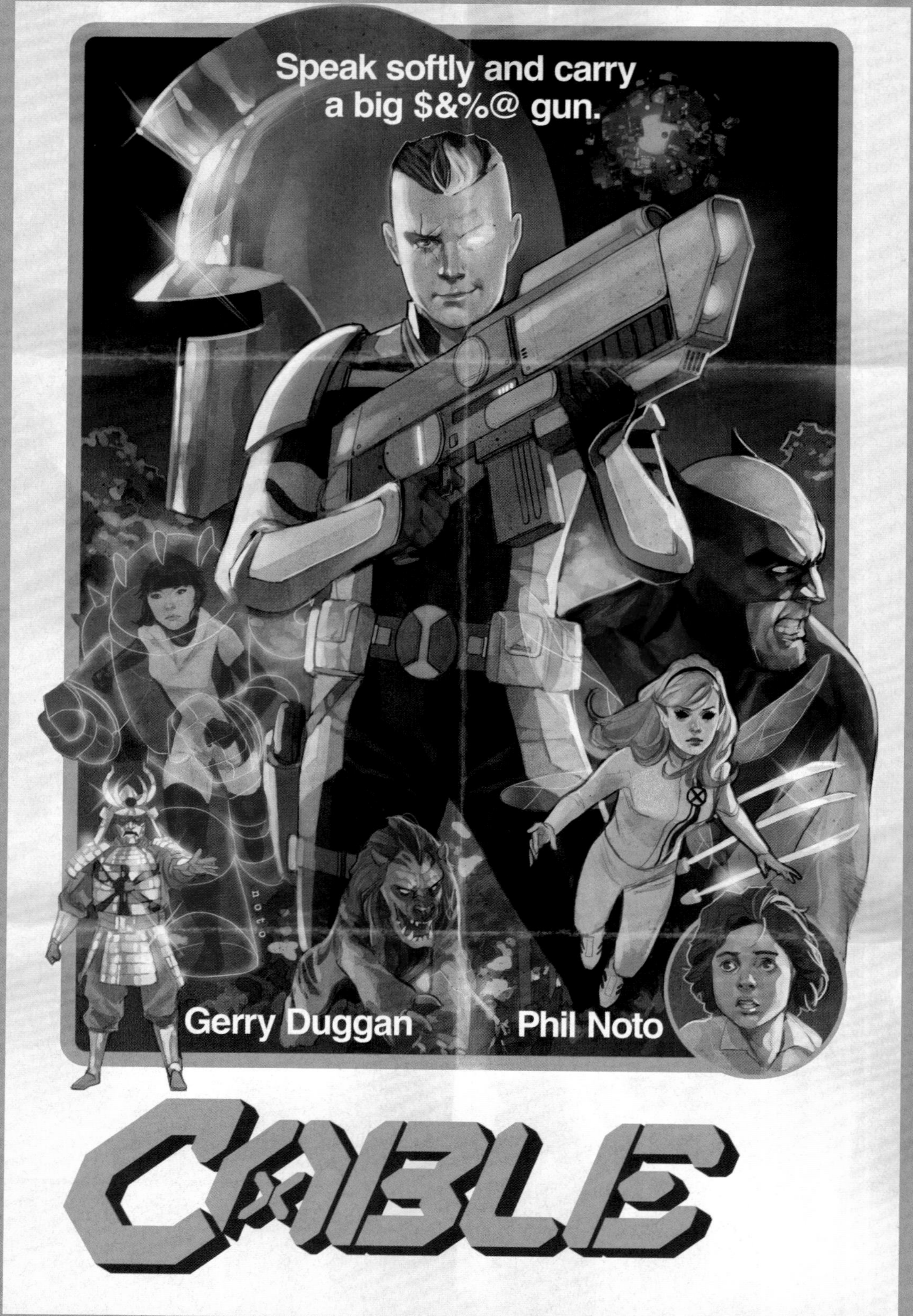
Speak softly and carry
a big $&%@ gun.
Gerry Duggan
Phil Noto
CABLE

by Phil Noto

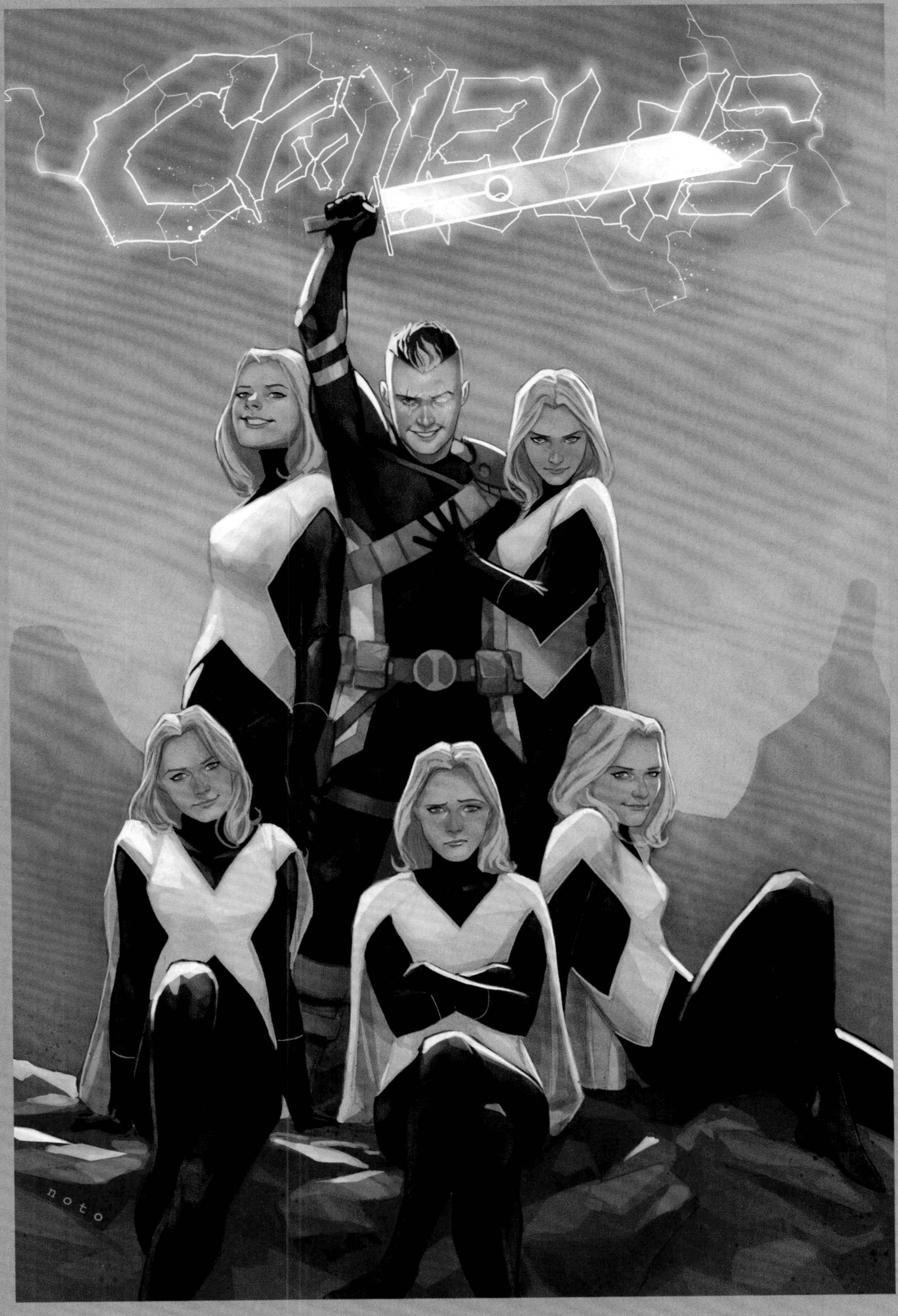
noto

Cable #2 by Phil Noto

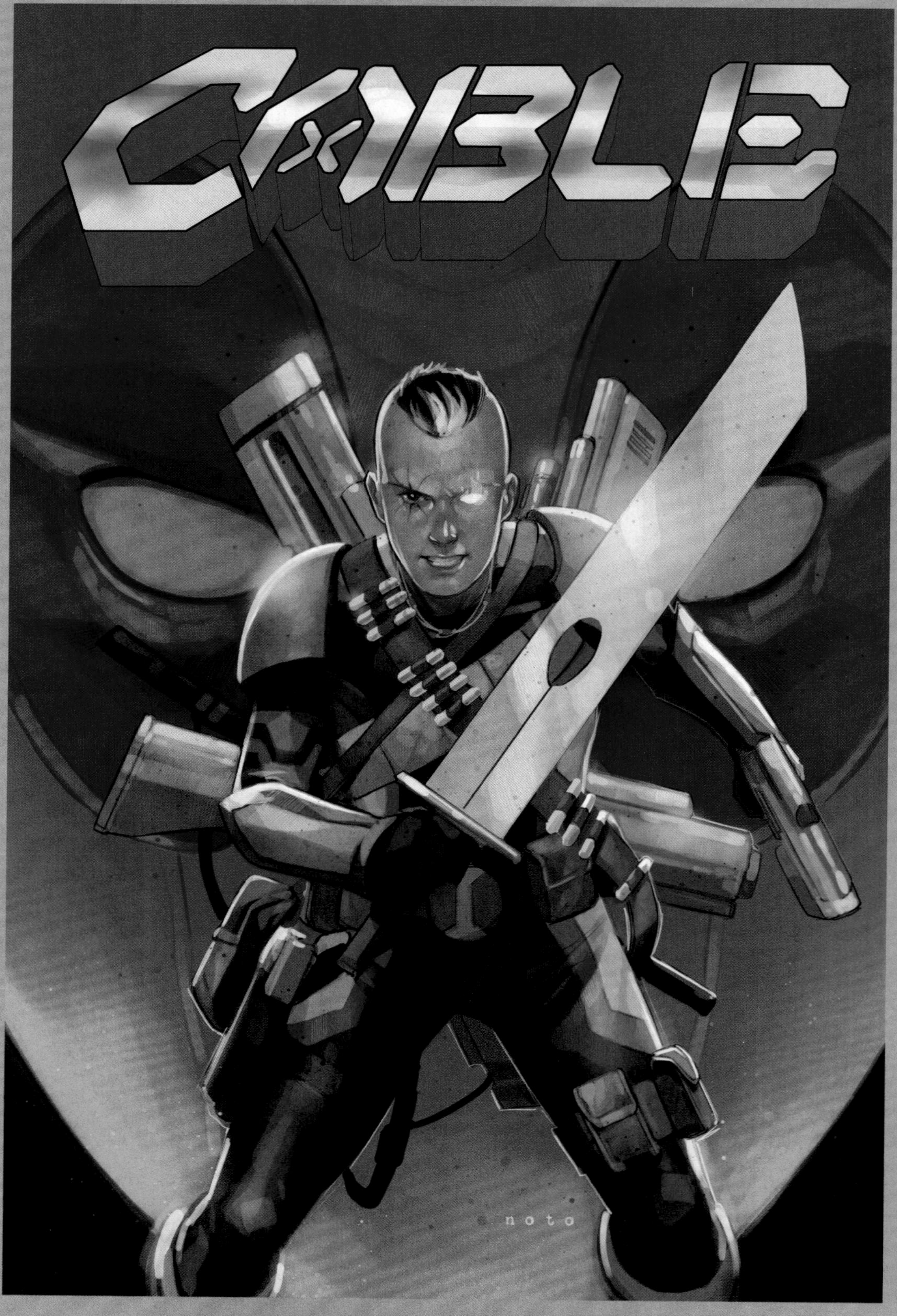
CABLE
noto

Cable #3 by Phil Noto

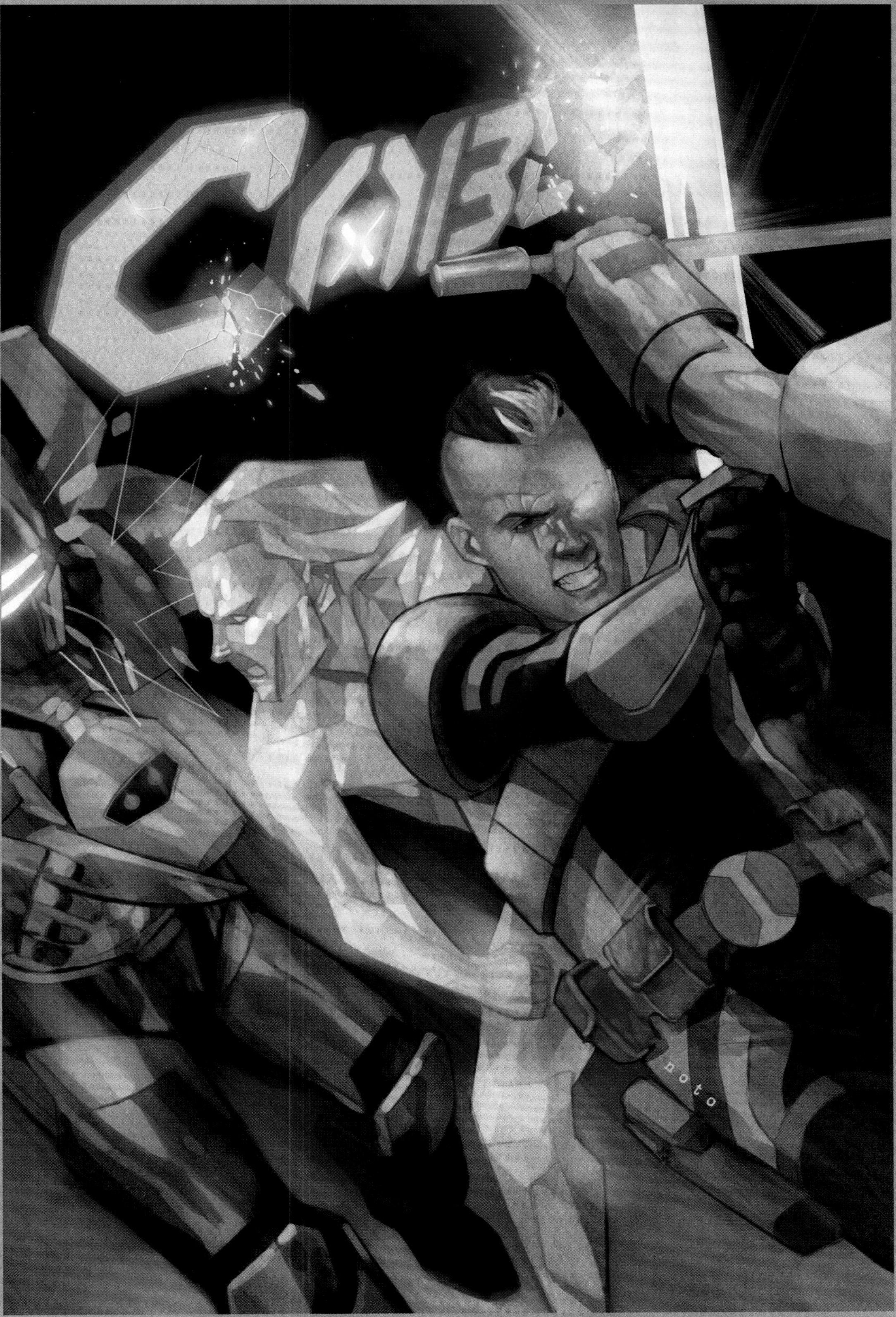
noto

Cable #4 by Phil Noto

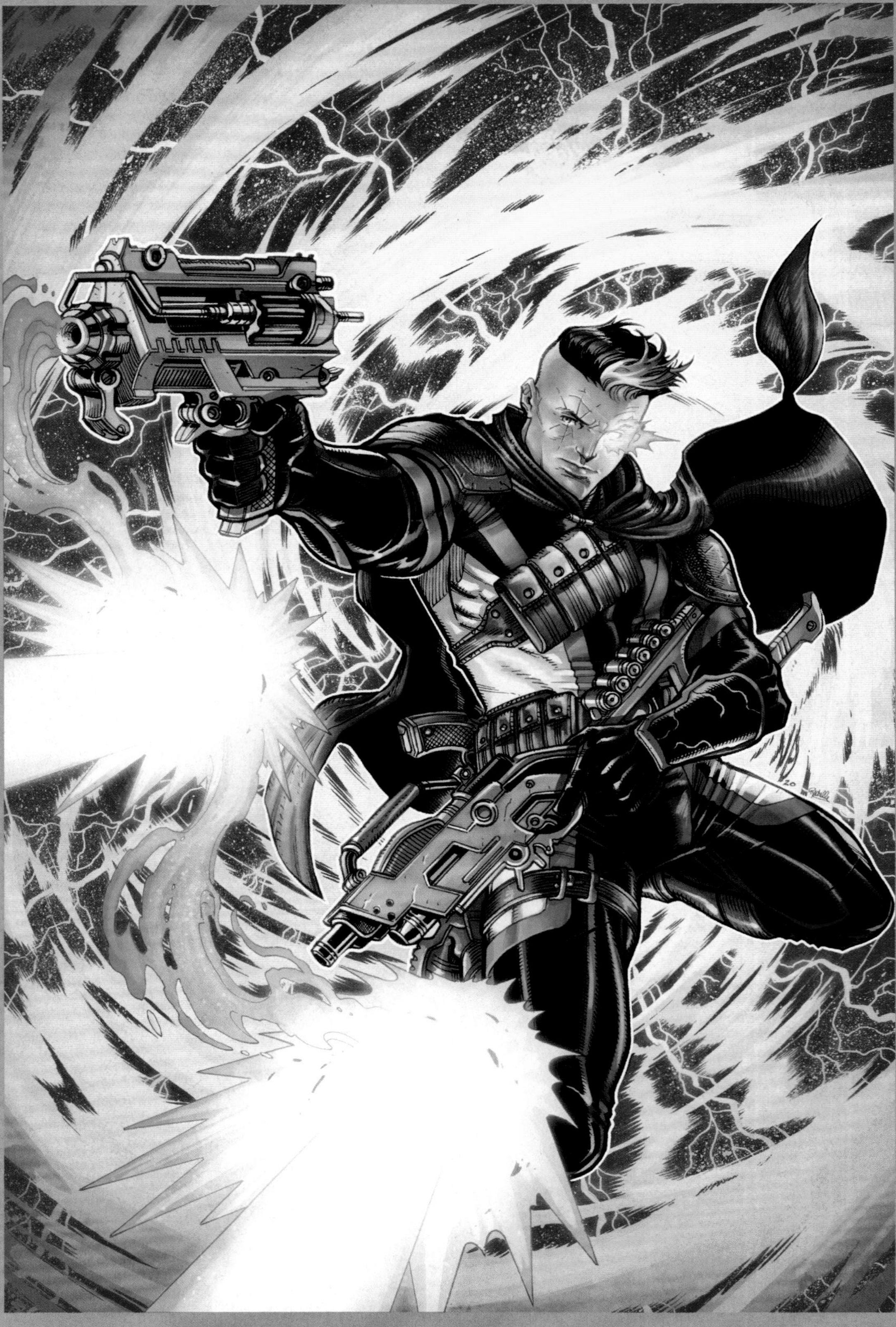

Cable #1 Variant

by Nick Bradshaw
& Rachelle Rosenberg

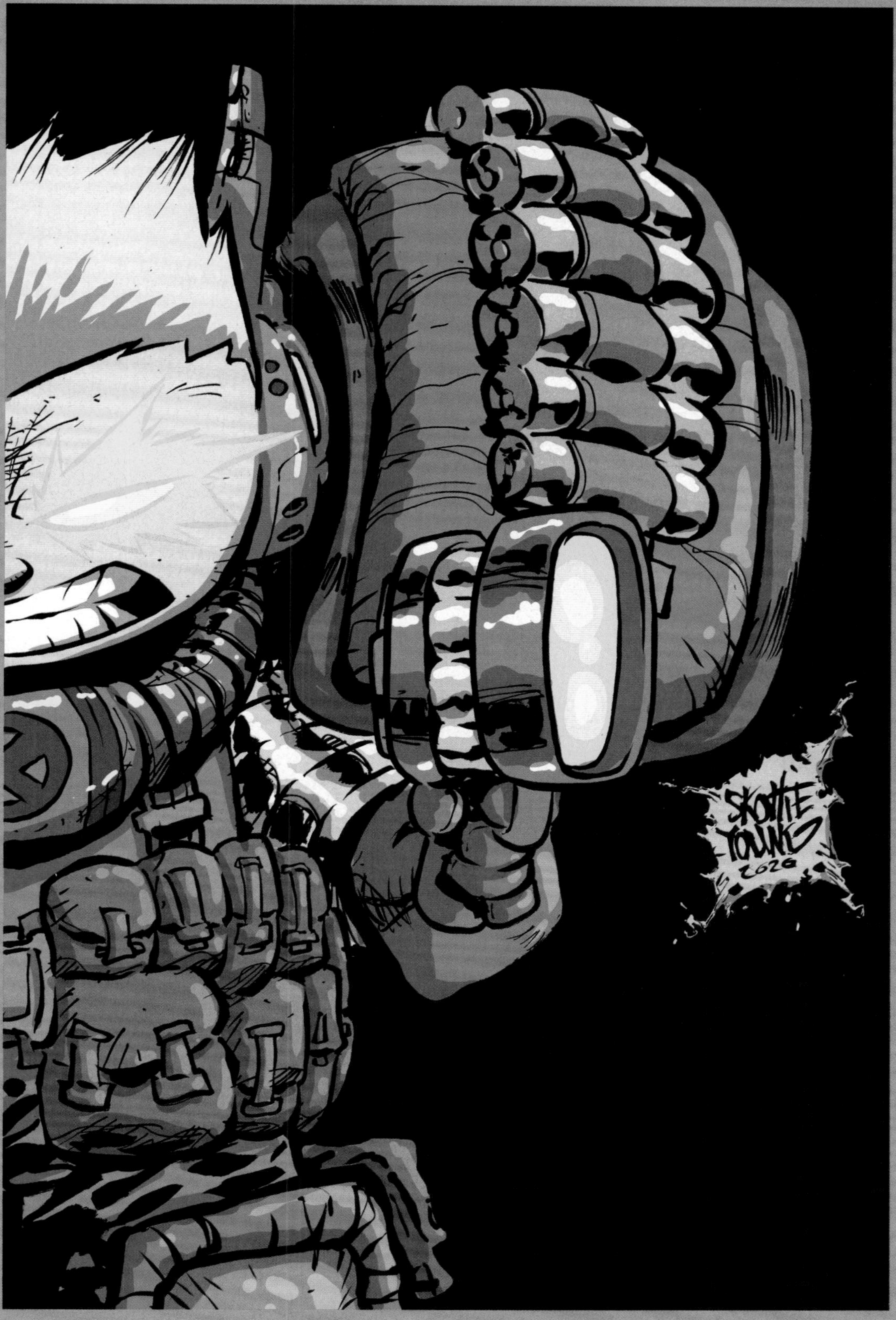
SKOTTIE
YOUNG
2020

Cable #1 Variant by Skottie Young

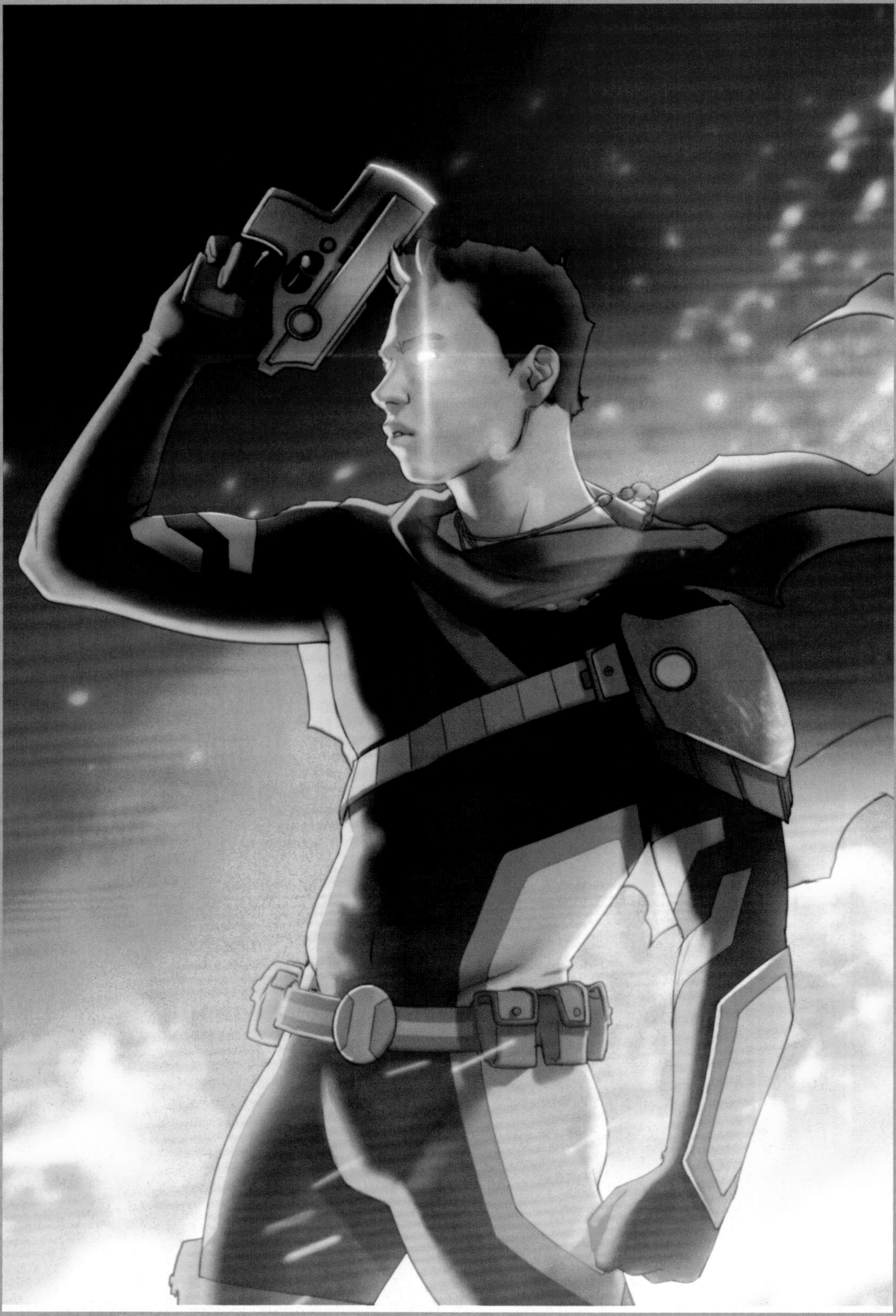

Cable #1 Variant by William Forbes

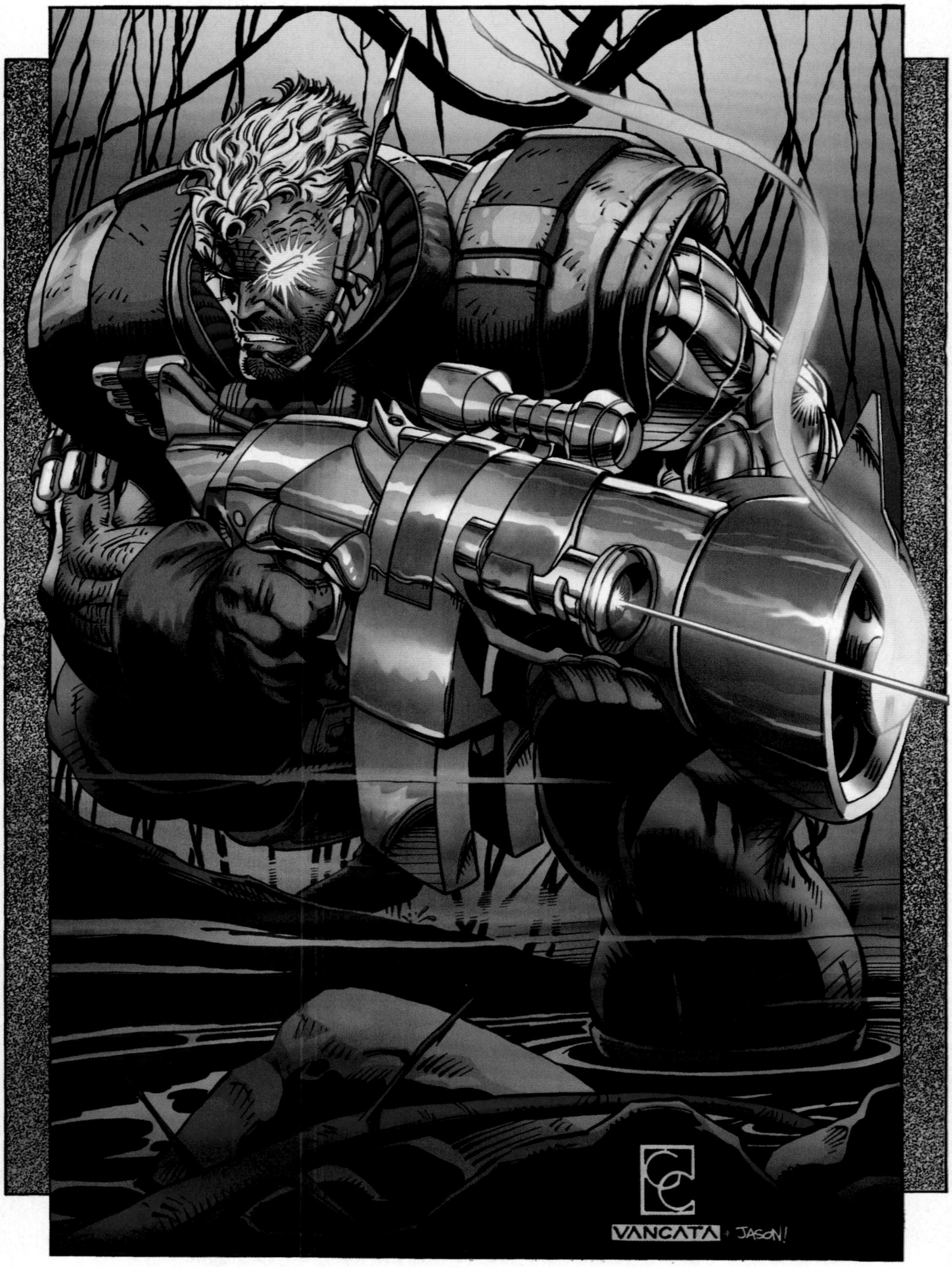
VANCATA + JASON!

Cable #1 Hidden Gem Variant

by Greg Capullo
& Jason Keith

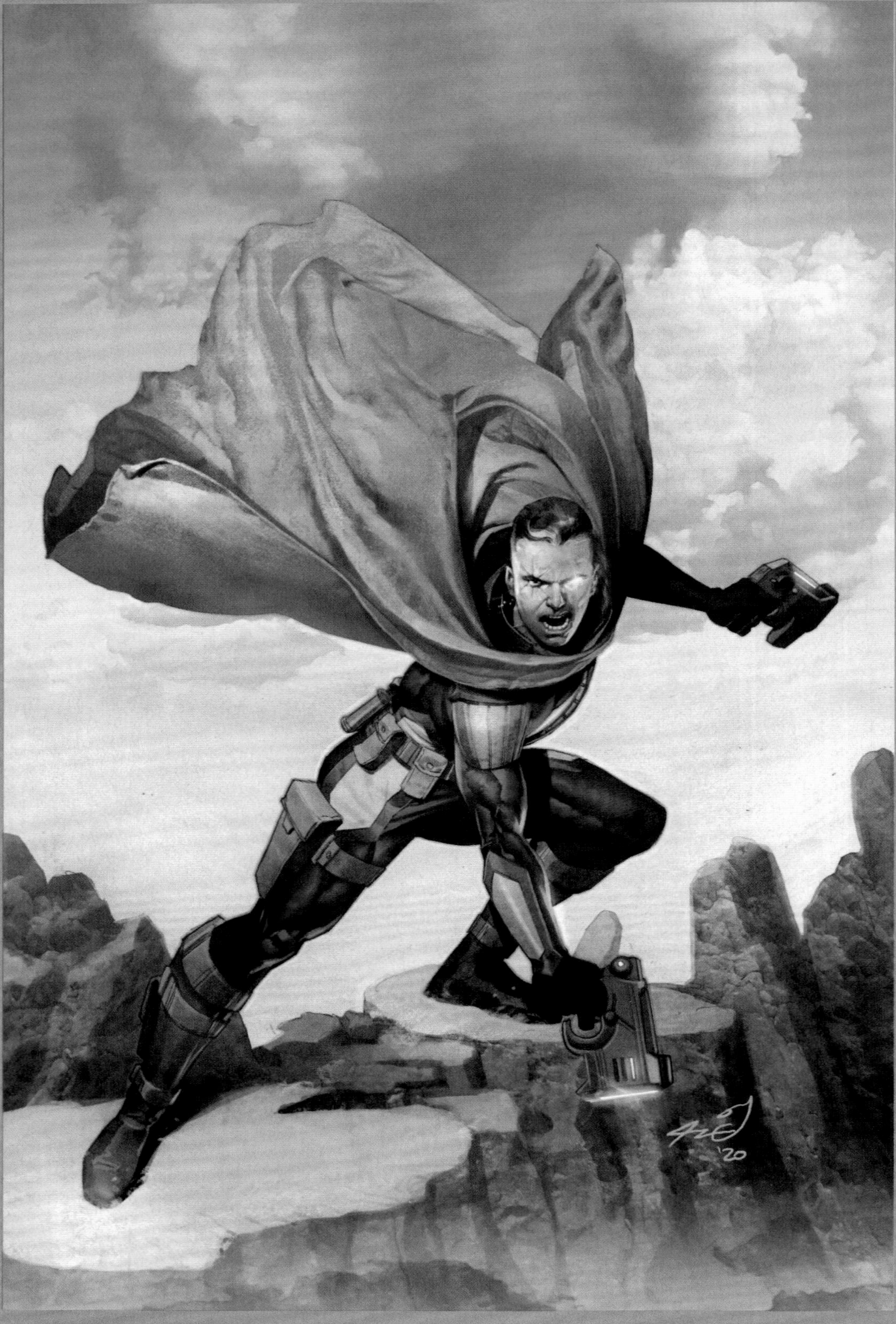

Cable #2 Variant by Ariel Olivetti

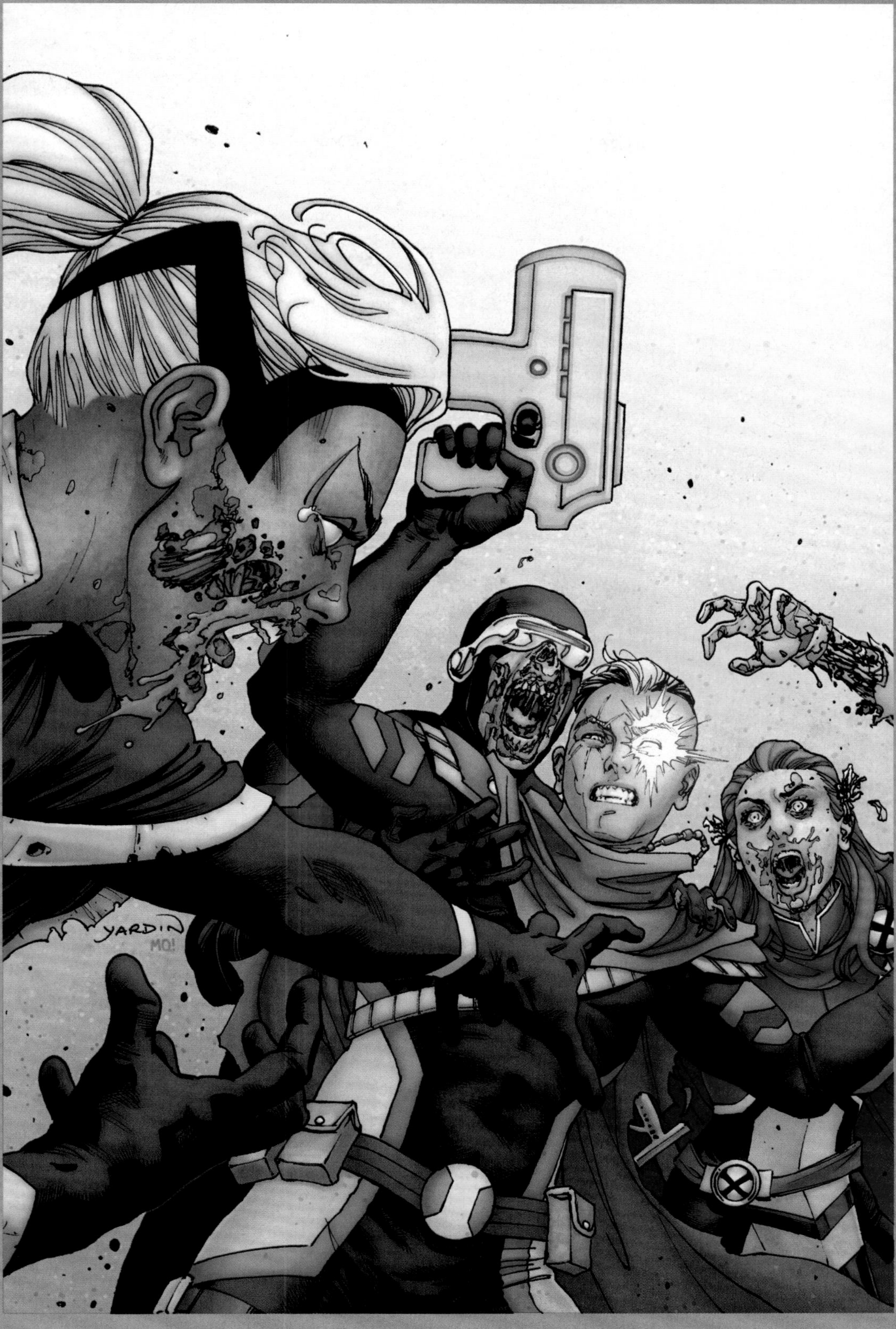
YARDIN
MQ!

Cable #2 Marvel Zombies Variant

by David Yardin
& Morry Hollowell

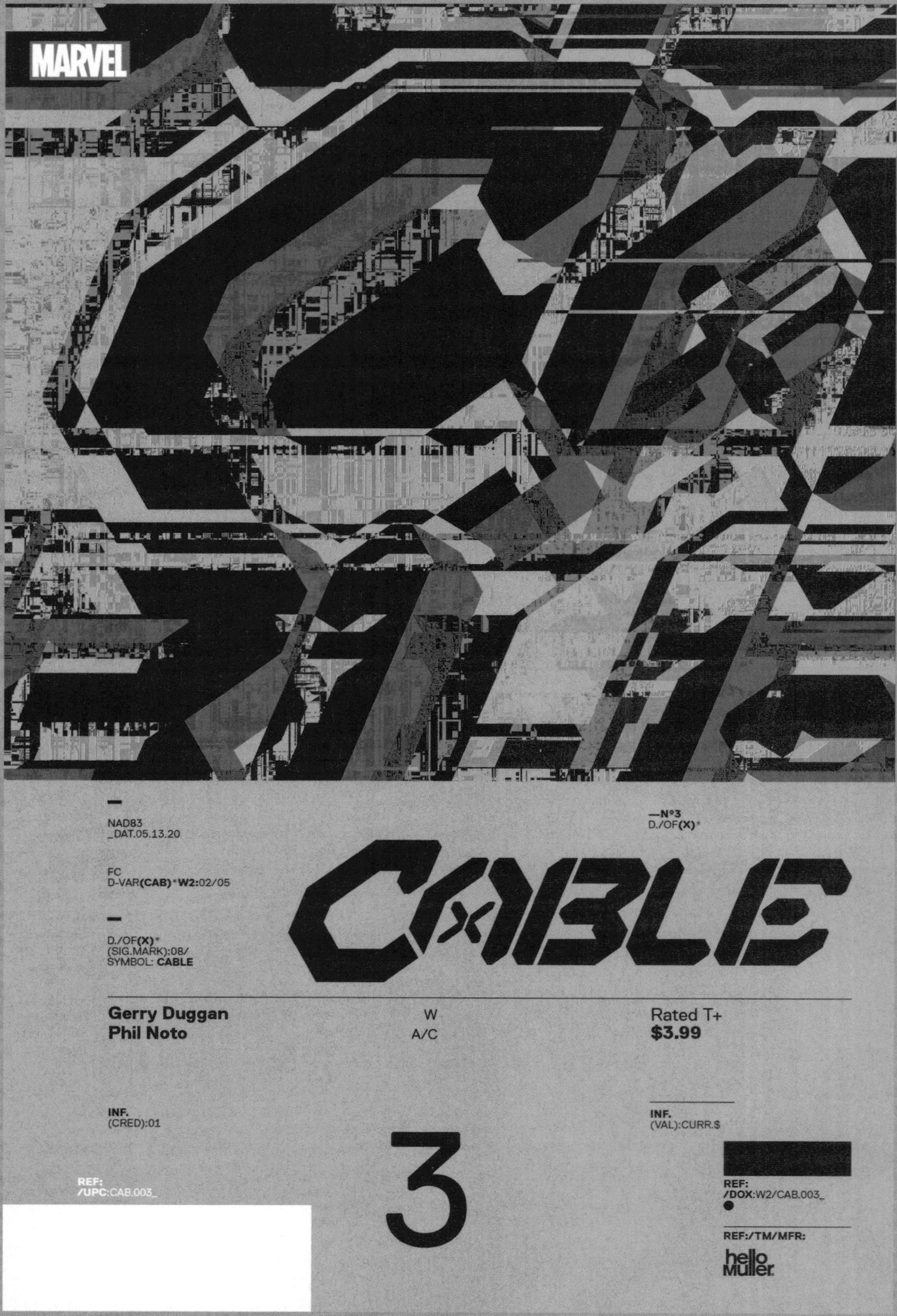
MARVEL
NAD83
_DAT.05.13.20
—Nº3
D./OF(X)*
FC
D-VAR(CAB)*W2:02/05
D./OF(X)*
(SIG.MARK):08/
SYMBOL: CABLE
CABLE
Gerry Duggan W
Phil Noto A/C
Rated T+
$3.99
INF.
(CRED):01
INF.
(VAL):CURR.$
3
REF:
/UPC:CAB.003_
REF:
/DOX:W2/CAB.003_
REF:/TM/MFR:
hello Muller.

Cable #3 Design Variant by Tom Muller

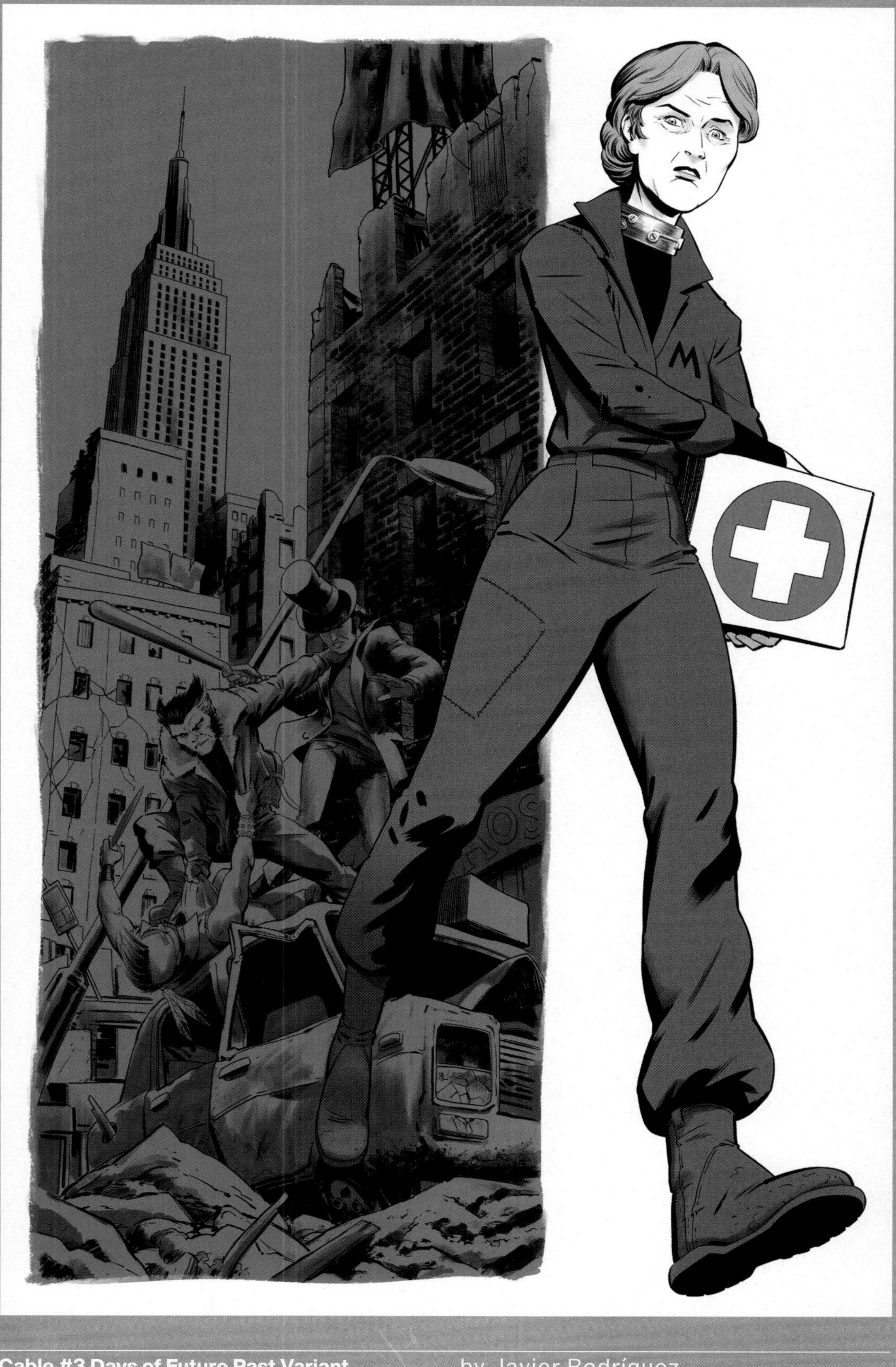

Cable #3 Days of Future Past Variant

by Javier Rodríguez
& Álvaro López